ENDORSEMENTS

"Todd Ahrend, in his book *The Abrahamic Revolution,* captures both God's heart for the nations as well as the Church's responsibility to make Christ's last command our first commitment. I found the book informative, practical, and inspirational."

Dr. Bill Jones
President
Columbia International University

"So many Christians think that missions begins with Jesus's Great Commission in the New Testament. The truth is, God was always interested in blessing the nations with his salvation. He's made that clear since the call of Abraham. In this book, Todd Ahrend has done a great job of showing the earlier initiation of God's plan for the nations and tracing its development through Scripture all the way to its culmination in Revelation. Readers are going to discover that mission cannot be just a hobby horse of a few interested people, it's the theme of the Bible and a part of every believer's responsibility."

Dr. Mike Pocock
Senior Professor and Chairman
World Missions and Intercultural Studies
Dallas Theological Seminary

"Todd has done a superb job exploring the depth of God's heart for the nations from Creation to Revelation. And he's coupled this careful study of the Word with the thoughtful passion of a long-term mission mobilizer. His treatment and survey of the peoples of our world are rich. His discussion of our personal options and roles clearly marks a path for every believer who captures the heart of God for His world."

Dr. William D. Taylor
Global Ambassador and Senior Mentor
Mission Commission
World Evangelical Alliance

"*The Abrahamic Revolution* is a much needed challenge to our self-absorbed culture to see the world from God's perspective. Todd has laid out in concise language that there is no *"plan B"* when it comes to reaching the nations with the gospel of Jesus Christ—we're it! Thanks, Todd, for a handbook on how to do what we were created to do: *Spread the glory of God to every tribe, tongue, and nation.*"

Lee Epstein
Global Pastor
New Heights Church, Arkansas

"Todd Ahrend has issued a call from God to put away the petty, distracted, and often self-serving brand of Christian faith that sees Jesus as the One who assists us toward self-fulfillment. Instead, *The Abrahamic Revolution* is a call toward the life-changing, world-changing mission of God. Every reader will finish this book with a greater sense of where he or she fits in the global, eternal purposes of God."

Dr. Paul Borthwick
International Mobilizer
and author of *How to Be a World-Class Christian*

"Todd guides us through the Scriptures, leaving us in no doubt what God's purpose is, and then gives us all very practical ways to personally live it out. Thank you for once again calling us away from the mediocre version of faith that we so easily settle for and challenging us to the revolutionary call to bless the nations. Thank you for not just preaching it but passionately living it out."

Andrew Scott
President/CEO
Operation Mobilization—USA

"Our parents used to exhort us to 'spend time with the best kind of friends who will inspire you to be all you're intended to be.' I urge you to 'spend time' with Todd absorbing the reality described in *The Abrahamic Revolution*. Ask the Father to 'lift up your eyes' beyond where you've been ... then 'go and do likewise.'"

Dr. Greg Livingstone
Founder
Frontiers

"If you simply desire a book that will lead you down the path of cultural Christianity—this is not it. If you are looking for a book that will simply endorse your self-centered ambition—this is not it. If you are looking for a message as old as Abraham that will lead you toward a crucifixion of your own agenda—this is it. The truth in this book will jump off the pages and challenge you to see your life as a part of the overarching, unchanging mission of God. My friend Todd Ahrend has written a book that will help you find your purpose and role in the never-changing grand plan of God."

Dr. Alex Himaya
Founder and Senior Pastor
The Church at BattleCreek, Oklahoma

"Herein you will find great encouragement! Your life matters ... You have a purpose on planet earth ... You can live that purpose ... You can make a difference! Herein you will also find great challenge. Like Abraham, this life will be a choice of radical leaps ... always from the security of the known into the unknown!"

Greg Lillestrand
U.S. Director — Campus Crusade for Christ International
City Ministries

"In a day when too many have lost sight of the definitive theme of God's Word, Todd's tracing of the desert-dwelling patriarch whose pursuit of Yahweh changed history forever will link your life purpose to the mission of God. This book will both expand the Church's vision and laser the Church's focus on the missional DNA of the Church. His retelling of the biblical story is based on solid scholarship but told in the vernacular of the times. This is mandatory reading for all committed Jesus followers who claim to want to be obedient to the big picture of Scripture."

Dr. Steve Hoke
Life Coach, Church Resources Ministries
and co-author of *The Global Mission Handbook*

"Caution! Ahrend's *Abrahamic Revoluton* is a deep river moving swiftly toward God's global purpose. Take the plunge only if you dare to impact the nations for Christ!"

Matt Burns
Managing Director, Perspectives Global
U.S. Center for World Mission

One of the most succinct books written on missions for this generation ... balancing theological depth with practical steps of application. If you are a believer unsettled in your understanding of what God's global purposes are, please read this book!

Joshua Rolf
Minister of Missions Mobilization
Prestonwood Baptist Church

Mission changes everything: how we read Scripture, how we think about God, how we worship, how we live our lives. *The Abrahamic Revolution* helps us see the startling truth that God's mission is *the* story of Scripture and *the* reason His people remain on the earth. What was once thought to be reserved for the few and the brave who left all to follow God's call to the remotest of places is now understood to be the privilege of each and every follower of Christ. This book will help you find your place in the mission of God. But, beware! You will be changed if you take it seriously.

Dr. Mark Young
President — Denver Seminary

The Abrahamic Revolution is a must-read book for every Christian, not just those who are interested in "missions." Todd Ahrend has balanced the biblical basis of mission with the essentials of different religious blocs to create an approachable read that will greatly enhance your understanding of God's global drama.

James M. Kim
Vice President of Mobilization
Pioneers — USA

the ABRAHAMIC REVOLUTION

GOD'S MISSION IN MOTION

TODD AHREND

Dawson**Media**

THE ABRAHAMIC REVOLUTION: GOD'S MISSION IN MOTION

© 2011 by Todd Ahrend

DAWSON MEDIA and the DAWSON MEDIA logo are registered trademarks of Dawson Media. Absence of ® in connection with marks of Dawson Media or other parties does not indicate an absence of registration of those marks.

ISBN-13: 978-1-93565-127-7

Cover design by Niddy Griddy Design, Inc. and Jason Miller
Interior design by Liquid Lotus, LLC

Maps used by permission, Jason Mandryk and GMI, all rights reserved.

Some of the anecdotal illustrations in this book are true to life and are included with the permission of the persons involved. All other illustrations are composites of real situations, and any resemblance to people living or dead is coincidental. Unless otherwise identified, all Scripture quotations in this publication are taken from the *Holy Bible, New International Version®* (niv®). Copyright © 1973, 1978, 1984 Biblica. Used by permission of Zondervan. All rights reserved. Other versions used include:

the New American Standard Bible® (nasb), Copyright © 1960, 1962, 1963, 1968, 1971, 1972, 1973, 1975, 1977, 1995 by The Lockman Foundation. Used by permission;

The Holy Bible, English Standard Version (esv), copyright © 2001 by Crossway Bibles, a division of Good News Publishers. Used by permission. All rights reserved.

Italics found in Scripture quotations reflect the author's own emphasis.

LCCN: 2011929004

Printed in United States of America

15 14 13 12 11/1 2 3 4 5 6 7 8

To Norman and Shelia

My parents. My mentors. My friends.

CONTENTS

FOREWORD

This book is about a powerful revolution—one that has been going on for a very long time. In fact, it is the oldest revolution in the world—and guess what—God started it! If we really listen to the message of this book, we will begin to understand that Ahrend is calling us to become part of this ancient revolution. Just as Abraham left behind the idols of his upbringing and his own tiny little world to follow the one true God and capture a global vision, Ahrend calls us to leave behind the minimalistic, low-bar version of our faith that has come to characterize so much of modern Christianity. In its place Ahrend calls for us to be set ablaze in a fresh way with the original fire which sweeps from the dramatic call of Abraham to the burning bush of Moses, to the weeping heart of the prophets, to the apostles who witnessed the Resurrection, and down to where you and I sit today. Ahrend calls this the Abrahamic Revolution—the divine call to be a blessing to all nations! This is a revolution which began in the heart of God but will someday reach its climax in that great scene recorded in the book of Revelation where John sees a multitude that no one can count, from every nation, tribe, people, and language standing before the throne, worshipping Jesus Christ. This is the great movement which we are called to participate in. All of us stand somewhere between Genesis 12 and Revelation 7:9-10; that is, between Abraham's call and that great vision of John the Apostle. The question is, are we going to join this great revolution?

If you are looking for a road map which begins with one lonely man in Ur of the Chaldees and shows us the way to the heavenly city and that great multitude from all nations that no one can count, you have found it. Having known the author for a number of years, I can say that his life is a moving mobilization machine. He is as inspiring in real life as he is in print. When you read this book, you will capture a sense of his own passion; this is no armchair author. Nor is this some stale book of information. Instead, inside this one book you will receive a thrilling and breathtaking crash course in mission theology, the history of Christian missions, and a practical guide as to how to mobilize missionaries, become a missionary, or support one who is going. In short, Ahrend gives us all a pathway to become part of the Abrahamic Revolution.

I used to laugh inside when I heard Christians mistakenly call the book of Revelation, the book of Revolution. Now, I see that the last laugh is on me, because that is precisely what Todd Ahrend's fine book helps us all to see: that the great biblical story which God is unfolding is nothing short of a revolution—one which I want to be a part of. When you read this book, you'll want to be a part of it too!

Timothy C. Tennent, PhD
President, Asbury Theological Seminary

ACKNOWLEDGMENTS

The way we spend our moments is the way we spend our lives. The measure of my life will be the sum total of all the little choices I make on a day-to-day, moment-by-moment basis. When I think of Christians who have kingdom impact, I picture those heroes who have packed up all their stuff, turned their back on a life of ease, and moved overseas, never to return. I also think of the guy who initiates spiritual conversations in line at the grocery store, the young mom who opens her home to the Muslims in her neighborhood, the little boy who gives his allowance to a missionary, and the grandma who prays for India. I've known my share of kingdom-impact Christians, and their everyday decisions to follow the heart of God have not gone unnoticed by me. No, they have shaped me, and for that I want to thank them.

Fred and Suzanne Ferguson made the everyday choice to model Jesus to me throughout my youth. They were like second parents to me, and I am indebted to them for their influence.

Bob Sjogren understood God's global purpose and was faithful to pursue his role in it—recruiting others. He traveled day after day to state after state, helping his hearers grasp a passion for missions. I was in one of his audiences. I was never the same.

John Barnett chooses to prize the Word of God above all else. He embodies the truth that those who love God's law are firmly planted and bear much fruit.

D. L. Moody said, "The world has yet to see what God can do with a man fully consecrated to Him." He obviously never met Andy Kampman. Just standing next to Andy makes you want to totally abandon yourself to the cause of Christ! He literally seizes every opportunity for kingdom impact.

Dave Riner is talented enough to be doing anything, but he has never wavered in two things: investing in people and striving to reach the world. He came beside me while I was the young founder of a new ministry and helped shape my paradigm of building into others in a strategic way.

I am thankful for Lee and Ruth Epstein who, having endured incredible hardship, are triumphant examples of joy. Their lives are a testimony that, in every situation, God is good and worthy to be praised by all nations. Daily they live out these realities.

Paul Van Der Werf has taught me that prayer should not only be first place in our lives but first, second, and third place. He truly lives the words of Andrew Murray, "The person who mobilizes the Church to pray will make the largest contribution in history to world evangelization." That is Vandy's clarion call!

Thanks to my good friend Adam Miller. His presence invites authenticity. He's able to distill deep Christian truths into a profound yet practical wisdom that he genuinely lives out.

My sister Alicia has made a lot of little decisions to put herself last in light of others. She reminds me that it is more blessed to give than to receive. And then there is Theresa, the oldest of my siblings, who died only months before this manuscript was finished. The fact that 700 people showed up to her funeral and waited for three hours to pay their respects proves that Theresa got it right when it came to impacting lives. She had thousands of little conversations that pointed others to Christ; she shined for Him. She was always so proud of me, and her affirmation keeps me going. Theresa had a beautiful voice, and I know that she's worshipping our Lord alongside the nations. I can't wait to join her.

My first known memory is of my mom teaching me how to tie my shoe. I remember her sitting on the floor with me, patiently waiting, giving her time and energy to not only me but to all her children. To this day she still endlessly gives! My father made the moment-by-moment choice to stand behind me in my every endeavor. My success was his success, and he has never stopped cheering.

And to the girl I married, Jess. She is truly a magnificent wife and mother. Thanks for saying "I do" at the altar and for saying it every day since. Indeed, "Many women do noble things, but you surpass them all" (Proverbs 31:29).

THE WORD

"We have not made the Revolution, the Revolution has made us."

— Georg Büchner

CHAPTER 1
WHERE IS MISSIONS NOT?

When I first became a believer, I zealously sought all that I perceived the Christian life required. I looked around and found that all the believers I knew did three basic things. First, they all listened to Christian music. I figured if I wanted to grow in Christ, this was step one in discipleship. I immediately threw away all my secular music in order to be a good Christian. Second, my committed friends wore Christian apparel. Since I had none, I quickly went shopping at the Christian bookstore and stocked up on a new wardrobe. Third, Christians put a silver fish on the back of their cars in order to clearly identify themselves with Christ. I decided to put one on the back *and* one on the front just to let people know that I was a solid believer. (I think it worked. I don't recall ever getting a ticket.) And then my world came crashing down.

As a college student walking across campus in my Christian T-shirt while listening to my Christian music, I was introduced to a guy with a completely different paradigm. He invited me to his 6 a.m. Bible study. I tried to decline, but I could offer no legitimate excuse. (I'm not all that busy at 6 a.m.) Not wanting to betray my Christian T-shirt and all it represented about my spiritual life, I said yes, fully intending to go only a few times and then slowly fade back into my life.

At the first Bible study, this guy I'd met laid out a map of the world and invited us to pick a country and pray for it. I tried to get dibs on the States. He asked me to pick another country. I scrambled, "Uh … Canada." Nope. North America was not an option for this guy. I looked down at the center and chose the largest country I saw—Saudi Arabia. My prayer lasted about ten seconds. I'm sure it went something like, "Lord, help Saudi. Amen." I was clueless about that country and how to pray for it. The leader challenged me to come back the next week and to know a little more. I did. Over those next few weeks, I hunted down all the information I could find on Saudi Arabia: How many Muslims? How many churches? How many Christians? How many missionaries? My research and prayer time for Saudi caused confusion at the most foundational level of my faith.

In Him, we actually possess the ability to live for a goal beyond ourselves—something global!

I realized that up to that point I had done a really good job of *Christianizing* my life: making sure I dressed the part, knew the lingo, and participated in a few good Christian activities. However, something slowly became apparent. God was not interested in me *Christianizing* my life; He was interested in me *crucifying* my life.

Most people want to live for something. I don't think I've ever met a person who aspired to futility. People crave purpose. We all want to be a part of something that will out-last us. We all want, at the end of the day—and more impor-tantly, at the end of our lives—to be able to say, "I contributed to that ... I made an impact on those people ... I spent my time significantly."

God's mission has been in motion from the beginning of time. It's a mission of eternal impact and a purpose of in-estimable significance. As believers, God has invited us into this purpose. In Him, we actually possess the ability to live for a goal beyond ourselves—something global! Many times, though, this potential is not realized in believers' lives.

Some Christians miss God's mission because they compartmentalize their spiritual life from the rest of their life. Others have never realized God's mission is all-encompassing and meant for every believer. Some miss it because they throw everything they've got at all the things our culture defines as "Christian," never realizing God has more for them. I know in my own life that has been true.

My problem was that when I became a believer, I just slapped a Christian name tag on my former ambitions. My plans, goals, and general orientation in life hadn't changed much except that I wore a Christian T-shirt while pursuing them. But after being confronted with another perspective, I began to see in Scripture that God's ambition is to redeem all nations. The biblical response is to lay down our purposes in exchange for His. In order for this great exchange to take place, three things must happen. First, we need to crucify our lives to Him. Paul declared, "I have been crucified with Christ and I no longer live, but Christ lives in me" (Galatians 2:20). Second, we need to learn about His overarching plan. And third, we must understand practically how to connect

His plan to our lives in what I call the Abrahamic Revolution.

Did you ever realize you'd be in any way connected to Abraham? That desert-dwelling patriarch whose pride was his herd of camels and the son born to him at age one hundred seems so far from today's world! Yet, you are inextricably linked to the founding father of our faith.

Abram (later Abraham) lived in a place called Ur. He was a normal guy leading a typical life for a man of his day and age. The fact that he and his wife had no kids was the only blip that made Abram stand out in any way. That is, until God spoke to him. God broke into Abram's ordinary life and invited him to do something extraordinary—something that would change the world. God told Abram to look out at the stars and said, "So shall your descendants be" (Genesis 15:5 nasb). Essentially, He was saying, *I am going to take your unfruitful, insignificant life and multiply it beyond your wildest dreams! I'm going to change your identity from Abram, "exalted father," and make you Abraham, "the father of many nations."* But there was a catch. In order to be used of God in such a mighty way, Abraham had to first lay down his own plans and take on God's agenda. Abraham accepted. Henceforth, his spiritual heritage has covered the globe.

The question of our connection with Abraham is critical because within its answer we find our own purpose, our link to God's mission. The word *revolution* means "a sudden, complete, or marked change in something." That's what happened to Abraham when God interrupted his life. That's what happened to me when I encountered the mission that God initiated only a few chapters into Scripture. As Georg Büchner said, "We have not made the Revolution, the Revolution has made us." When we say yes to God's purpose, a sudden and marked change occurs. We take on His agenda, we read His Word in a new context, we see the world with new eyes, and we take on a new lifestyle—the Revolution makes us. A revolutionized person has taken hold of a new understanding that changes his whole life—he no longer grasps for self-preservation and self-promotion, but a life defined by faith. He is convinced there is no greater story to be a part of and no other movement yielding greater impact. Such people are ordinary men and women being used by God for extraordinary things. Let's take a closer look at His mission and see if our life purpose doesn't undergo the same revolution that has transformed lives for two thousand years.

THE MISSION OF GOD

From Genesis to Revelation God has one plan—reaching all nations—and one method—using people. What verses come to mind when you think of the word *missions*? Most of us are hard-pressed to name more than the good ol' Great Commission (Matthew 28:18-20).[1]

God has one plan—reaching all nations—and one method—using people.

For years our church culture has singled out this passage to be the theme of our missions conferences and the

---

[1] Matthew 28:18-20 "Then Jesus came to them and said, 'All authority in heaven and on earth has been given to me. Therefore go and make disciples of all nations, baptizing them in the name of the Father and of the Son and of the Holy Spirit, and teaching them to obey everything I have commanded you. And surely I am with you always, to the very end of the age.'"

motivation for those who go. It's no wonder our obedience is slow. Who wants to hang their future on one verse? Actually, we see God's heart for the world way before the Great Commission. It's evident all the way back in the life of Abraham. As we will discover, God invited Abraham in Genesis 12 to lay down his plans and follow Him in faith. Abraham was the first in the historic line of men and women who stepped out to follow God in reaching the nations. This set the mission of God into motion and is the foundation for how we interpret the rest of the Bible.

More than simply picking out a string of verses and making a case for the biblical basis of missions, "the whole Bible renders to us the story of God's mission through God's people in their engagement with God's work."[2] God is a missional God, and His mission has been called the *missio Dei* (literally translated the "sending of God"). The *missio Dei* is God's self-revelation as the One who loves the world. It includes His work in the world involving the participation of God's people in proclaiming the good news that God loves all.[3] In other words, the Church is a missionary Church not because it existed first. No, the mission (*missio Dei*) existed and has involved the Church as its privileged instrument.

---

[2] History shows that a person can take the Bible and prove about anything. Scripture passages can be found to support just about any claim. For example, there is a biblical basis for marriage, a biblical basis for work, and I have even heard of a biblical basis for bread making! The difference, however, is that there is not a marital basis for the Bible, nor is work what the Bible is all about (or bread making). In contrast, the whole of Scripture finds its focus in Christ and in the mission to all nations. Christopher J. H. Wright, *The Mission of God: Unlocking the Bible's Grand Narrative* (Downers Grove, IL: InterVarsity Press, 2006), 29-30, 51.

[3] David J. Bosch, *Transforming Mission: Paradigm Shifts in Theology of Mission* (MaryKnoll, NY: Orbis Books, 2005), 10.

Thus it is no surprise that the Bible portrays Israel as having a mission, Jesus as having a mission, and the Church as having a mission. David Bosch, in *Transforming Mission*, said:

> It is not the Church that has a mission of salvation to fulfill in the world; it is the mission of the Son and the Spirit through the Father that includes the Church. Mission is thereby seen as a movement from God to the world; the Church is viewed as an instrument for that mission. There is Church because there is mission, not vice versa.[4]

If you don't believe that all sixty-six books of the Bible can be reduced to one theme, keep reading. You will see that missions is not your pastor's idea, your campus minister's idea, or even your idea ... it is God's idea. The question is not *Where is missions in the Bible?* The question is *Where is it not!* Since Creation, God has been moving toward a promise that He will ultimately fulfill—a representation of every nation before His throne. As Christians, we must see things according to the global plan He lays out in Scripture. Let us look at the Bible in light of God's heart for the world, and we will see that from Genesis to Revelation, He beckons you and me and all of His people to join Him in reaching every nation. The Bible is not a collection of random books with no common connection. It is one book with an introduction (Genesis 1–11), a plot (Genesis 12 – Jude), and a conclusion (Revelation). What began with Abraham now comes to us. Come learn about this *Abrahamic Revolution!*

---

4 Bosch, 390.

CHAPTER 2
MISSIONS IN THE FIRST FIVE BOOKS

I can remember when I was in high school there was one day I looked forward to all year. As the day approached, the anticipation grew. It was the talk of the cafeteria, hallways, and classrooms—the day the yearbooks arrived. As teachers passed them out to their classes, like synchronized swimmers, we all simultaneously turned to the back, found our names, and counted how many pages had our picture on them. I remember my devastation year after year when the index only listed one page number beside my name—my stock photo with the generic blue background. It was the only one of me. All my suspicions were confirmed in that moment: I was a loser. Then, the year came when I had two numbers! I turned as fast as I could to the other page. My eyes scanned all over. Where was I? I did not immediately stand out on the page so I kept searching. Finally, in a group picture of about fifty, I spotted myself. What a glorious day!

Isn't it interesting how we are wired? We naturally tend to scan a picture and look for ourselves first, checking our hair, smile, and outfit. Only after zooming in on ourselves do we zoom out to take notice of others. When someone pointed out to me that we often read the Bible like a yearbook, I was immediately convicted. What does the Bible say about *me*? What does it say about *my* promises? Very rarely do we ask, "Lord, where are *You*? What are *Your* desires? What is *Your* ultimate goal?" Over the next few chapters, I would like to explore those exact questions. Let's take our eyes off ourselves and see what God is doing.

Like any good book, the Bible contains three compelling parts: an introduction, a plot, and a conclusion. Found in Genesis 1–11, the introduction sets the stage, acquaints us with the problem, and whets our appetite for the plot. The plot runs from Genesis 12 to Jude and introduces us to the Bible's main characters. We follow along as they work toward solving the dilemma created in the first eleven chapters. The conclusion is found in Revelation when God achieves the goal toward which He has moved for the whole of Scripture: the redemption of all nations. So let's begin with the intro. Let's look at Genesis.

IN THE BEGINNING

When God created mankind, He commanded Adam and Eve to fill the earth. "God blessed them, and God said to them, 'Be fruitful and multiply; fill the earth'" (Genesis 1:28 nkjv). This command should come as no surprise since only two people existed on the planet. Adam and Eve were obviously meant to populate physically, but God also intended they reproduce a spiritual heritage. Can you picture that? The planet covered with worshippers? As people distanced themselves geographically, they would naturally have separated into different clusters. Various customs would surely have developed. Cultures would have been created, individualizing their own distinct worship style of the one true God. Isaiah tells us, "for the earth will be full of the knowledge of the Lord as the waters cover the sea" (Isaiah 11:9). God's desire from the beginning was that mankind would worship Him all over the globe in diverse ways. How is that for glorifying God!

However, by Genesis 3 sin had crept in, and by Genesis 6 man's heart was filled with all kinds of evil. As Scripture explains, "The Lord saw how great man's wickedness on the earth had become, and that every inclination of the thoughts of his heart was only evil all the time" (Genesis 6:5). Consequently, God flooded the earth and started over with one family: Noah's. The command God issued Noah should sound very familiar. "So God blessed Noah and his sons, and said to them: 'Be fruitful and multiply, and fill the earth'" (Genesis 9:1 nkjv). When we come to Genesis 10–11, one question should be on our minds: Does God get the earth filled?

FROM ONE TO MANY

Now that I am a dad, I find my conversations with people often center on kids. I recently heard a story regarding a mother and her son. The boy had been caught in a defiant act. His mother went to the drawer for a wooden spoon while the son ran to his room. By the time his mother found him, the young boy had stacked no fewer than twelve pairs of underwear under his pants! Similarly, in Genesis 11, God's children prepare themselves for His consequences while they respond to His command in blatant defiance:

Now the whole world had one language and a common speech. As men moved eastward, they found a plain in Shinar and settled there. They said to each other, "Come, let's make bricks and bake them thoroughly." They used brick instead of stone, and tar for mortar. Then they said, "Come, let us build ourselves a city, with a tower that reaches to the heavens, so that we may make a name for ourselves and not be scattered over the face of the whole earth." (Genesis 11:1-4)

We read that the whole earth had one language. There was no "us" and "them" mentality. Contrary to God's command to fill the earth, people decided to settle and make a name for themselves—their blatant defiance. We don't know what the plain in Shinar looked like, but it was appealing enough that the people chose to stay and be disobedient. When they set out to build their homes, "they used brick instead of stone, and tar for mortar." Why include this detail? The story would still make sense even if we were unaware of the blueprints for early mankind's construction. But the writer, Moses, included this detail because it reveals the people's heart—they were stacking on the underwear! Remembering how God punished sin up to this point, with a flood, the people got ready. The bricks and tar would withstand a large force of water more effectively than stones. In case they didn't, surely a high tower would provide a place of shelter if God chose the same form of judgment on their sin of rebellion. Steve Hawthorne, a mission strategist, suggests, "The Babel people united in disbelief. They saw rainbows in the sky which signified that 'never again will the water become a flood to destroy all life' (Genesis 9:15). But they didn't believe it. They wanted to be really sure ... So the folks at Babel built a tower. They like most people had two basic needs: security and significance by groping for glory."[1]

The end of the passage sheds light on their true intentions. They were more interested in making a name for themselves. In direct disobedience, they chose not to be scattered, not to fill the earth (Genesis 11:4). God responded in a way they did not anticipate. They felt prepared for a flood, but instead He touched their tongues and accomplished what He desired from the beginning: the scattering of the nations. The diversification of languages at Babel was God's merciful way of avoiding the destruction of the whole human race who rebelled against Him.[2]

> "Come, let us go down and confuse their language so they will not understand each other." So the Lord scattered them from there over all the earth, and they stopped building the city. That is why it was called Babel—because there the Lord confused the language of the whole world. From there the Lord scattered them over the face of the whole earth. (Genesis 11:7-9)

What should have happened naturally over time took place in a moment as *seventy* languages instantly came into being.[3] How do we know God created seventy languages?

---

[1] Steve Hawthorne, "Mercy to Babel: God Answers Man's Desire for Security and Significance." Available from thetravelingteam.org.

[2] Arthur Glasser, *Announcing the Kingdom: The Story of God's Mission in the Bible* (Grand Rapids, MI: Baker Academic, 2003), 52.

[3] One of the most prominent scholars of the first five books of the Bible is John Sailhamer. He writes, "There are exactly seventy nations represented in the list.... In other words, 'all nations' find their ultimate origins in the three sons of Noah.... It is not without purpose the author reminds his readers that the total number of Abraham's 'seed' at the close of Genesis is also 'seventy' (Genesis 46:27)." John H. Sailhamer, *The Pentateuch as Narrative* (Grand Rapids, MI: Zondervan, 1992), 130-131.

The writer of Genesis lists every nation created by God in Genesis 10 and then explains how this diversity was achieved at the Tower of Babel in Genesis 11:1-9 (as Genesis 10 and Genesis 11 are not in chronological order). Let's read a portion of Genesis 10:5-32 to gain insight into the formation of the nations.

> From these the maritime [coastland] peoples spread out into their territories by their clans within their nations, each with its own language) ... Mizraim was the father of the Ludites, Anamites, Lehabites, Naphtuhites, Pathrusites, Casluhites (from whom the Philistines came) and Caphtorites. Canaan was the father of Sidon his firstborn, and of the Hittites, Jebusites, Amorites, Girgashites, Hivites, Arkites, Sinites, Arvadites, Zemarites and Hamathites. (Genesis 10:5, 13-18)

That is a lot of "ites." It might be helpful to think of the "ites" in terms of today's "ans." We call people from America, Americans; Brazil, Brazilians; India, Indians; Egypt, Egyptians; and so on. The use of an denotes a certain nationality, and ite represents the same concept. The chapter concludes with, "These are the clans of Noah's sons, according to their lines of descent, within their nations. From these the nations spread out over the earth after the flood" (Genesis 10:32). Genesis 10 is called the Table of the Nations and has major ramifications for the rest of Scripture—for it is the Table of the Nations God desires to reach. Its creation brings the introduction of the Bible to a close and leaves the reader with tension. How will God reach these nations scattered all over the globe speaking completely different languages? Here the plot begins as God calls one man from one nation of the seventy to reach the rest. Abraham is invited to the greatest revolution of all time.

THE ABRAHAMIC DILEMMA

At first glance, Abraham was an unlikely revolutionary. As mentioned previously, he lived in Ur, about 220 miles southeast of Baghdad. So in modern times he would have been Iraqi.[4] Abraham was a quiet sojourner, obscure and unknown, brought up by parents who worshipped idols (Joshua 24:2), and his chosen bride, Sarah, was barren. Scripture even fills us in on some situations when Abraham lacked faith and blatantly lied (Genesis 12:10-13; 20:1-2). But, one thing is clear from Scripture: God is not concerned with ability but with availability. God spoke to Abraham,

The Lord had said to Abram, "Leave your country, your people and your father's household and go to the land I will show you.

I will make you into a great nation and I will bless you; I will make your name great, and you will be a blessing. I will bless those who bless you, and whoever curses you I will curse; and all peoples on earth will be blessed through you." (Genesis 12:1-3)

Abraham was called to commit to a Person, not a country.

God's promise to Abraham has three main parts. First, God would bless Abraham personally through

---

[4] Bill Stearns and Amy Stearns, *20/20 Vision: Practical Ways Individuals and Churches Can Be Involved* (Minneapolis, MN: Bethany House, 2005), 63.

descendants and land. God instructed him to leave his place of security and venture out with no indication of where to go. Abraham was called to commit to a Person, not a country.[5] Second, through Abraham's descendants a great nation would emerge. This is an interesting reversal. In contrast to the Tower of Babel where the people determined to make a name for themselves apart from God, Abraham's name would be made great *by* God.[6] Third, he would be the source of blessing to all peoples of the earth. God's call is universal and will have worldwide implications.[7] The unbroken thread running through the entire Bible is this global promise, based on God's closing remarks to Abraham that "all peoples on earth will be blessed through you" (Genesis 12:3). John Stott, one of the leading evangelical scholars in Europe, says about the opening verses of Genesis 12, "These are perhaps the most unifying verses in the Bible; the whole of God's purpose is encapsulated here."[8] In Abraham and his descendants, God answers the question of how He will reach the Table of the Nations. Keep in mind that Abraham had no idea where he was to go and no idea how long he was to stay in this new place. More importantly, Abraham had no idea the name of this God beckoning him to move out. Abraham had a choice: stay in Ur, follow his personal plans and choose to direct

---

[5] David M. Howard, *Student Power in World Evangelism* (Downers Grove, IL: InterVarsity Press, 1970), 11.

[6] Timothy C. Tennent, *Invitation to World Missions: A Trinitarian Missiology for the Twenty-first Century* (Grand Rapids, MI: Kregel, 2010), 107.

[7] David Filbeck, *Yes, God of the Gentiles, Too: A Missionary Message of the Old Testament* (Wheaton, IL: Billy Graham Center, 1994), 60.

[8] John Kyle, ed., *Should I Not Be Concerned? A Mission Reader* (Downers Grove, IL: InterVarsity Press, 1987), 32.

his own life, or step out in faith. The story continues, "So Abram left, as the Lord had told him" (Genesis 12:4). He left everything familiar—his home, his people, his stuff—and so the *plot* begins.

Four more times throughout Genesis God promises to reach all nations: two more times to Abraham, once to his son Isaac, and once to Isaac's son Jacob.[9] Consider the following passages:

> Abraham will surely become a great and powerful nation, and *all nations on earth* will be blessed through him. (Genesis 18:18)

> I will surely bless you and make your descendants as numerous as the stars in the sky and as the sand on the seashore. Your descendants will take possession of the cities of their enemies, and through your offspring *all nations on earth* will be blessed. (Genesis 22:17-18)

> The Lord appeared to Isaac and said, "… For to you and your descendants I will give all these lands and will confirm the oath I swore to your father Abraham. I will make your descendants as numerous as the stars in the sky and will give them all these lands, and through your offspring *all nations on earth* will be blessed." (Genesis 26:2-4)

> There above it stood the Lord, and he said: "I am the Lord, the God of your father Abraham and the God of Isaac. I will give

---

[9] When God repeats the covenant with Isaac and Jacob it follows the same threefold pattern of blessing—having descendants and land, becoming a great nation, and blessing "all the nations on earth" through his seed. See Tennent, 109.

you and your descendants the land on which you are lying. Your descendants will be like the dust of the earth, and you will spread out to the west and to the east, to the north and to the south. *All peoples on earth* will be blessed through you and your offspring." (Genesis 28:13-14)

For the rest of Scripture God will identify Himself as "the God of Abraham, Isaac, and Jacob." John Zumwalt explains,

Why not include some other, more noteworthy individuals like Moses, or Joseph or Samuel?... Why not? Because the deal was signed between God and these three in person. These three heard the covenant stated to them directly from God. Every time Jesus referred to the God of Abraham, Isaac and Jacob, it was a reminder to the children of Israel. These were the people with whom God made that covenant: "I will bless you, and through you all nations will be blessed."[10]

Jesus speaks about the day Abraham, Isaac, and Jacob will see this vision fulfilled: "I say to you that many will come from the east and the west, and will take their places at the feast with Abraham, Isaac and Jacob in the kingdom of heaven" (Matthew 8:11; Luke 13:29 adds the north and south). God called out these three men for this final day. Israel must understand that because of the connection with their forefathers, the blessing comes with the responsibility to pass it on to all peoples.

---

[10] John Willis Zumwalt, *Passion for the Heart of God* (Choctaw, OK: HGM Publishing, 2000), 28.

A NATION TO REACH ALL NATIONS

Have you noticed that from Genesis 12 all the way to the last book of the Old Testament, Malachi, you follow one nation—Israel? Where they go, you go. The only reason you read of the Ninevites, Hittites, or Amorites is because they crossed paths with the Israelites. This relates back to God having chosen Abraham, Isaac, and Jacob as His agents. In Genesis 32:28 God changed Jacob's name to Israel, and from that point forward Israel was the nation that represented the continuation of God's purpose. Their identity was now as a nation to bless all nations.[11] God told the Israelites, "You yourselves have seen what I did to Egypt, and how I carried you on eagles' wings and brought you to myself. Now if you obey me fully and keep my covenant, then out of all nations you will be my treasured possession" (Exodus 19:4-5). God elected Israel but it was not *just* for Israel! God elected them to be His representatives among the nations, His mediator of the blessing. Christopher Wright, author of *The Mission of God's People,* states, "One nation is chosen, but all nations are to be the beneficiaries of that choice."[12] The passage continues, "You will be for me a kingdom of priests and a

---

[11] This is actually how the book of Genesis concludes. Arthur Glasser correctly observes, "When we think of Joseph, the descendant of Abraham who brought deliverance from famine and social distress to the greatest nation of the ancient world (Egypt), we see anticipatory fulfillment of the promise of Abraham's seed blessing the nations. This seems to be symbolized by the account of Joseph bringing his father, Jacob, into the court of Pharaoh that Jacob might twice bless him (Genesis 47:7, 10).... Indeed, the Israelite people were kept alive because God's worldwide redemptive purpose through them had yet to be fulfilled on behalf of Egypt and all other peoples (Galatians 3:8)." Glasser, 67-68.

[12] Christopher J. H. Wright, *The Mission of God's People: A Biblical Theology of the Church's Mission* (Grand Rapids, MI: Zondervan Publishing, 2010), 71.

Israel was meant to extend God's blessing throughout the world.

holy nation" (Exodus 19:6). The role of the priest was to serve God personally and to serve others on His behalf, to mediate. Israel was to represent God to the nations as a kingdom of priests. God's desire to establish a holy nation was the purpose behind Israel being God's treasured possession. Bill Stearns says, "He chose them, not to bless them at the exclusion of every other family of the earth, and not to single them out because of their superiority. Rather, He chose them to take on the responsibility of serving as priests whose parish was the entire world."[13]

One example of Israel being a nation to reach all nations is the Exodus of Israel from Egypt. God rained down ten plagues on Pharaoh and the Egyptians, but it was not solely to loosen Pharaoh's grip on the Israelites. The plagues also acted as a testimony of God's greatness to the Egyptians and the rest of the world. The God of the Israelites loved the Egyptians, and He intended to use this event to reveal Himself to them. He said to Pharaoh, "For by now I could have stretched out my hand and struck you and your people with a plague that would have wiped you off the earth. But I have raised you up for this very purpose, that I might show you my power and that my name might be proclaimed in all the earth" (Exodus 9:15-16). As we see from other passages, "The Lord Almighty will bless them, saying, 'Blessed be Egypt my people, Assyria my handiwork, and Israel my

---

[13] Stearns, 90.

inheritance'" (Isaiah 19:25). God loves Egypt, Assyria, and Israel. If you read the rest of the Exodus story, you notice there were Egyptians who believed in God and even followed them into the desert. "The Israelites journeyed from Rameses to Succoth. There were about six hundred thousand men on foot, besides women and children. *Many other people* went up with them, as well as large droves of livestock, both flocks and herds" (Exodus 12:37-38).[14] Throughout the story of the Exodus the phrase "that the Egyptians will know that I am the Lord" actually occurs more than the phrase "that Israel may know."[15]

After leaving Egypt, God took Israel to the Promised Land and bid them to claim their blessings. Israel's lack of faith in God's ability to deliver His promise resulted in them circling the desert for forty years. When the next generation prepared to enter the Promised Land under Joshua, Moses reminded the people of God's laws and requirements. At first glance it may seem like the sole purpose of the Ten Commandments, and all of the Mosaic law, was to restrain bad behavior. However, there is a major missionary dimension attached to the Law of God, as seen in the following verses:

> See, I have taught you decrees and laws as the Lord my God commanded me, so that you may follow them in the land you are entering to take possession of it. Observe them carefully, *for this will show your wisdom and understanding to the nations,* who will hear about all these decrees and say,

---

[14] Walter C. Kaiser, *Mission in the Old Testament: Israel as a Light to the Nations* (Grand Rapids, MI: Baker Books, 2000), 21.

[15] "That the Egyptians [and Pharaoh] will know that I am the LORD" and its equivalent is found in Exodus 7:5; 8:10, 22; and 14:18. Glasser, 78.

"Surely this great nation is a wise and understanding people."
(Deuteronomy 4:5-6)

What God began in Genesis with Abraham, Isaac, and Jacob, He was preparing Israel to fulfill as a nation that blessed all nations.

A friend of mine contacted me about his Bible study of ten young Christian businessmen that met once a week to study the book of Matthew. They had come across this concept of the Great Commission and many in the group were excited. They reasoned, if a "good commission" is 15-20 percent, what is a "Great Commission"? He invited me to come speak on the subject. I asked everyone to open their Bibles to Genesis 12:1-4 and began to show them how God blessed Abraham, Isaac, and Jacob to bless all nations. We were not even out of Genesis yet when my friend spoke up. "Todd, so far you have mentioned eight times the fact that God blessed Israel. What exactly does the blessing of God look like in the context of the Old Testament?" I explained that when God blessed Israel there were consistent components involved: an increase in land, family, finances, and a great name as well. As you recall, God gave Israel the land between the Nile and Euphrates (Genesis 15:18). He promised Abraham his descendants would be like the sand on the seashore (Genesis 22:17). He forbade Abraham from taking anything from kings to show God's provision for him (Genesis 14:22-23). And finally, Abraham would be blessed with a great name (Genesis 12:2).

As my friend pondered this concept of blessing, he made a very personal connection: *land*—his house, yard, and fence; *family*—his two young boys and wife; *finances*—

he made a good salary and had a healthy savings account; *a great name*—he'd established a good reputation in his city. My friend looked up from the table after a moment of processing and said, "Todd, it is an eighty-hour work week just to manage my blessings. I don't have time to pass them on to the nations! I'm trying not to drown in them!" I started to think—maybe this is the problem with the Church. After managing our blessings, no time or energy is left to extend God's kingdom beyond our walls. We are trying to stay afloat. For the rest of the Old Testament, Israel will deal with this tension: hoard the blessing or obey the Blesser?

CHAPTER 3
MISSIONS IN THE LIVES OF THE KINGS AND PROPHETS

As I travel speaking in churches, I am occasionally asked to give my opinion of the state of the American Church. My response is always the same: "If you want to know the state of the Church in America, all you have to do is go to the Christian bookstore. There you will gain an accurate pulse as to our status." Why is this my staple answer? Because the Christian bookstore caters to its customers—American Christians.

Christian bookstores have been a great resource in my walk with God. I do find it fascinating, though, how many trinkets we can think up. Christian bracelets. Christian coffee cups. Christian plants. The list keeps going. One of my most memorable life lessons actually took place in a Christian bookstore. I was walking by the Christian stationery when I saw the section of Christian pictures. One particular picture caught my eye. It depicted a man fishing early in the morning, sun rising in the background. His tackle box lay open, and I believe a deer was even in the distance. Huge gold calligraphy at the bottom of the picture proclaimed the verse, "Be still, and know that I am God ..." (Psalm 46:10). I had seen this verse before embroidered on tea towels and inscribed on the sides of bowling balls and such, but this time was different. I noticed something that had always eluded my attention—the three dots at the end. For the first time I realized there was more to this verse. What could possibly make the rest of the verse so bad that it had to be cut? I tracked down the Bible section of the store to find out. I turned to Psalm 46:10 and read the whole verse: "Be still, and know that I am God; *I will be exalted among the nations, I will be exalted in the earth*." How was it possible that after all those years, all those tea towels, all those bowling balls, not once had I seen the complete verse? I knew the first half by memory. I even had it underlined in my Bible—it was about *me*. I'd never heard the second half, the part about God. His exaltation among the nations just wasn't good enough for the fishing picture.

As it turns out, lots of Scripture gets overlooked because we focus on the part about us. These stories fill the Old Testament, stories we are familiar with but may never have fully heard or understood. I think you will be amazed to find all of these examples have one thing in common: the portions overlooked focus on God being exalted. Take a look.

THE BIGGER PICTURE

Since Israel was chosen by God to be His missionary nation to all nations, the rest of the Old Testament takes shape around this *missio Dei* (the sending of God). When Moses passed the leadership of the nation on to Joshua and Israel headed into the Promised Land, their reputation preceded them. The parting of the Red Sea and the separating of the Jordan River had served their purpose of showing God's glory to the nations. Joshua reminds the people,

> The Lord your God did to the Jordan just what he had done to the Red Sea when he dried it up before us until we had crossed over. He did this *so that* all the peoples of the earth might know that the hand of the Lord is powerful and so that you might always fear the Lord your God. (Joshua 4:23-24)

Notice the "so that"? God's motive behind such a dramatic display was that news of His greatness would spread abroad. We know it worked because when Joshua sent spies into the land, the Gentile woman who hid them, Rahab, stated, "I know that the Lord has given this land to you and that a great fear of you has fallen on us, so that all who live in this country are melting in fear because of you. *We have heard* how the Lord dried up the water of the Red Sea for you when you came out of Egypt" (Joshua 2:9-10).

The establishment of the Davidic kingship in Israel was critical for God's rule and blessing to be passed on. In David's youth, he delivered food to his brothers stationed on the front lines of battle with the Philistines. Scripture says, "As he was talking with them, Goliath, the Philistine champion from Gath, stepped out from his lines and shouted his usual defiance, and David heard it" (1 Samuel 17:23). Enraged that this Philistine would dare profane God's name, David stepped up and shouted back at Goliath, "This day the Lord will hand you over to me, and I'll strike you down and cut off your head. Today I will give the carcasses of the Philistine army to the birds of the air and the beasts of the earth, *and the whole world will know that there is a God in Israel"* (1 Samuel 17:46). The story ends with David's triumph over Goliath and God's name lifted up among the nations.

PSALMS AND THE NATIONS

King David ruled Israel for forty years. In studying his life, it's clear David grasped the role Israel was to play in blessing all nations. This perspective permeates his writings.

On one occasion recorded in the book of Chronicles, David summoned Israel and all the nations to worship God through a song he had written. Here is a portion of that song which later became parts of Psalms 96, 105, and 106:

Psalms is one of the greatest missionary books in the Bible, though it's rarely recognized for that.

Give thanks to the Lord, call on his name; make known among the nations what he has done.... Sing to the Lord, all the *earth*; proclaim his salvation day after day. Declare his glory among the *nations*, his marvelous deeds among *all peoples*.... Ascribe to the Lord, O families of *nations*, ascribe to the Lord glory and strength, ascribe to the Lord the glory due his name.... Let the heavens rejoice, let the *earth* be glad; let them say among the *nations*, "The Lord reigns!" (1 Chronicles 16:8, 23-24, 28-29, 31)

David wrote seventy-three of the psalms, and other writers such as Asaph and the sons of Korah also contributed. Their psalms also affirm God's rule over all the earth. When the nations behold Yahweh's deeds, they are called to acknowledge Him. Such missionary vision can be supported in the psalms by more than 175 references to Israel and its testimony to the nations of the world.[1] Psalms is one of the greatest missionary books in the Bible, though it's rarely recognized for that. Take a look at these few examples:

All the ends of the earth will remember and turn to the Lord, and *all the families of the nations* will bow down before him, for dominion belongs to the Lord and he rules *over the nations.* (Psalm 22:27-28)

May God be gracious to us and bless us and make his face shine upon us, that your ways may be known on *earth,* your salvation among *all nations.* May the *peoples* praise you, O God; may all the peoples praise you. May the *nations* be glad and sing for joy, for you rule the *peoples* justly and guide the *nations* of the earth. May the *peoples* praise you, O God; may all the *peoples* praise you. Then the land will yield its harvest, and God, our God, will bless us. God will bless us, and all the *ends of the earth* will fear him. (Psalm 67:1-7)

All the nations you have made will come and worship before you, O Lord; they will bring glory to your name. For you are great and do marvelous deeds; you alone are God. (Psalm 86:9-10)

---

[1] George W. Peters, *A Biblical Theology of Missions* (Chicago: Moody Press, 1972), 116.

> The Lord has made his salvation known and revealed his righteousness *to the nations*. He has remembered his love and his faithfulness to the house of Israel; all the ends of the earth have seen the salvation of our God.... Let the sea resound, and everything in it, the world, and *all* who live in it.... He will judge the world in righteousness and the *peoples* with equity. (Psalm 98:2-3, 7, 9)

In one of the most fascinating psalms, written by the sons of Korah, we learn of a unique book that God possesses. Growing up I was familiar with the Lamb's Book of Life mentioned in Revelation 20:12, and even heard sermons about it. Why? Because the Book of Life revolved around me and my personal salvation. The Bible speaks of another book, the Register of the Peoples. I was clueless as to what it was or why it was important. Listen to the words of the sons of Korah and the importance of the Register of the Peoples:

> "I will record Rahab and Babylon among those who acknowledge me—Philistia too, and Tyre, along with Cush—and will say, 'This one was born in Zion.'" Indeed, of Zion it will be said, "This one and that one were born in her, and the Most High himself will establish her." *The Lord will write in the register of the peoples*: "This one was born in Zion." (Psalm 87:4-6)

God is counting. He desires for a representation from every nation to worship Him, and He is keeping track. Babylon has a witness, Philistia as well. Tyre and Cush have been recorded in the Register of the Peoples. They are now in Zion, the kingdom of God. "God registers every distinct ethnic group that has ever existed because He made a promise to Abraham to reach every one of them, and He's going to be faithful in tracking that promise."[2]

A HOUSE FOR ALL PEOPLES

David taught his son Solomon Israel's missionary purpose. Under Solomon Abrahamic promises came to pass: the Promised Land came under Israelite control to the greatest extent, Israel was a great nation, and "The people of Judah and Israel were as numerous as the sand on the seashore" (1 Kings 4:20).[3] It is also under Solomon's kingship that the temple was built (2 Samuel 7:12-13).

As the day approached for Solomon's crowning achievement, the temple of God, to be dedicated, the celebration was nothing shy of elaborate. Solomon stood before the nation of Israel, lifted his hands to the sky, and prayed for the various needs of his people, asking the Lord to be gracious when they cried out to Him. Solomon then, led by the Holy Spirit, anticipated the coming of foreigners to the temple to pray. He prayed,

> **As for the foreigner who does not belong to your people Israel but has come from a distant land because of your name—for men will hear of your great name and your mighty hand and your outstretched arm—when he comes and prays toward this temple, then hear from heaven, your dwelling place, and *do***

---

[2] Bob Sjogren, *Unveiled at Last: Discover God's Hidden Message from Genesis to Revelation* (Seattle, WA: YWAM Publishing, 1992), 34.

[3] Andreas J. Köstenberger and Peter T. O'Brien, *Salvation to the Ends of the Earth: A Biblical Theology of Mission* (Downers Grove, IL: InterVarsity Press, 2001), 40.

whatever the foreigner asks of you, so that *all the peoples of the earth* may know your name and fear you. (1 Kings 8:41-43)

Surely some in his audience got nervous. "Did he just say that when Philistines come from their distant land and pray to our God he wants our God to do whatever they ask? What if we don't like what they pray?" A modern-day equivalent would be if your pastor closed a sermon with, "Father, allow Muslims to come to our church and lift up their requests to You. *Whatever* they ask, we want You to answer—so they will know You are the one true God." No doubt there would be an emergency elder meeting following the service! Solomon rightly perceived the truth that George Peters summarizes, "The temple was God's monument of His relationship to the earth and the accessibility to God by all nations."[4]

Israel's history is littered with people of other nations who were attracted by their example and took steps to experience the blessing of Yahweh (Ruth 1:16-17 and 2 Kings 5:1-19).[5] The encounter between Solomon and the queen of Sheba details one such instance. Solomon knew God had bestowed such abundant blessings on Israel that the nations would come to see God's goodness. "King Solomon was greater in riches and wisdom than all the other kings of the earth. *The whole world* sought audience with Solomon to hear the wisdom God had put in his heart" (1 Kings 10:23-24). The queen traveled 1,200 miles from modern-day Yemen to visit Solomon. She presented him a gift equivalent to $50,000

---

[4] Peters, 117.

[5] Arthur Glasser, *Announcing the Kingdom: The Story of God's Mission in the Bible* (Grand Rapids, MI: Baker Academic, 2003), 63.

(1 Kings 10:10). We are told, "When the queen of Sheba heard about the fame of Solomon and his relation to the name of the Lord, she came to test him with hard questions" (1 Kings 10:1). I wish I could have been a fly on the wall for those sessions. Wouldn't it be great to know what she asked him? Whatever the questions were, we know they were answered in such a way that this Yemeni queen spontaneously declared, "Praise be to the Lord your God, who has delighted in you and placed you on the throne of Israel. Because of the Lord's eternal love for Israel, he has made you king, to maintain justice and righteousness" (1 Kings 10:9). We can be sure that before the queen of Sheba started her journey back to Yemen, Solomon left her with one theme echoing in her head—the same theme he declared over and over again in his book of Proverbs: "The fear of the Lord is the beginning of wisdom" (Proverbs 9:10).

DESCENDING INTO DISOBEDIENCE

The rule of King Solomon represented the high point of Israel's obedience to the call to be a nation that blessed all nations. As previously mentioned, under Solomon they controlled the most land. Under Solomon the temple was constructed. And under Solomon the nations sought Israel's audience. Unfortunately, near the end of Solomon's life, the spiral downward began. His heart no longer remained fully devoted to the one true God (1 Kings 11:4). Israel quickly descended into disobedience, and instead of being a light for the nations, they actually became the prototype of wickedness among them. So along came the prophets.

The prophets can be broken up into three categories:

pre-exilic (those who spoke to the nation before they were taken into exile or captivity), exilic (the prophets who prophesied to the nation during exile), and post-exilic (those who spoke after they were released from bondage).

Pre-exilic: All the prophets had one thing in common. They never stopped reminding Israel's people of their larger purpose—to bless all nations. Here are some reminders to them before they were taken into exile:

> The Lord will be awesome to them when he destroys all the gods of the land. *The nations on every shore* will worship him, everyone in its own land. (Zephaniah 2:11)

> Give thanks to the Lord, call on his name; *make known among the nations* what he has done, and proclaim that his name is exalted. Sing to the Lord, for he has done glorious things; let this be known *to all the world.* (Isaiah 12:4-5)

> *Foreigners* who bind themselves to the Lord to serve him, to love the name of the Lord, and to worship him, all who keep the Sabbath without desecrating it and who hold fast to my covenant—*these I will bring to my holy mountain* and give them joy in my house of prayer. Their burnt offerings and sacrifices will be accepted on my altar; for my house will be called a house of prayer *for all nations.* (Isaiah 56:6-7)

> O Lord, my strength and my fortress, my refuge in time of distress, *to you the nations will come* from the ends of the earth and say, "Our fathers possessed nothing but false gods, worthless idols that did them no good." (Jeremiah 16:19)

One of the most recognizable pre-exilic prophets in the Old Testament is Jonah. Unfortunately, what made him famous was his disobedience to take God's call of repentance to the Ninevites. In the time of Jonah (787 – 746 BC), Israel had become so preoccupied with herself that she lost all desire to be God's kingdom of priests. Jonah refused to deliver God's message to the Ninevites because he felt they did not deserve God's love. The Ninevites were a vicious, shameful, and brutal people known for their violence, and Jonah saw no value in saving them.[6] But God did. God said to Jonah, "Go to the great city of Nineveh and preach against it, because its wickedness has come up before me" (Jonah 1:2). Jonah refused and made famous these three words: "But Jonah ran" (Jonah 1:3). Look at what obeyed God throughout the four chapters of this book: the storm, the lots the sailors cast, the sailors themselves, the big fish, the Ninevites, the vine Jonah sat under, and the worm that ate the vine! Ironically, the prophet of God was the only one who disobeyed Him. The reason for this disobedience was Jonah's frustration that God

The indictment against Israel is that they chose to hoard the blessings and deny the Blesser.

would extend compassion and blessings on the nations and not just on Israel. Some of Jonah's last words were, "I knew that you are a gracious and compassionate God, slow to anger and abounding in love, a God who relents from sending

---

[6] Gary V. Smith, *The Prophets as Preachers: An Introduction to the Hebrew Prophets* (Nashville, TN: Broadman and Holman Publishers, 1994), 90.

calamity" (Jonah 4:2-3). The book of Jonah actually has no conclusion, and the final question of the book has no answer. God reached his goal with Nineveh; they repented. But what about Jonah? Does he ever come to grips with God's goodness extended to others? No one knows. Thomas Carlisle's poem *You Jonah* closes with these lines:

> And Jonah stalked
> To his shaded seat
> And waited for God
> To come around
> To his way of thinking.
> And God is still waiting for a host of Jonahs
> To come around
> To his way of loving.[7]

Jonah shows us the greatest hindrance to the spread of the gospel is not persecution or other religious paradigms, but it is the failure and disobedience of those God has redeemed. Like Jonah we too can be judgmental, lazy, and apathetic, not heeding God's command. Every believer who wants the blessings of salvation but refuses to offer the same opportunity to others may have Jonah as his spiritual father.

The indictment against Israel is that they chose to hoard the blessings and deny the Blesser. The prophet Habakkuk warned that God would raise up a nation to take them into exile. If the nation continued in rebellion against God, consequences were eminent. He warned,

[7] Jonathan Lewis, ed., *World Mission: An Analysis of the World Christian Movement, Part 1: The Biblical Historical Foundation* (Pasadena, CA: William Carey Library, 1987), 39.

Look at the nations and watch—and be utterly amazed. For I am going to do something in your days that you would not believe, even if you were told. *I am raising up the Babylonians*, that ruthless and impetuous people, who sweep across the whole earth to seize dwelling places not their own. (Habakkuk 1:5-6)

Exilic: Between 597 – 581 BC Habakkuk's prophecy came to pass when the Babylonians, led by King Nebuchadnezzar, reduced every town to rubble, including Jerusalem and the temple. Hundreds of thousands were slain and others were taken captive. The nation as a political and religious entity came to an end.[8]

The deeper you move into the Old Testament, the more the vision of worldwide spiritual blessing through Abraham's descendants diminishes in the consciousness of the people of God.[9] Scripture says,

And *wherever they went among the nations* they profaned my holy name, for it was said of them, "These are the Lord's people, and yet they had to leave his land." I had concern for my holy name, which the house of Israel *profaned among the nations* where they had gone. (Ezekiel 36:20-21)

God blessed Israel beyond what they could have asked. He provided for them so they could represent Him to the nations. He gave them offspring, a great name, finances, the priests, the temple, the Law, prophets to guide them, and His presence and protection. He also gave them

---

[8] Glasser, 108.

[9] Glasser, 64.

prime property in the center of the nations to make them more accessible. But they did not care. Yet, despite Israel's rebellion, God's plan would not be thwarted. Ezekiel said,

> This is what the Sovereign Lord says: This is Jerusalem, *which I have set in the center of the nations,* with countries all around her. Yet in her wickedness she has rebelled against my laws and decrees more than the nations and countries around her. She has rejected my laws and has not followed my decrees. (Ezekiel 5:5-6)

While in captivity Shadrach, Meshach, and Abed-nego's devotion to God resulted in King Nebuchadnezzar's declaration to the ends of the earth,

> *To the peoples, nations and men of every language, who live in all the world:* May you prosper greatly! It is my pleasure to tell you about the miraculous signs and wonders that the Most High God has performed for me. How great are his signs, how mighty his wonders! His kingdom is an eternal kingdom; his dominion endures from generation to generation. (Daniel 4:1-3)

The prophets who spoke during the exile assured Israel that God had not abandoned her. God would preserve His plan.

Post-exilic: After release from captivity, the post-exilic prophets reaffirmed the people of the same message, as in the following examples:

> This is what the Lord Almighty says: "*Many peoples* and the inhabitants of many cities will yet come, and the inhabitants

of one city will go to another and say, 'Let us go at once to entreat the Lord and seek the Lord Almighty. I myself am going.' And *many peoples and powerful nations* will come to Jerusalem to seek the Lord Almighty and to entreat him." (Zechariah 8:20-22)

"My name will be great among the nations, from the rising to the setting of the sun. In every place incense and pure offerings will be brought to my name, because *my name will be great among the nations*," says the Lord Almighty. (Malachi 1:11)

My wife and I have spent the last decade traveling to college campuses challenging Christian students to use their degrees to extend God's kingdom throughout the world. At one point, our travels took us to Utah. It just so happened that the same town where we were meeting with believers was also the location of Brigham Young University, the premier institution for Mormonism. While touring the campus, we stumbled upon a chapel service. The auditorium was full. Thousands of people were in attendance! The speaker used biblical passages to challenge the student body to use their talents and gifts for God. He reminded them that they had been blessed for a purpose beyond themselves. I noticed everyone around me was following along and diligently taking notes. The speaker concluded and dismissed the audience. I sat, unable to move and astonished at what I had experienced: thousands in the audience, a challenging message to use your influence, and everyone taking notes. To my amazement, we also learned that 46 percent of the student body will go on a mission trip before they are 25.[10] Whoa ... I was overwhelmed. I was grieved.

Have you ever tried to talk a Mormon out of going on his or her two-year mission trip? It just doesn't happen. Have you ever tried to talk a Christian into going on one? It is incredibly difficult. How is it that Mormons, devoid of the saving truth of Jesus Christ, assume a general obligation to take the teachings of Joseph Smith to the ends of the earth while Christians can be indifferent? As Scott Martin says, "Mormons give two years; Christians give excuses." Granted, the motivation for Mormon missions is entirely different from that of Christian missions. They go in effort to gain merit with God and earn salvation through their good works. We go out of a grateful response to the free gift of salvation. How much more compelled ought we to be?

It is so easy to follow in Israel's disobedience. Our God is so lavish with His blessings that the temptation still today is to happily receive them without a second thought. May we recognize the weight of responsibility that comes with having access to the Word of God while many on the planet do not.

[10] I double-checked this figure from Brigham Young University. Not only is 46 percent accurate, but if you only look at the males who go, the percentage is as high as 78 percent. "Y Facts," *Percentage of Students Who Have Served Missions*. Brigham Young University. Available at yfacts.byu.edu.

CHAPTER 4
MISSIONS IN THE LIFE OF CHRIST

My friend Hudson invited an international student to his home for spring break when he was a college student. The family rolled out the red carpet for this foreigner: cooked a full breakfast every morning, washed and ironed his clothes, and I believe even included him in their family picture! One night this international student did something unexpected: he cleaned up after dinner. Then he started helping every night. Not only that, he also made his own bed and tackled other chores around the house. The family insisted he stop; after all, he was the honored guest. But the international student remained resolute about his desire to contribute in order to feel a part of the family. He could not merely be a recipient. As we transition to the New Testament, we will see that as part of the family of God, we too have a contribution in what God began with Abraham.

The biblical theme of missions continues through the life of Christ, the disciples' ministry, and the early Church. Don't make the mistake of assuming that only minutes before Jesus's ascension He commissioned the disciples just to give them something to do. Actually, quite the opposite is true. If the words of the Great Commission (Matthew 28:18-20) had never been spoken, we would still have a command and responsibility to take part in blessing all nations. Indeed, Jesus's emphasis on the mission of God as seen in the Gospels is but an extension of the theme already established in the Old Testament.

The nations (Gentiles) play a prominent role throughout the entirety of Matthew: the four non-Israelite women mentioned in Jesus's genealogy (Matthew 1), the visit of the magi (Matthew 2:2-12), the healing of the centurion's servant (Matthew 8:5-13), the deliverance of the two demon-possessed men in the district of Gergesenes (Matthew 8:28), the healing of the Canaanite's daughter (Matthew 15:21-28), the feeding of the four thousand Gentiles (Matthew 15:32-39), and the healing of the blind and lame in the Court of the Gentiles (Matthew 21:12-14).[1] His entire ministry, Jesus communicated that God was not just the God of Israel, but equally the God of the nations.

Have you ever wondered what the first words spoken over you were? I think the first words spoken over me were, "Oh … doesn't he look like his father?" A bit anticlimactic. Just after His birth, Joseph and Mary took Jesus to Jerusalem to present Him to God in the temple as the Law required. When they arrived, an old prophet named Simeon saw Joseph, Mary, and the baby and walked intentionally over to them. He took Jesus in his arms,

Missions is not simply on the periphery in the Gospels.

---

[1] David J. Bosch, *Transforming Mission: Paradigm Shifts in Theology of Mission* (MaryKnoll, NY: Orbis Books, 2005), 60.

lifted up his eyes to heaven, and, in the middle of the temple courts, declared, "For my eyes have seen your salvation, which you have prepared in the sight of all people, *a light for revelation to the Gentiles* and for glory to your people Israel" (Luke 2:30-32). Translation: the Gentile nations will be drawn to the grace God will provide. This Child will be a Servant of the Lord who brings salvation to all nations.

THE BEGINNING OF HIS MINISTRY

Missions is not simply on the periphery in the Gospels. Jesus began His ministry by going into the desert for forty days and being tempted by Satan. Afterward, He went to Nazareth, His hometown, and entered the synagogue as was His custom. The leaders handed the scroll of the prophet Isaiah to Him and He read, "The Spirit of the Lord is on me, because he has anointed me to preach good news to the poor. He has sent me to proclaim freedom for the prisoners and recovery of sight for the blind, to release the oppressed, to proclaim the year of the Lord's favor" (Luke 4:18-19). Astonished, all in the synagogue spoke well of Him. Jesus continued,

> I assure you that there were many widows in Israel in Elijah's time, when the sky was shut for three and a half years and there was a severe famine throughout the land. Yet Elijah was not sent to any of them, but to a widow in Zarephath in the region of Sidon. And there were many in Israel with leprosy in the time of Elisha the prophet, yet not one of them was cleansed—only Naaman the Syrian. (Luke 4:25-27)

After reading this passage do you have a sudden urge to throw someone off a cliff? Honestly, I don't. So why did they get so mad? What in these words caused the spontaneous rage of those in the synagogue? "All the people in the synagogue were furious when they heard this. They got up, drove him out of the town, and took him to the brow of the hill ... in order to throw him down the cliff" (Luke 4:28-29).

The core of Jesus's message communicated that God's redemptive purpose was not solely tied to Israel. He explained that it was not for lack of Israelite need that God sent His prophets to minister in Zarephath—approximately 100 miles north of Israel—and in Syria. No, God skipped over these needs in order to intentionally reach out to the nations. To those in the synagogue, this was blasphemous! Yahweh blessing non-Israelite nations was an unfathomable concept, and they wanted nothing to do with it, nor would they tolerate its promotion. His hearers grabbed Jesus and took Him to one of the highest cliffs in Nazareth, hoping to throw Him off, yet, "He walked right through the crowd and went on his way" (Luke 4:30). Jesus's mission and the mission He was calling the disciples to was global. His purpose was clear.

We find this global message reiterated as Jesus's earthly ministry drew to a close. One week before the cross, He tried to prepare the disciples for the imminent destruction of the temple and persecution of Israel. This prompted the disciples to ask a question and, as He commonly did, Jesus answered it in a bigger context. Matthew relates, "As Jesus was sitting on the Mount of Olives, the disciples came to him privately. 'Tell us,' they said, 'when will this happen, and what will be the sign of your coming and of the end of the age?'" (Matthew 24:13). Jesus replied that there would be an increase in wars, false prophets, famines, earthquakes, and persecution (Matthew 24:4-12). However, in keeping with the promise to Abraham, He answers the question by saying, "And this gospel of the kingdom will be preached in the whole world as a testimony to all nations, and then the end will come" (Matthew 24:14; see also Mark 13:10). Christopher Wright explains, "Jesus is not setting a timetable; he is simply stating an order of events that lies within the prophesied plan of God."[2] In light of this being the end goal, missions should not be reduced to the March missions minute or something the Church does in its free time. Instead it is the heart of the gospel and the very sign of the approaching end when Christ will return and set all things new. The missionary movement stands uniquely within an end-times context, and only when it has been completed to His satisfaction will the end come.

THE GREAT COMMISSION TEXTS

In light of all the stories and similarities in the Gospels, it is hard to imagine there are only three events recorded by all four gospel writers. How important was the virgin birth? I'd say it's pretty important in showing Jesus as the God-man, yet only Matthew and Luke record it. What about the Mount of Transfiguration where Peter, James, and John witness the full, unveiled deity of Christ and hear the Father speaking audibly to Jesus? John's gospel leaves this story out completely. The only three things found in all four gospels

---

[2] Christopher J. H. Wright, *The Mission of God: Unlocking the Bible's Grand Narrative* (Downers Grove, IL: InterVarsity Press, 2006), 511.

are the feeding of the five thousand, the crucifixion, and the commissioning of the disciples.

It is important to understand that the term "Great Commission" does not refer to one single passage (Matthew 28:18-20); instead, it designates an entire range of passages found elsewhere in the Gospels. Jesus actually never used the phrase "Great Commission." Neither did the apostle Paul or, for that matter, William Carey, who sailed to India in 1793. Actually A. T. Pierson coined the term in 1893 in his book *The Divine Enterprise of Missions.* Pierson, a prominent mission spokesman in the nineteenth century, used the term to encompass all five of the commission texts (Matthew 28:18-20, Mark 16:15, Luke 24:46-48, John 20:21, and Acts 1:8), not just the one in Matthew.[3] Each commission communicates a key idea. In Matthew it is to *make disciples*, in Mark it is to *preach*, in Luke the key idea is *witness*. In John, it is *being sent.* And in Acts it is the *power of the Holy Spirit.*

The first and most well known Great Commission text is Matthew's, which reads,

> Then Jesus came to them and said, "All authority in heaven and on earth has been given to me. Therefore go and make disciples of all nations, baptizing them in the name of the Father and of the Son and of the Holy Spirit, and teaching them to obey everything I have commanded you. And surely I am with you always, to the very end of the age." (Matthew 28:18-20)

Those who are familiar with this passage may be tempted to skip the first part of the passage and move straight

---

[3] Arthur Tappan Pierson, *The Divine Enterprise of Missions* (London: Hodder and Stoughton, 1893), 20.

to the "Go." However, before the Great Commission comes the Great Foundation, which represents the theological basis the Great Commission texts are built upon: "All authority in heaven and earth has been given to me." No one else in history can claim to have all authority, and when He who possesses it speaks, He should be obeyed. The emphasis of this passage is on making disciples (one word in Greek—*matheteuo*) and is supported by three specific actions: going, baptizing, and teaching. Because of the form these verbs take, it is as if Jesus is saying, "As you are going ... make disciples, as you are baptizing ... make disciples, as you are teaching ... make disciples." One of the most striking observations about the passage is that the disciples are not to focus only on making disciples of just *individuals,* but of entire *nations,* and *all* nations. This is as startling as it is grand! How can the disciples be expected to embark on a job of this magnitude? Surely this is a hopeless ambition beyond man's reach. But, the passage ends with the Great Promise: Jesus will actually be with the disciples, and with us.[4] Based on the authoritative foundation, we have our commission as well as the promise of His abiding presence.

---

[4] Mission scholar Peter Kuzmic should be attributed with the observation regarding the three-part understanding—Great Foundation, Great Commission, and Great Promise.

[5] It is a common understanding among scholars that the original ending of Mark was lost or simply never written. The thought is that the early church added Mark 16:9-20 to make the ending less abrupt. It is beyond the scope of this book to provide a detailed argument either for or against Mark's anonymous ending. For more information regarding the argument for the authenticity of the ending, Samuel Zwemer designates an entire chapter to the debate in his book *Into All the World.* Samuel Zwemer, *Into All the World* (Grand Rapids, MI: Zondervan, 1943), 69-86. See also Arthur Glasser, *Announcing the Kingdom: The Story of God's Mission in the Bible* (Grand Rapids, MI: Baker Academic, 2003), 232-233.

Mark's Great Commission text mirrors his gospel's message: "Proclaiming the good news of God" (Mark 1:14). Mark quotes Jesus saying, "Go into all the world and preach the good news to all creation. Whoever believes and is baptized will be saved, but whoever does not believe will be condemned" (Mark 16:15-16).[5] The emphasis in this commission is preaching. Mark clarifies the breadth of who should be preached to—*all creation.* This reveals the all-encompassing nature of God's glory, since not only should all mankind praise Him, but all creation as well. The passage continues to explain that those who reject this good news will not simply be less satisfied with life, but will be condemned.

The gospel of Luke presents yet another angle on the commission. His emphasis is on fulfillment, as seen in the following passage:

> He said to them, … "Everything *must be fulfilled* that is written about me in the Law of Moses, the Prophets and the Psalms." Then he opened their minds so they could understand the Scriptures. He told them, *"This is what is written: The Christ will suffer and rise from the dead on the third day, and repentance and forgiveness of sins will be preached in his name to all nations, beginning at Jerusalem. You are witnesses* of these things. I am going to send you what my Father has promised; but stay in the city until you have been *clothed with power* from on high." (Luke 24:44-49)

Jesus states that His ministry is in conjunction with and fulfills the prophecies of the Old Testament. He does not quote any specific verse from the Old Testament but claims that all of Scripture "finds its focus and fulfillment *both* in

The Church's mission is in the context of the entire Bible.

the life, death, and resurrection of Israel's Messiah, *and* in the mission to all nations."[6]

Luke reveals continuity between the Great Commission and all the rest of Scripture when he quotes Jesus saying, "Everything must be fulfilled that is written about me in the Law of Moses, the Prophets and the Psalms" (Luke 24:44). This is the heart of the gospel message. This is the *misseo Dei*—the sending of God. The Church's mission is in the context of the entire Bible. A. T. Pierson stated, "It seems ... that if, at the outset, we desire to grasp the divine idea of missions, here we shall find our starting point toward the most advanced goal. It is like God to be simple; and in that one word, *witness*, is condensed the whole wisdom of God as to this worldwide work."[7] A final unique emphasis of Luke's commission is the importance of the Holy Spirit. The warning to the disciples is not to go out on their own but to wait until the power of the Holy Spirit comes on them. The Spirit drives missions.

John refers to Jesus as the *sent One* forty times in his gospel.[8] On the actual fortieth time, something interesting happens—Jesus looks at the disciples and sends them. He says, "Peace be with you! As the Father has sent me, I am

---

[6] Wright, 29-30.

[7] Pierson, 25.

[8] For a few references to Jesus as the *sent One,* see John 4:34; 5:24; 6:38; 7:16, 28, 33; 8:26; 12:44-45; 13:20; 15:21. Timothy C. Tennent, *Invitation to World Missions: A Trinitarian Missiology for the Twenty-first Century* (Grand Rapids, MI: Kregel, 2010), 155.

sending you" (John 20:21). Just as Christ was sent from the Father, so now the Church is sent out to continue the mission. Jesus was the ultimate sent One. He knew the Father intimately (John 7:29), and He lived in close relationship with Him (John 8:16). He desired to do the Father's will (John 4:34), the Father's work (John 5:36), and speak the Father's words (John 3:34). He followed the Father's example (John 13:16) and bore witness to Him (John 12:44-45).[9] Jesus's life provides a blueprint for His followers. In John 20:21 Jesus sends the disciples (and us)! The question is not *if* we are sent but *where!* The authors of *Salvation to the Ends of the Earth* state,

> Jesus' followers are to embody the qualities characteristic of their Lord during his earthly mission. As Jesus did his Father's will, they have to do *Jesus'* will. As Jesus did his Father's works, they have to do *Jesus'* works. As Jesus spoke the words of his Father, they have to speak *Jesus'* words. Their relationship to their sender, Jesus, is to reflect Jesus' relationship with *his* sender.[10]

Jesus gave the final Great Commission text before He ascended to heaven as recorded in the book of Acts. In light of Luke and Acts being written by the same person, the related emphasis in both accounts should be no surprise. The gospel of Luke highlights the disciples' role as witnesses empowered by the Holy Spirit. Similar terminology is used in the book of Acts, which quotes Jesus saying, "But you

---

[9] Andreas J. Köstenberger and Peter T. O'Brien, *Salvation to the Ends of the Earth: A Biblical Theology of Mission* (Downers Grove, IL: InterVarsity Press, 2001), 209.

[10] Köstenberger and O'Brien, 222.

will *receive power* when the Holy Spirit comes on you; and you *will be my witnesses* in Jerusalem, and in all Judea and Samaria, and to the ends of the earth" (Acts 1:8).

The final command the disciples heard their Lord give implied that the message of salvation would move out and gradually affect all. Darrell Bock, a leading scholar on the book of Acts, suggests, "The church exists, in major part, to extend the apostolic witness to Jesus everywhere. In fact, the church does not *have* a mission; it is to be missional and *is* a mission."[11] It is of this end that we must never lose sight—it's the theme of the rest of the New Testament!

COMMISSIONED ON DIFFERENT OCCASIONS

In college I read the Great Commission texts in Matthew, Mark, Luke, and John and assumed they all referenced one single account. Upon further study I realized a truth that made the commissions even more compelling: there were at least three different commissions! In Matthew's account we read, "Then the eleven disciples went to Galilee, to the mountain where Jesus had told them to go" (Matthew 28:16). All the events leading up to Christ's death and resurrection took place in Jerusalem. It would have taken the disciples at least a few days (if not weeks) to make their way north to Galilee; therefore, this could not have happened on the night of the resurrection when Mark, Luke, and John's Great Commission texts take place. Theirs all occurred in Jerusalem. The Acts account took place south of Galilee on the Mount

---

[11] Darrell Bock, *Acts* (Grand Rapids, MI: Baker Academic, 2007), 66.

of Olives, and immediately following this commission Jesus ascended to the Father. Timothy Tennent explains,

> Not only is the language between the accounts remarkably distinct, but they are also set in diverse settings. This means that Jesus repeats various versions of the Great Commission in various places, with different emphases. Matthew's commission takes place in Galilee some weeks after the Resurrection.... Mark's commission has distinctive language not shared by any of the other Gospels. Luke's and John's commissions both occur in Jerusalem on the very night after the Resurrection. Interestingly, although Luke's and John's commissions occur on the same night, there is not a single verbal overlap between the two, which means that they are distinct sayings of Christ. The commission in Acts takes place forty days after the Resurrection in Bethany, not in Jerusalem.[12]

The last few hours spent with those you love are sacred. No words fall to the floor. The context of death sharpens the mind, and those who hear those final words vividly recall them for the rest of their lives. Recently my oldest sister passed away. Every time I have seen my mother since then, she has reminded me of Theresa's last words to her. I'm confident my mother is constantly assured and comforted by them. Jesus, before he departed from the earth, inspired in the hearts of His disciples one mission—the same mission God gave to Abraham, Isaac, and Jacob—to bless all nations. Just as my sister's memory is felt and her heart is revealed by her last words, so in the hearts of those who

---

[12] Tennent, 129.

love Him, Jesus's last words should carry such significance, sustaining us daily in purpose.

A new marine recruit arrived at boot camp.[13] Before the recruit put his bags down, the drill sergeant ordered all in the platoon to line up. At the top of his lungs the sergeant yelled, "Forward march!" A few hundred yards into the march, the sergeant looked back to check the recruits. One had not moved. Rubbing his eyes in disbelief, he sprinted back to the stagnant recruit. "Boy, did you hear me when I said 'forward march'?" The recruit shouted, "Yes, sir!" The officer yelled back, "Then kindly tell me why in the world you haven't budged?" The young man looked right in the eyes of the commanding sergeant and said, "You didn't call my name."

Jesus reiterated our marching orders—not once, not twice, but throughout His life. Yet, how many in God's Church stand stagnant, waiting to hear their name? The Great Commission is reduced to the Great Suggestion. Indeed if you have been taught that God's missional heart is revealed once in Scripture, in the Great Commission of Matthew 28, then it *is* merely a suggestion! What we have seen, however, is the Old Testament and the Gospels teem with this truth: God's purpose is to reach all nations. So far, from the biblical evidence we have surveyed, God has orchestrated each event toward the completion of His promise. Let's look now to the Epistles and the Church's early foundation to see how the apostles carry on the mission God set in motion with Abraham.

---

[13] This story is adapted from John Willis Zumwalt, *Passion for the Heart of God* (Choctaw, OK: HGM Publishing, 2000), 70.

CHAPTER 5
MISSIONS IN THE EARLY CHURCH

My wife and I spent two weeks crisscrossing Sweden speaking about missions. The night before our departure, I was packing our bags and noticed the news report on the TV. A volcano had just erupted in Iceland. I think I yawned and flipped to the sports channel. Early the next morning, as we left for our flight, the hotel manager informed us the airport was closed. Actually, all of Europe's airports were shut down due to the volcanic ash that was slowly making its way across the continent. Seven million travelers were stranded without hope. I was a statistic. Initially the reports indicated planes would not be allowed in the air for a month. Then we started hearing about the possibility of a second eruption from the neighboring volcano, Mount Katla. This eruption would dwarf the first one. In the past the smaller eruption had triggered Mount Katla, and if it were to blow again, there would literally be a worldwide climate change. Ash would float in global airspace for over a year![1] Sweden would become my new home. Luckily, no second eruption occurred and, after being stuck almost

---

[1] Doug York, "Eyjafjallajökull Is Considered a Small Volcano? What Happens If the Big One Erupts?" April 17, 2010. Available at news.gather.com.

two weeks, we made it home. As we look at missions in the early Church, we see a similar chain reaction. When Cornelius encountered the gospel in Acts 10, an eruption shook his culture, setting off a second, much larger explosion. As a result the Church experienced a climate change that is still felt today!

The Holy Spirit descended at Pentecost in Acts 2, and the people of God were filled with power. Peter preached public sermons to a Jewish audience and thousands joined the church (Acts 2:22-41; 3:12). This fulfilled what Jesus had stated in Acts 1:8, "You will be my witnesses *in Jerusalem*, and in all Judea and Samaria, and to the ends of the earth." The second move of the gospel commanded here (to Judea and Samaria) was fulfilled after the first martyr, Stephen, was killed in Acts 7. "On that day a great persecution broke out against the church at Jerusalem, and all except the apostles were scattered throughout Judea and Samaria" (Acts 8:1). At this point the disciples began to comprehend more regarding the mission of God. Their understanding of Christ's desire to reach all nations continued to mature as the book of Acts progresses.

In accordance with the Acts 1:8 commissioning, we should naturally see the gospel going forth next to the nations. Picking up in Acts 10, we are introduced to Cornelius and the first eruption that achieves a step toward Gentile peoples. Cornelius was not a Jew, but he definitely fell into the category "God-fearer" (Acts 10:2). Darrell Bock explains, "Cornelius has not become a full Jewish proselyte but as a Gentile has been exposed to the God of Israel. The description means that he has responded positively to this exposure without embracing in any detailed way elements of Jewish legal practice.... This openness to Judaism would be rare among such soldiers."[2] He gave generously to the poor, fasted, and prayed regularly. God heard his prayers. In response to the vision, Cornelius sent emissaries to retrieve Peter. Peter, being a devout Jew, would find it impossible to enter a non-Jewish home. So, God prepared Peter's heart for the encounter by giving him a vision that culminated with God saying, "Do not call anything impure that God has made clean" (Acts 10:15).

When Peter entered Cornelius's house, he reminded him, "You are well aware that it is against our law for a Jew to associate with a Gentile or visit him. But God has shown me that I should not call any man impure or unclean. So when I was sent for, I came without raising any objection. May I ask why you sent for me?" (Acts 10:28-29). This is a totally different Peter than the man who so passionately preached to thousands of Jews in Acts 2. Now he's confused and far from his comfort zone. Christopher Wright suggests,

> It took angels and visions, however, to move Peter beyond theological conviction to practical action. A worldview shaped by a lifetime lived within the rules of Jewish food laws and the paradigm of segregation they symbolized was not easily set aside.... Peter had long ago confessed Jesus as "the Christ, the Son of the living God" and understood something of the universal significance of that. But it was only through the encounter with Cornelius and his testimony that he was

---

[2] Darrell Bock, *Acts* (Grand Rapids, MI: Baker Academic, 2007), 386.

converted to the recognition that "God does not show favoritism but accepts people from every nation" (Acts 10:34-35).[3]

Cornelius shared his vision with Peter about the angel who appeared and prompted him to summon Peter (Acts 10:30-33). According to Acts, "Then Peter began to speak: 'I now realize how true it is that God does not show favoritism but accepts men from every nation who fear him and do what is right'" (Acts 10:34-35). The Holy Spirit fell on the household of Cornelius. The story continues, "Then Peter said, 'Can anyone keep these people from being baptized with water? They have received the Holy Spirit just as we have'" (Acts 10:46-47). This meeting between Peter and Cornelius was equally monumental for both men. The world was now different. Lesslie Newbigin, author of the missions theology book *The Open Secret,* writes,

At the end of the story, which runs from Acts 10:1 to 11:18, the church itself became a kind of society different from what it was before Peter and Cornelius met. It had been a society enclosed within the cultural world of Israel; it became something radically different, a society that spanned the enormous gulf between Jew and pagan and was open to embrace all the nations that had been outside the covenant by which Israel lived.[4]

---

[3] Christopher J. H. Wright, *The Mission of God: Unlocking the Bible's Grand Narrative* (Downers Grove, IL: InterVarsity Press, 2006), 515.

[4] Lesslie Newbigin, *The Open Secret:An Introduction to the Theology of Mission* (Grand Rapids, MI: Eerdmans, 1995), 60.

THE SECOND VOLCANO ERUPTS

The encounter between Peter and Cornelius cracked open the door for a new face of the people of God. But over the next few chapters of Acts, the door will be blown off its hinges! A second monstrous volcano erupts to cause a climate shift among God's people. We are not even given the names of those responsible, although we do know their work:

> Now those who had been scattered by the persecution in connection with Stephen traveled as far as Phoenicia, Cyprus and Antioch, telling the message only to Jews. *Some of them,* however, men from Cyprus and Cyrene, went to Antioch and *began to speak to Greeks also*, telling them the good news about the Lord Jesus. (Acts 11:19-20)

Christians in Jerusalem fled their homes because of the persecution and traveled to Phoenicia, Cyprus, and Antioch. They began sharing Christ with Jews. Some of them, however, these unnamed trailblazers, took a risk and went to Antioch and spoke to the Greeks about Jesus. In the previous story, Cornelius feared God. Even though he was not a Jew, he followed Jewish customs: fasting, praying, and giving to those in need. The step of faith for him to trust Christ was smaller than those unfamiliar with these customs. The Greeks, for example, had no concept of the Jewish traditions.[5] If it was difficult for Peter to approach Cornelius, who was at least familiar with their religious rituals, consider now the greater leap of faith for these unknown men and women

---

[5] F. F. Bruce, *The Book of Acts* (Grand Rapids, MI: Eerdmans Publishing, 1988), 225.

to go to those who were totally removed from Jewish culture! Yet, the groundbreaking mission was a success. "The Lord's hand was with them, and a great number of people believed and turned to the Lord" (Acts 11:21). The Greeks attempted to find meaning through wisdom, cults, and pagan gods, which all fell short. Early Christ followers told them how the Son of God had become man and conquered the grave. Some believed. This marked the beginning of the full-scale conversion of the Greek (or Gentile) world. This momentous step forward marks a critical event in Christian history. The Church henceforth would never look the same.

The emergence of both Jewish and Greek believers created internal conflict, however. The Greek believers did not value circumcision. They did not care about the future of the nation of Israel. They had no attachment to the temple of the past or to observing the Sabbath. These issues became problematic because the predominance of Gentiles in the church at Antioch made it impossible to categorize it as a messianic movement within Judaism.[6] Something had to change in describing this community. It is no wonder that in Antioch the community of believers is first called *Christians* (Acts 11:26). A new name was necessary to describe this new people of God! As Andrew Walls, author of *The Cross -Cultural Process in Christian History*, observes,

> In principle, the fact that Gentiles would be saved was not very new, or very secret; Jews had always believed that the other nations would be blessed by means of Israel's Messiah. The

---

[6] Timothy C. Tennent, *Invitation to World Missions: A Trinitarian Missiology for the Twenty-first Century* (Grand Rapids, MI: Kregel, 2010), 438.

novel element, strikingly, indeed devastatingly, demonstrated in the impact of the gospel ... was the sheer scale of Gentile salvation, the huge significance of the Gentiles' role in the story of Israel.[7]

REACHING ALL THE WAY BACK

The disciples did not quote the Great Commission in any form for the rest of the New Testament. How is that possible? They were the last words of Christ, repeated at least three different times, and yet not one time do they even refer to it from Acts 2 through Revelation. The reason is that the apostles did not see their commission as having its origin in those last words of Christ. They knew the mandate stretched further back. It began with Abraham! This is the case they brought to bear on their audiences when they challenged them to heed God's global cause. Consider the following:

Next to Christ, Abraham is the most important figure in Paul's understanding of the gospel.

And you are heirs of the prophets and of the covenant God made with your fathers. He said to Abraham, "Through your offspring all peoples on earth will be blessed." (Acts 3:25)

---

[7] Andrew Walls, *The Cross-Cultural Process in Christian History: Studies in the Transmission and Appropriation of Faith* (Maryknoll, NY: Orbis Press, 2002), 75.

He is the father of us all. As it is written: "I have made you a father of many nations." He is our father in the sight of God, in whom he believed—the God who gives life to the dead and calls things that are not as though they were. (Romans 4:16-17)

When God made his promise to Abraham, since there was no one greater for him to swear by, he swore by himself, saying, "I will surely bless you and give you many descendants." And so after waiting patiently, Abraham received what was promised. (Hebrews 6:13-15)

Next to Christ, Abraham is the most important figure in Paul's understanding of the gospel.[8] God's promise to Abraham guided Paul's mission. In one of the most straightforward passages connecting the Church to the Abrahamic blessing, Paul states in Galatians,

The Scripture foresaw that God would justify the Gentiles by faith, and announced the gospel in advance to Abraham: "All nations will be blessed through you."… He redeemed us in order that the blessing given to Abraham might come to the Gentiles through Christ Jesus, so that by faith we might receive the promise of the Spirit. (Galatians 3:8, 14)

Paul reminds the Galatians that the reason for their redemption was to extend the blessing to the nations.

The commission to reach the nations finds its foundation not in the life of Christ, or in the establishment of the

---

[8] Christopher J. H. Wright, *The Mission of God's People: A Biblical Theology of the Church's Mission* (Grand Rapids, MI: Zondervan Publishing, 2010), 75.

Church, but in the institution of God's plan in Genesis—the very beginning of the plot. The authors of the New Testament stood on the solid ground of the Hebrew Scripture and on over two thousand years of history as they sought to prove to their readers the responsibility of all to bless the nations.

A MISSIONARY LETTER

Romans is Paul's masterpiece. Martin Luther called it "the most important document in the New Testament."[9] Mostly seen as a theological treatise of the Christian faith, Romans reveals the lostness of man and the goodness of God. During Paul's third missionary journey, it was becoming apparent that his work in the eastern Mediterranean was ending.[10] He wanted to make his way to Spain (the equivalent to the ends of the earth in his day), and Rome was one of the few places that could provide a needed base of operations. Paul wrote to the Roman church hoping that they would accept and support his missionary endeavors.

Paul began with his calling, saying, "Paul, a servant of Christ Jesus, called to be an apostle and set apart for the gospel of God ... Through him and for his name's sake, we received grace and apostleship to call people from among *all the Gentiles* to the obedience that comes from faith" (Romans 1:1, 5). For Paul, individual salvation was linked to a general obligation to reach all nations (Gentiles) for Christ.

---

[9] John Dillenberger, ed., *Martin Luther: Selections from His Writings* (Garden City, NY: Anchor Books, 1961), 19.

[10] Arthur Glasser, *Announcing the Kingdom: The Story of God's Mission in the Bible* (Grand Rapids, MI: Baker Academic, 2003), 321.

Unfortunately, today there is a tendency to separate the call of salvation from passing it on to the nations. Erwin McManus, in his book *An Unstoppable Force,* relates his experience growing as a new Christian. After his decision to follow Christ, he was faced with another altar call—a calling to Lordship. A few weeks later, there was another altar call—a calling to the ministry. After that, two more "calls"—a calling for home ministry and a calling to foreign ministry. He explains:

> So now I had discovered five levels of callings from God—a calling to be saved, a calling for Jesus to be Lord, a calling to ministry, a calling to home missions, and a calling to foreign missions…. Why are there so many levels of Christian calling in our contemporary Christian community? Where are they found in the biblical text? I have a strange suspicion that the nuances of these "callings" have less to do with theology and more to do with the condition of the church. Paul seemed to think there was only *one* calling…. The one call is to lay your life at the feet of Jesus and to do whatever he asks.[11]

In Romans chapters 1–8, Paul covers incredible theological ground for his Jewish readers to prove that salvation is for all nations, not just the Jews. In Romans 9 he reminds Israel that God indeed chose them for a special purpose—not to be an end in themselves, but for the purpose of extending worldwide blessing. He quotes the Lord, saying, "I will call them 'my people' who are not my people; and I will call her 'my loved one' who is not my loved one" (Romans 9:25; see

---

[11] Erwin Raphael McManus, *An Unstoppable Force: Daring to Become the Church God Had in Mind* (Loveland, CO: Group Publishing, 2001), 201.

also Hosea 2:23). Paul encourages the church at Rome to be faithful as messengers of the good news, stating,

> How, then, can they call on the one they have not believed in? And how can they believe in the one of whom they have not heard? And how can they hear without someone preaching to them? And how can they preach unless they are sent? As it is written, "How beautiful are the feet of those who bring good news!" (Romans 10:14-15)

The final chapters deal with practical matters concerning spiritual life, but Paul does not close the letter without making the Roman church decide if they will be a part of his mission to take the gospel to Spain. True to form, Paul reaches back to the Old Testament to prove and to celebrate the fulfillment of God's promise to Abraham. "Therefore I will praise you among the Gentiles; I will sing hymns to your name.... Rejoice, O Gentiles, with his people.... Praise the Lord, all you Gentiles, and sing praises to him, all you peoples.... The Root of Jesse will spring up, one who will arise to rule over the nations; the Gentiles will hope in him" (Romans 15:9-12; Paul quoting Psalm 18:49; Deuteronomy 32:43; Psalm 117:1; Isaiah 11:10). Then he challenges the church at Rome, saying,

> So from Jerusalem all the way around to Illyricum, I have fully proclaimed the gospel of Christ. It has always been my ambition to preach the gospel where Christ was not known, so that I would not be building on someone else's foundation.... I urge you, brothers, by our Lord Jesus Christ and by the love of the Spirit, to join me in my struggle. (Romans 15:19-20, 30)

From the beginning of this great letter to its conclusion, one thing presses on Paul's heart: "That all nations might believe and obey him—to the only wise God be glory forever through Jesus Christ! Amen" (Romans 16:26-27). Romans has rightly been extolled as one of the greatest doctrinal pieces of literature ever written. No doubt one of its most valued elements is its missional theme. Steve Hawthorne echoes Paul's heart and ambition when he says, "You can do something other than working with God in His purpose, but it will always be something lesser, and you couldn't come up with something better."

THE MYSTERY REVEALED

In Ephesians Paul speaks of the mystery of God that is now made known. He proclaims, "In reading this, then, you will be able to understand my insight into the mystery of Christ, which was not made known to men in other generations as it has now been revealed by the Spirit to God's holy apostles and prophets" (Ephesians 3:4-5). What is this mystery? For two thousand years the Jews had known God's plan to bless the nations; this was *not* so puzzling. The mystery, however, lies in the fact that the Gentiles would be brought into *unity* with God's chosen people. Paul explains, "This mystery is that through the gospel the Gentiles are heirs together with Israel, members together of one body, and sharers together in the promise in Christ Jesus" (Ephesians 3:6). Bill Stearns elaborates, "God's chosen Hebrew–Jewish people would not only pass on His blessing but would have as fellow family members those from every tribe, tongue, and nation who were saved by grace. This equal status was uncomfortable news; this was a head-scratching mystery."[12] Paul challenged the Ephesians to embrace this truth, to be unified in their diversity, and to be active in outreach to all peoples as they function as one body.[13]

The authors of the Epistles took passages of the Old Testament and made personal and present-day application to the mission of the Church. When Paul and Barnabas were in Pisidian Antioch, they took the Old Testament promise of the Messiah from Isaiah 49:6 and expounded the Church's corresponding responsibility, saying, "For this is what the Lord has commanded us: 'I have made you a light for the Gentiles, that you may bring salvation to the ends of the earth.' When the Gentiles heard this, they were glad and honored the word of the Lord" (Acts 13:47-48). Peter also recalled when God told the people of Israel in Exodus 19:3-6 that they were to be a royal priesthood and a holy nation.[14] He wrote of the Church's duty to be the same, saying, "But you are a chosen people, a royal priesthood, a holy nation, a people belonging to God, that you may declare the praises of him who called you out of darkness into his wonderful light" (1 Peter 2:9).

---

[12] Bill Stearns and Amy Stearns, *20/20 Vision: Practical Ways Individuals and Churches Can Be Involved* (Minneapolis, MN: Bethany House, 2005), 145-146.

[13] Andrew Walls, Professor Emeritus of the Study of Christianity in the Non-Western World at the University of Edinburgh, has explored this "Ephesians Moment" thoroughly in his book *The Cross-Cultural Process in Christian History.*

[14] Then Moses went up to God, and the LORD called to him from the mountain and said, "This is what you are to say to the house of Jacob and what you are to tell the people of Israel: 'You yourselves have seen what I did to Egypt, and how I carried you on eagles' wings and brought you to myself. Now if you obey me fully and keep my covenant, then out of all nations you will be my treasured possession. Although the whole earth is mine, you will be for me a kingdom of priests and a holy nation.'" (Exodus 19:3-6)

We all have a part to play in extending salvation to the nations. John reminds us, "He is the atoning sacrifice for our sins, and not only for ours but also for the sins of the whole world" (1 John 2:2). Salvation has come to us because it's on its way to someone else. Unfortunately, much like Israel, today's Church forgets and, at times, rejects its identity as God's distinct people, His mediator to the nations.[15] Thankfully, the Epistles offer consistent reminders of and insight into our role as the Church in participation with the *misseo Dei*. May each believer draw strength from the Epistles to become "a workman who does not need to be ashamed and who correctly handles the word of truth" (2 Timothy 2:15). Finally, our assurance that God's plan will be fulfilled is found in Revelation.

REVELATION — THE CONCLUSION

We've made it through the plot of Scripture and find ourselves at the conclusion. The book of Revelation gives us a peek behind the curtain as John writes from the vantage point of God's throne. In God's right hand is a scroll which no one is found worthy to open. Then Christ, portrayed as the Lamb, takes the scroll.

> Then I saw a Lamb, looking as if it had been slain, standing in the center of the throne.... He came and took the scroll from the right hand of him who sat on the throne. And when he had taken it, the four living creatures and the twenty-four elders

[15] Gailyn Van Rheenen, *Missions: Biblical Foundations and Contemporary Strategies* (Grand Rapids, MI: Zondervan Publishing, 1996), 30.

fell down before the Lamb. Each one had a harp and they were holding golden bowls full of incense, which are the prayers of the saints. (Revelation 5:6-8)

Immediately the living creatures and elders explain to John,

And they sang a new song: "You are worthy to take the scroll and to open its seals, because you were slain, and with your blood you purchased men for God from every tribe and language and people and nation. You have made them to be a kingdom and priests to serve our God, and they will reign on the earth." (Revelation 5:9-10)

This song echoes all the way back to the beginning of Scripture, testifying to the consistency of the worldwide purpose of salvation God initiated with Abraham. Three elements point us back to Genesis 12: First, God's purpose is *redemptive*—Jesus' death rescues a people for God. Second, it is *universal*—people come from "every tribe and language and people and nation." Finally, it is *victorious*—the redeemed will reign on earth![16] The climax of this vision is a worshipping multicultural host in the fulfillment of the Abrahamic Revolution.

After this I looked and there before me was a great multitude that no one could count, from every nation, tribe, people and language, standing before the throne and in front of the Lamb. They were wearing white robes and were holding palm

---

[16] Wright, *The Mission of God,* 250.

branches in their hands. And they cried out in a loud voice: "Salvation belongs to our God, who sits on the throne, and to the Lamb." (Revelation 7:9-10)

John saw them in unity, but also in their particularity. Every culture was there, and he recognized this. What God began in Genesis we see fulfilled in Revelation! God will do it. A representation from every nation, tribe, people, and language will bow and worship at His feet. God is a missionary God, and from cover to cover of the Bible, He reveals and invites us into His mission. Will you join His revolution and participate with Him in drawing men and women from every people group to His throne?

God is a missionary God, and from cover to cover of the Bible, He reveals and invites us into His mission.

For better or worse, "missions people" almost always have a reputation. It's because missions is something typically associated with a great deal of passion, which is manifested in various ways—sleeping on the floor, going barefoot, dogs named after missionaries, canned-food drives, world-map wallpaper, you name it. In my experience, when passion comes first, it fades. It's dependent on the next thing—the upcoming retreat, missions speaker, or the next short-term trip. It's an incessant effort to keep the drive alive. People led by passion prove inconsistent at best in their missions vision. Passion has its place, and that is grounded in the foundation of God's Word.

The sixty-six books of the Bible bleed God's heart for the world. If we want to be consistent in our purpose to reach the nations, it's going to have to come from God and the Word. That's why we have started with Scripture. So saturate yourself with the biblical foundation of His purpose, His passion, and His promise—and then go plaster the world map on your wall!

When my wife and I began dating, one obvious chasm stood between us—my deep devotion to coffee and her total lack of it. If you love coffee, you know how devastating this was to me. I begged her, "Jess, please try to come toward me in this!" At first she'd order hot chocolate. But gradually she advanced to mochas and lattes. Then she graduated to coffee with cream and seventeen sugar packets stirred in. Finally, that thrilling day came when Jess ordered straight coffee! Jess didn't start out loving coffee; she started by loving me. Because she desired to move toward me in my passions, she developed a love for coffee. If loving the nations feels too radical, redirect your love to God. He loves the nations and we love Him. That is enough. Through His Word we are assured of His purpose and we are assured of its victorious fulfillment. The only question is: *Will you be a part?*

SECTION 2

THE WORLD

"All roads lead to the judgment seat of Christ."

\- Keith Green

CHAPTER 6
THE FINAL FRONTIER

never played football growing up. I guess I couldn't get past the fact that most football players get hurt. Instead, I stuck to checkers. I only sustained one injury to my left thumb; I was one of the lucky ones. I do enjoy watching football though. One thing that makes football so exciting is an area of the field known as the "red zone." All the drama centers around each team's effort to drive the ball one hundred yards to score, and the last twenty yards before the end zone (the red zone) are always the hardest to break through. This is because the defense is packed in so tight that it is a tremendous feat for the offensive team to score and finish the drive they started. How frustrating to go so far and not be able to finish! Similarly, a red zone exists in missions.

Great progress has been made toward reaching the first eighty yards of the world with the gospel. Stories of

---

[1] For further study on Europe, see Kenneth Scott Latourette, *A History of Christianity, vol.* 1 (New York: Harper Collins, 1953). For North America, see Mark A. Noll, *A History of Christianity in the United States and Canada* (Grand Rapids, MI: Eerdmans Publishing, 2003). For South America, see Ondina E. González and Justo L. González, *Christianity in Latin America: A History* (New York, NY: Cambridge University Press, 2008), and for Sub-Saharan Africa see Klaus Fiedler, *The Story of Faith Missions from Hudson Taylor to Present Day Africa* (Oxford: Regnum Books International, 1994).

those who have given their lives to see the gospel planted in places like Europe, North America, South America, and Sub-Saharan Africa are voluminous.[1] However the enemy, Satan, is defending the red zone with all he has got. This final frontier includes the regions that today, for one reason or another, have not had the opportunity to hear the gospel to the same degree other areas have. In this section we will focus on the state of the world, with specific emphasis on the red zone. It's imperative as we pursue penetration of the red zone that our strategy aligns with God's.

THE FORGOTTEN SHIPS

Imagine there are five cruise ships simultaneously sinking off the coast.[2] They are spaced at five-mile increments and the ship closest to the shore floats five miles out. This means you have sinking cruise ships five, ten, fifteen, twenty, and twenty-five miles away from the coast. The Coast Guard dispatches rescuers as hundreds aboard each cruise ship await relief. The rescuers must make a choice. Which cruise ship do they go to first? The one five miles out seems the most logical since valuable time and energy would seemingly be wasted in going to the ship twenty-five miles out. Rescuers would necessarily pass over perishing lives as they head to the farthest ship. Even after the first decision of who to help, every subsequent rescue would involve a difficult choice of who to help next. These would be tough choices *if* no definition had been given as to the end

---

[2] This illustration is adapted from John Piper, *Let the Nations Be Glad! The Supremacy of God in Missions* (Grand Rapids, MI: Baker Books, 1993), 168-169.

goal. If the desired end is to save as many people as possible—simply a numeric issue—then it makes sense to focus solely on the closest cruise ship. But if the definition was *not* numeric in nature, the rescue strategy would conform to another desired end. God has expressed His end goal of missions. John Piper explains how the mission of God is not numeric in nature:

> God may have in mind that the aim of the rescue operation should be to gather saved sinners from every people in the world, even if some of the successful rescuers must leave a fruitful *reached people*, in order to labor in a (possibly less fruitful) *unreached* people. The task of missions may not be merely to win as many individuals as possible from the most responsive people groups of the world, but rather to win individuals from *all* the people groups of the world.[3]

Piper utilizes a definition of the final goal of missions dictated by Revelation 5:9, which says, "And they sang a new song: 'You are worthy to take the scroll and to open its seals, because you were slain, and with your blood you purchased men for God *from every tribe and language and people and nation.*'" God desires to have a representation from every tribe, tongue, and nation, and therefore, we participate in the completion of this goal by engaging in missions. Our outreach efforts, energy, money, and time need to be poured into seeing this become a reality. Given that God's desire is to save some from every people, rescuers necessarily have to go to every cruise ship, not just the ones that yield the

---

[3] Piper, 168-169.

When missions includes everything, it becomes nothing.

most fruit or are most convenient. Unfortunately, in an effort to avoid the super-spiritual stereotype that seems to follow missions around, churches and Christian organizations have been willing to put the day-care center, softball league, and Bible translation in Indonesia booths side by side at the missions conference.[4] The inevitable damage this equal-opportunity approach causes is a loss of contrast between "monoculture evangelism" and "cross-cultural missions."[5] Though I wholeheartedly endorse every outreach effort—softball league and otherwise—without a clear definition of missions, everything and everyone gets lumped into one mushy pile. The result is the whole mission enterprise is robbed of its distinctive emphasis. If the goal is to see all peoples, nations, tribes, and languages represented before God's heavenly throne, this loss is more than just a nuance of terms. When missions includes everything, it becomes nothing.

CLARIFYING THE TASK

In 1792, just before sailing to India, William Carey wrote a book, entitled *An Enquiry,* that sparked mission activity for centuries to come. One key component in this eighty-six-page book is how Carey viewed the world. He divided the

---

[4] Carlos F. Cardoza-Orlandi, *Mission: An Essential Guide* (Nashville: Abingdon, 2002), 24-25.

[5] Timothy C. Tennent, *Invitation to World Missions: A Trinitarian Missiology for the Twenty-first Century* (Grand Rapids, MI: Kregel, 2010), 24.

planet into four parts (Europe, Asia, Africa, and America) and looked at their respective populations, civilizations, and religions.[6] He labeled the major religions as Christian, Jewish, Mahometan (Muslims), and Pagan. In trying to summarize their cumulative population, Carey writes:

> The inhabitants of the world according to this calculation amount to about seven hundred and thirty one million; four hundred and twenty million of whom are still in pagan darkness; a hundred and thirty million followers of Mahomet; a hundred million Catholics; forty-four million Protestants; thirty million of the Greek and Armenian churches, and perhaps seven million Jews.[7]

Amazingly, his calculations proved quite accurate. Through *An Enquiry,* Carey sought to awaken the Church to the major religious blocs of the world and motivate it to action. He put faces on distant people. Because of Carey, would-be goers now had direction and a light for their path.

Cameron Townsend was another who made great strides toward clarifying the task. Born in California, he attended Occidental College in Los Angeles. In 1917, as a junior, he learned of an opportunity to go to South America to sell Bibles. Fluent in Spanish, he decided to apply.[8] He was accepted and enroute to Guatemala before graduating.

---

[6] William Carey, *An Enquiry into the Obligations of Christians to Use Means for the Conversion of the Heathens* (England: Ann Ireland, 1792), reprint edition. Dallas, TX: Criswell Publications, 1988, 62.

[7] Carey, 49.

[8] James Hefley and Marti Hefley, *Uncle Cam* (Huntington Beach, CA: Wycliffe Bible Translators, 1984), 25.

Townsend worked in Guatemala distributing Spanish Scriptures, but someone soon pointed out to him that the indigenous populations did not speak Spanish and could only be reached in their own language.[9] One Indian asked him, "If your God is so smart, why can't He speak my language?" This so motivated Townsend that he gave the rest of his life to translating the Bible for these indigenous peoples. Townsend went to Guatemala with a reach-every-country perspective, but he left Guatemala with a new understanding of the imperative for every language group within every country to be reached. This new outlook so radically impacted him that he went on to found Wycliffe Bible Translators.

A contemporary of Townsend and another key player was Donald McGavran. Raised in India, he spent an additional thirty years as an adult doing mission work there. Through his church-planting efforts, McGavran recognized the social and cultural barriers present in the region.[10] McGavran realized that "people become Christians as a wave of decisions for Christ sweeps through the group mind."[11] He called this process a "People Movement" and became the proponent of a new way of thinking about missions.

Though the change in perspective spread slowly, Townsend and McGavran's cumulative contribution to missions thinking was an emphasis on ethno-linguistic groups over geopolitically defined countries. Such a group came to be called a *people group*—"the largest group through which

---

[9] Hefley, 39.

[10] Donald Anderson McGavran, *Bridges of God: A Study in the Strategy of Missions* (London: World Dominion Press, 1957), 1.

[11] McGavran, 12.

the gospel can spread without encountering significant barriers of understanding and acceptance." Out of this new understanding arose an emphasis on the term *ethne*. Mission enthusiasts began to recognize the very explicit definition of the term *ethne* in Scripture.[12] It became important to see if the biblical definition of *ethne* went deeper than just "all countries."

> The "nations" to which Jesus often referred were mainly ethnic groups within the single political structure of the Roman government. The various nations represented on the day of Pentecost were for the most part not *countries* but *peoples.* In the Great Commission as it is found in Matthew, the phrase "make disciples of all *ethne* (peoples)" does not let us off the hook once we have a church in every country—God wants a strong church within every people![13]

Pockets of people followed their lead in this understanding.[14] A focus on people groups who had never heard the gospel emerged. However, this new paradigm was not fully introduced or explained until 1974 when Billy Graham

---

[12] Ralph D. Winter and Steven C. Hawthorne, eds., *Perspectives on the World Christian Movement,* 4th ed. (Pasadena, CA: William Carey Library, 2009), 275.

[13] J. D. Douglas, *Let the Earth Hear His Voice: International Congress on World Evangelization: Lausanne, Switzerland* (Minnesota: World Wide Publications, 1975), 221.

[14] In 1963 Leslie Lyall of Overseas Missionary Fellowship wrote a world survey called *Missionary Opportunity Today.* In 1968 another global survey identifying unreached peoples by Missions Advanced Research and Communications Center was released, and in 1972 Patrick Johnstone wrote *Operation World.* Patrick Johnstone, *The Church Is Bigger Than You Think: The Unfinished Work of World Evangelism* (Great Britain: Christian Focus Publications, 1998), 91-92.

hosted a world evangelization conference in Lausanne, Switzerland. Christians from all over the world met for this international discussion about reaching the world. Ralph Winter, founder of the U.S. Center for World Mission, challenged the participants through a document entitled, "The Highest Priority: Cross-Cultural Evangelism." In it, he showed that if anyone considered the world to be reached, it was because he or she peered through the wrong lens. He asserted that it is false and misleading to proclaim the world has been evangelized simply because a church exists in every country. Dr. Winter's influence at this convention ignited an understanding among participants of what he called the "hidden peoples" of the world—those who have no access to the gospel. As Ralph Winter said,

> I'm afraid that all our exultation about the fact that every *country* of the world has been penetrated has allowed many to suppose that every *culture* has by now been penetrated. This misunderstanding is a malady so widespread that it deserves a special name, let us call it "people blindness" that is, blindness to the existence of separate *peoples* within *countries*.[15]

This conference helped erect a new foundation stone that would eventually become the bedrock of missions thinking. Following the event, Dr. Winter and others agreed to use the term "unreached peoples" in describing the ethnolinguistic groups not yet reached.[16] Several publications created on the issue resulted in precise definitions of what were

---

[15] J. D. Douglas, 221.

[16] Johnstone, 103.

once vague ideas: an *unreached people group* is "a people group within which there is no indigenous community of believing Christians with adequate numbers and resources to evangelize this people group without outside (cross-cultural) assistance."[17] To be considered unreached, the people group must be less than 2 percent evangelical Christian. The original seventy people groups created in Genesis 10 and 11 have developed into today's 16,000 people groups. Approximately 6,000 of these remain categorized as unreached—a total of 2.5 billion people.[18] We must be careful that statistic does not fall off our lips too flippantly. It is hard to fathom such a number. Put into perspective, it would take 200 years to read the names of 2 billion people aloud. Sobering, isn't it?

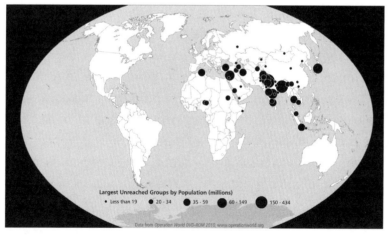

Unreached people groups

---

[17] Ralph Winter, "Momentum Is Building: Many Voices Discuss Completing the Task by 2000 A.D.," *International Journal of Frontier Missions*, no. 1-4 (1986): 71.

[18] Joshuaproject.net

Another important clarification made in the last three decades involves the difference between unreached people groups and *unengaged people groups.* An unreached people group may have a small population of Christians (less than 2 percent) and missionary teams currently working there, but they remain unreached because the gospel has yet to take root. Unengaged people, however, have no Bibles, no workers, and no active church planting initiative directed at them. There are approximately 600 unengaged people groups today with a total population of 500 million people.[19]

PANTA TA ETHNE

John Piper, in his book *Let the Nations Be Glad,* presents one of the most thorough works on the Bible's use of the word *ethne.* He contends in the eighteen times the phrase *panta ta ethne* (all the nations) appears in the New Testament, it favors the idea of people groups the majority of times.[20] He points back to the promise given to Abraham in Genesis 12:3 (and by you *all the families* of the earth shall be blessed) to show the Hebrew word *Mishpaha* (family) can be, and usually is, even smaller than a tribe. This, Piper says, proves that the blessing of Abraham was meant to reach small groupings of people. Based on his evidence, he concludes that to read Matthew 28:19 in light of people groups is a solid interpretation.

---

[19] These 600 unengaged people groups are within the 6,000 unreached people groups.

[20] Piper, 180-182.

The singular use of *ethnos* in the New Testament always re-fers to a people group. The plural use of *ethnos* sometimes must be a people group and sometimes must refer to Gentile individuals, but usually can go either way ... The combination of these results suggests that the meaning of *panta ta ethne* leans heavily in the direction of "all the nations (people groups)."[21]

Piper further writes, "Dr. Winter reached up and pulled the unseen rope called 'unreached peoples' that rang a bell which reverberates to this day."[22]

The implication of this people group understanding for today is that strategy must take higher priority. The responsibility to preach the gospel stays constant, but the scope of the task changes as it becomes more clearly defined.[23] Today, missions mobilizers focus in on the exact task remaining—enabling us to see with precision where missionaries are, who is yet to have a witness, and where to send those who desire to serve on the front lines. India provides a good example of this. In the past,

> *The responsibility to preach the gospel stays constant, but the scope of the task changes as it becomes more clearly defined.*

---

[21] Piper, 180.

[22] John Piper, "Personal Tribute to the Late Ralph Winter." Desiring God Ministries. Available from desiringgod.org, 2009.

[23] Alan Johnson, "The Frontier Mission Movement's Understanding of the Modern Mission Era," *International Journal of Frontier Missions* 18, no. 2 (2001): 82.

if God laid on someone's heart to go to India, they could end up anywhere in the country. In fact, that's exactly what happened. Though they might have known where pockets of Hindus, Sikhs, and Christians were, they had no idea how many people groups existed or how to strategize to get teams of workers into each of them. Today, because of our shift in thinking, we now discern our efforts in India to be among the 2,500-plus distinct people groups speaking 438 languages instead of in India as a whole.[24]

Today when someone plans to go overseas, they might tell you *where* they are going—"to India," "to Sudan," "to Korea," or "to Kazakhstan." But, in light of this people-group understanding, it is more important, more accurate, and increasingly more common to hear someone say to *whom* they are going—"to the Uighurs," "to the Hausas," "to the Ansaris," or "to the Betawis."

The vast majority of unreached and unengaged people live in a section of the world known as the 10-40 window. An Argentinean mission strategist, Luis Bush, coined this phrase. He and his wife could see the redwood trees framed through a window of their home and connected this view with a passion to see the evangelization of unengaged and unreached people groups.[25] Bush called it the 10-40 window because these people dwell in the geographic region between 10 degrees and 40 degrees north latitude from West Africa to China.

---

[24] For more information on people groups see joshuaproject.net or thetravelingteam .org/stateworld. Jason Mandryk, *Operation World,* 7th ed. (Colorado Springs, CO: Biblica Publishing, 2010), 406.

[25] Alan Johnson, "The Frontier Mission Movement's Understanding of the Modern Mission Era," Part I and Part II, *International Journal of Frontier Missions* 18, no. 2 (2001).

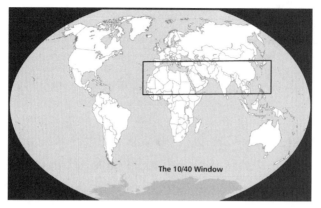

The 10/40 Window

The 10-40 Window

Today the 10-40 window is home to just over 4 billion people and 8,800 people groups. Every major world religion was founded here. It's the location of the world's least reached peoples. A memorable and transferable way to understand the spiritual context of the 10-40 window is the acronym THUMB. The *T* stands for Tribal, *H* is for Hindu, *U* (turn it on its side for a C) is for Chinese, *M* is for Muslim, and *B* is for Buddhist.[26]

As we've seen throughout Scripture, what God began with Abraham will eventually reach every world religion, every country, every people group. May our study of the world's peoples not only serve to educate us as to the task and make us better strategists, but may it also solidify our resolve to join in the revolution, offering our lives with a willingness to leave our people, our country, and everything familiar to be used by God to bless all nations.

---

[26] Bob Sjogren coined the acronym THUMB in order to succinctly remember the 10-40 window. However, for U he uses Unreligious instead of China. By Unreligious, he means essentially the same as what I mean by China. Only the category's title has been changed. Bob Sjogren, *Unveiled at Last* (Seattle, WA: YWAM Publishing, 1992), 138.

CHAPTER 7
THE TRIBAL WORLD

I pursued my wife for two years before she agreed to date me. As providence would have it, two weeks after our first date, I left the country for a five-month trek across Asia while she worked among tribal people in Papua New Guinea. Our experiences were totally different, but I gained a whole new love and intrigue for the tribal world through her stories. Jess and her team lived among and studied tribes in the highlands of Papua New Guinea. They learned how to phonetically record an unwritten language, how to chart and strategize to most effectively reach a tribal area, and how to share the gospel with people who have never seen a Bible or heard of Israel. Jess played with the kids, ate food cooked in a hole in the ground, slept in a hut, made bead purses with her favorite local girl, watched tribesmen hunt for dinner with bows and arrows, swam in the river they bathed in, got an amoeba, and bought a spear.

But one of the most fascinating experiences she shared with me occurred in a village she visited. Located high in the mountains of the country, this particular village would by 5 p.m. be completely shrouded in cloud cover. The clouds began to roll in around 4 p.m. They were so thick that, if you were indoors with the door open, you could literally see an opaque white substance spilling in from outside. Jess and her teammates would go out to the small plane runway in this village at about 4:30 in the afternoon, when the cloud was thick but not quite all-consuming. Jess told me it looked like the world completely dropped off the edge of the runway. It was impossible to see beyond just a hundred yards ahead. For the rush of it, they would run as fast as they could toward the end of the runway and into what looked and felt like an abyss. Of course, the ground remained underfoot as they dove into the white void, but for a second Jess plunged into the end of the world.

That's a good picture of the tribal world; so unknown, so unseen—it feels like the end of the world. Let's run head-long into this mysterious demographic of our world and see what lies behind the shroud.

Tribal religions go by a variety of names. They may be referred to as primal religions, which simply means "being first in time."[1] Their umbrella title is *animism*, which means "soul" or "breath." This title usually applies to belief systems which operate from an assumption that the spirit world con-trols our physical world.[2] Tribal religions focus primarily on ancestor veneration and a strong belief in good and evil spir-its. For the tribal–primal–animistic world, the question is not *what* has occurred? But *who* has beseeched the spirits in order for this curse or blessing to occur? And, what have I done to either anger or delight those spirits?

---

[1] Michael McDowell and Nathan Robert Brown, *World Religions at Your Fingertips* (New York: Penguin Group Publishing, 2009), 6.

[2] Dean Halverson, *The Compact Guide to World Religions* (Minneapolis, MN: Bethany House Publishers, 1996), 37.

There are approximately 250 million adherents to tribal religions. This amounts to 3 percent of the world's population.[3] People in this group can be difficult to reach for several reasons. Of the world's 6,913 languages, 5,100 are spoken among tribes.[4] So, 71 percent of the languages are spread out among 3 percent of the world's population. What a daunting task! Another difficulty is that though there exist a few common denominators of faith between tribes, the rituals proceeding from these beliefs differ from tribe to tribe. In many cases the tribal world remains cut off from the rest of the world. Tribes are not only difficult to get to physically, but their way of life is totally removed from our own. The majority of the tribal world is located in Africa, Papua New Guinea, and parts of South America.

A TRIBE FINDS PEACE

While I was in college, I decided to attend a summer project in Florida where I would grow spiritually. I had just started taking my faith seriously, and this seemed like the perfect opportunity—living with over one hundred students learning about the Word, prayer, fellowship, and evangelism. I knew no one. Two weeks into the project, the project organizers announced that they needed someone to manage the project's "mini-bookstore" and promote various books in front of the students each week. Someone volunteered me,

---

[3] David Barrett, George Kurian, and Todd Johnson, *World Christian Encyclopedia: A Comparative Survey of Churches and Religions in the Modern World,* vol. 1 (New York: Oxford University Press, 2001), 582.

[4] David Sitton, *To Every Tribe With Jesus: Understanding and Reaching Tribal Peoples for Christ* (Sand Springs, OK: Grace and Truth Books, 2005), 4.

but up to this point I don't think I had ever read a complete book, much less a Christian one. I was now the official book guy. I decided I would try to read a book per week and share a snapshot of it at the meeting. The first one I chose was called *Peace Child* by Don Richardson. To this day I do not know why I grabbed that one off the shelf as my first read. Little did I know, years later it would still be one of my favorites! *Peace Child* tells the story of Don and his wife, Carol, taking the gospel to the Sawi people of New Guinea. The incredible story of this family who risked their lives among an unknown tribal people captivated me. The Sawi esteemed treachery so much that when Richardson explained the gospel, they responded by celebrating the most unlikely character in the narrative. Richardson says,

> At the climax of the story, Maum whistled a birdcall of admiration. Kani and several others touched their fingertips to their chests in awe. Still others chuckled. At first I sat there confused. Then the realization broke through. *They were acclaiming Judas as the hero of the story!* Yes, Judas, the one whom I had portrayed as the satanically motivated enemy of truth and goodness![5]

Richardson wondered, in light of how they valued warfare, if the peace of God would ever come to the Sawi. He then found what he later termed a "redemptive analogy." A redemptive analogy is some local practice or understanding which can be used to demonstrate the gospel. It's something Richardson suggests is embedded in many cultures.

---

[5] Don Richardson, *Peace Child* (Ventura, CA: Regal Books, 1974), 177.

For the Sawi the only guarantee of peace between villages is what they call the *Tarop Tim* or peace child. When Richardson stumbled on this tradition, he knew he'd found his redemptive analogy. The ritual included the exchange of infants between warring tribes. As long as this peace child lives, peace is guaranteed.

> Among the Sawi, every demonstration of friendship was suspect except one. If a man would actually give his own son to his enemies, that man could be trusted! That, and that alone, was a proof of good will no shadow of cynicism could discredit. And everyone who laid his hand on the given son was bound not to work violence against those who gave him.... I perceived its message and gasped! This was the key we had been praying for![6]

Don Richardson related the story of the ultimate Peace Child, Jesus. The message transformed the Sawi and a church was established. This was my first Christian book to read! I quickly finished Richardson's second book, *Lords of the Earth,* which tells the story of the Yali people of Irian Jaya.[7] I am sure many on the Florida project thought the bookstore only sold books on tribal missions! Needless to say, my new knowledge of the actual people at the end of the world—people so loved and obviously pursued by God—deeply impacted me.

---

[6] Richardson, *Peace Child,* 206.

[7] Don Richardson, *Lords of the Earth* (Ventura, CA: Regal Books, 1977). Also see his landmark book entitled *Eternity in Their Hearts* in which Richardson seeks to show that a supreme God has existed for centuries in cultures all over the world. Don Richardson, *Eternity in Their Hearts* (Ventura, CA: Regal Books, 1981).

TRIBAL BELIEFS

Most tribal people groups do not have a holy book detailing their belief system. Therefore, it's difficult for an outsider to understand the worldview driving each member of the tribe. Many animistic cultures not only lack this written history but also the architectural history seen in the majestic temples and shrines of many other religious cultures.[8] The core of tribal belief is transferred orally from generation to generation through myths and legends. A shaman (witch doctor) usually exists and attempts to provide protection and leadership to the tribe: healing, advising, and hoping to manipulate spiritual powers. The shaman is a personal diviner who seeks to understand and give a spiritual diagnosis as to which spirit or impersonal force has caused a sickness or catastrophe. The shaman undertakes this by a variety of methods depending on the tribe's location.

The African shaman typically divines by analyzing sticks thrown onto the ground or through the texture and content of stomachs, intestines, and the livers of sacrificial sheep, goats, or chickens. The Tungus shaman of Siberia divines by means of possession.... [others] by leading the sick person to confess his sins and thus gain release.[9]

---

[8] Though incredible monuments have been discovered whose origins are considered primal people (for example, England's Stonehenge, Mexico's Chichén Itzá, the ruins of Machu Picchu in Peru, and Easter Island's monoliths), these structures are not the norm for the average tribal culture.

[9] Gailyn Van Rheenen, *Communicating Christ in Animistic Contexts* (Pasadena, CA: William Carey Library, 1991), 148.

Each set of specific beliefs is unique to the tribe itself, but many tribes share some common characteristics. First, they have a concept of one supreme being or reverence a single spirit as the highest spirit. But this being exists beyond the spirit world. The role of the spirit world is to mediate between humans and this supreme being. For the spirits to respond benevolently, they must be given homage. These spirits also move from place to place and have the ability to enter a living person and possess them to work good or evil.[10] The tribal member is less concerned about offending the supreme being but devotes all energy to appeasing the intermediate spirit world with which he interacts constantly.

Second, while animists recognize a connection between what they do and reward and punishment, they believe the intermediate spirits dole it out, not the supreme being. Eating the wrong foods or doing the wrong things opens them up to punishment. The attempt to peacefully co-exist with the spirit world consumes their everyday lives, and thus the supreme being is forgotten. Much of one's life is pre-occupied with the quest to discover which spirits dominate one's life and in seeking to appease those spirits with the acceptable magic rituals.[11] If a ritual fails it means the people have either misdiagnosed the problem or they are simply dealing with a spirit stronger than their magic. Failure is never met by questioning the system; rather, failure induces an endless quest for the *right* ritual.

Third, not only do spirit beings exist, but many tribal

---

[10] Alan Neely, *Christian Mission: A Case Study Approach* (New York: Orbis Books, 1997), 92.

[11] Sitton, 8.

groups believe impersonal spiritual energy pervades objects and rituals. This energy is called *mana*.[12] Objects may possess mana because of their distinctiveness (a specific rock, bush, or tree). It can also be found in personal beings such as people, ancestors, or spirits.

A man comes by chance upon a stone which takes his fancy; its shape is singular, it is certainly not a common stone, there must be *mana* in it. So he argues with himself, and he puts it to the proof; he lays it at the root of a tree or he buries it in the ground when he plants his garden; an abundant crop on the tree or in the garden shows that he is right, the stone has mana, it has power in it. Having that power, it is a vehicle to convey mana to other stones.[13]

If a tribesman experiences success in hunting or fighting, it is because of mana, since it is thought that mana empowers one to prosper. Failure simply means the *absence* of mana. Tribes believe this spiritual energy gives them power to accomplish what they need for survival.[14] Without a proper understanding of mana, an outsider cannot grasp the beliefs and practices of the tribal world.

---

[12] R. H. Codrington was the first to study impersonal spiritual powers in depth in 1891. The Melanesians called it *mana;* however, other tribes use other words. For example, in parts of Indonesia it is called *toh* and the Muslim world would say *baraka*. R. H. Codrington, *The Melanesians: Studies in Their Anthropology and Folklore* (Oxford: Clarendon, 1891), 118-120.

[13] Codrington, 118-120. Also see David Burnett, *World of the Spirits* (Grand Rapids, MI: Monarch Books, 2000), 75-80.

[14] Though far from a tribal culture, the belief in mana is very prevalent in the United States. A basketball coach may wear the same tie if he realizes every time he wears it, the team wins. Before a test, students at Harvard University will rub the toe of the statue of John Harvard located at the center of campus.

The tribal worldview differs vastly from the Western worldview, and there are three primary areas where this is most apparent.[15]

Relationships: Harmony is sought and dissension is avoided at all cost. Arguments are not private matters but relate to everyone in the community. This means decision making is consensus based. Expulsion from the tribe is the worst punishment one could be given.

Phobias: Tribal people are suspicious of everyone because of their underlying fear of spirits as the driving force behind all events. Alan Neely, veteran missionary in Latin America, explains,

> Primal religions, for example, teach that the rains can come or the rains can be stopped, depending on the gods and whether they are appeased or satisfied. Moreover, misfortune, suffering, and even death can be inflicted on another person or group, regardless of their past behavior, if the power of a spirit, usually an evil spirit, is harnessed and utilized to afflict such malevolence.[16]

Time: Time is measured not by hours or days but by significant events. A tribesman told one friend of mine, "We will listen to you because you were here for the birth of my son and here at the death of my father." This man had earned his audience not by being present for decades, but by being present for the events that meant most to the tribe's leader.

---

[15] These observations were taken from Sitton, 23-27.

[16] Neely, 93.

LAYING DOWN YOUR BOARD

One of my modern-day heroes is a surfer from California named Brad Buser. Challenged by his youth minister to give his life for world evangelization, Brad turned his back on professional surfing and headed to the tribal world. He was eighteen when he left to spend twenty years with the Iteri tribe in Papua New Guinea, translating the Bible into their language and planting a church. While home on a two-year furlough, the neighboring tribe began to write letters to him. Here is a portion of one:

Wapia Sainaki
Sinou Village
Sandoun Province

What's going on? Where is our help? Have you forgot about us? We of Sinou haven't forgot about wanting a missionary, we carry a huge heavy constantly about this. We carry this heavy because we fear for our lives. We know the paipel [Bible] says you should come and tell us. Us dark ones need it. How will we go to God's place if not? Only those who know will go, how will we know if no one teaches us? That's my worry, we want a missionary now to give us God's talk.

The last time I talked to Brad, he was on his way back to Papua New Guinea to build a house for his son, who had decided to reach another tribal people group. When asked what it was like to give up surfing and other dreams in order to obey God, Buser responded,

The hardest step is the first one.

The hardest step is the first one. You know, I had been a Christian three months. It was just toward the end of my senior year of high school. I was surfing my brains out. But when I finally made the decision that I was done, I was doing it, I was going until God stopped me—it was a tremendous relief. You know, giving up surfing, cutting my hair, leaving the beach, those were all difficult days, but the hardest decision is the first one—saying "That's it, I'm doing it! I don't know what I'm getting into, I don't have hardly any answers, but I'm going for it."[17]

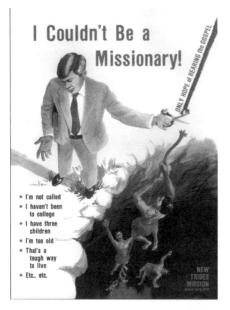

While many of his friends chased the American dream, Buser chased God to the unreached tribal world. He wouldn't trade it for anything.

Early recruiting poster for New Tribes Mission[18]

---

[17] The Traveling Team, "From Surfing the Beach to Serving in the Jungle: A Brad Buser Interview," *Ignition Magazine,* 2010, 25.

[18] New Tribes Mission works solely among tribal peoples. Founded in 1942 by Paul Fleming, their vision remains the same: planting churches among tribal unreached people groups. For more information see New Tribes Mission, ntm.org.

THE REALITY OF THE SPIRIT WORLD

Many Westerners imagine tribal people to be "noble savages," untainted by Western civilization. We think of cultures that have somehow achieved perfect spiritual, environmental, and relational peace. Nothing could be further from the truth. Let's take a closer look at a specific tribe and see what truly lies beneath the peaceful veneer.

The Yanomamo people live in the Amazon rain forest, hidden in the hills between Brazil and Venezuela. In light of their remote location, they remain largely uncontacted by the outside world.[19] The Yanomamo are harsh, savage, and aggressive in their protection and vengeance of fellow tribesmen. More than a third of Yanomamo males die in battle. Violence, fear of the spirits, insecurity, and death characterize the Yanomamo. White people (known to them as *nabas*) made their way into the village seeking natural resources, and a dilemma intensified among the tribesmen. How should they respond? They desired to utilize the white people's resources, but were unsure if there would be negative ramifications in building that relationship. The Yanomamo's practice was to invite the spirits into their physical bodies to reside there and protect them from everything, including the new

---

[19] In his book, *Spirit of the Rainforest,* Mark Ritchie teams up with a missionary named Gary Dawson to study the Venezuelan tribe called the Yanomamo. Dawson, who grew up among them, knew the language and people better than anyone. This book sets forth two main goals: first, to build an objective platform for the longstanding debate between missionaries and anthropologists about which party offers more benefit to a culture. It does this by consulting not the missionaries nor the anthropologists, but the culture itself. Second, it attempts to unmask the reality of sin and spiritual warfare to a modern world where it seems that with enough moral and spiritual crutches we can ignore these realities. Mark A. Ritchie, *Spirit of the Rainforest: A Yanomamo Shaman's Story* (Chicago: Island Lake Press, 1996).

Those exposed to the missionaries and their message discovered a completely new way of life.

white people. The white people had come to share something interesting with them: a new message about the Great Spirit (*Yai Pada*/God). The nabas told the Yanomamo that Yai Pada wanted them to throw all their other spirits away. The favored young shaman named Shoefoot responded positively to the gospel. Everyone in the tribe watched to see if Shoefoot, known for his loyalty and closeness with the spirits, would be killed for his decision to abandon them. Not only did Shoefoot survive conversion, but God transformed his heart and life before the doubtful eye of the tribe. His living example resulted in others in the tribe desiring to experience the same freedom and renewal. More began to give up their spirits. Shoefoot had become a follower of Christ and was adamant other Yanomamo do the same.[20] He saw how the old tribal ways and rituals were a detriment to his people and culture.

Those exposed to the missionaries and their message discovered a completely new way of life: fear of the spirits was replaced by confidence in the one Spirit, superstition gave way to knowledge, women gained dignity, children were nurtured, the extreme violence and compassion

---

[20] Ritchie, 251.

replaced the consuming thirst for revenge of traditional Yanomamo. Most importantly, and in contrast to what some anthropologists assert, the tribe happily let go of its base practices and was grateful for the new way of life. Shoefoot states, "The spirits are evil. The only hope for my people is to stop following those spirits."[21]

The tribal world feels like the end of the world—remote, hidden, veiled behind strange spiritual rituals, and shrouded in mystery. But God desires to be known and worshipped by each tribe. He is counting. Don and Carol Richardson, Brad Buser, and the unknown missionaries among the Yanomamo—these represent but a few of the great heroes who have given their lives to see the tribal world reached.[22] They, like Abraham, decided to exchange their own ambitions for God's. They surrendered to the revolution and were used by Him to impact the eternal destiny of otherwise unknown tribal peoples at the end of the world. Will you be used to reach the remaining unreached tribal world? May the legacy of the revolutionaries inspire us to advocate for these hidden peoples, and may the words of Isaiah ring true in this generation:

---

[21] Ritchie, 251.

[22] For anyone interested in more stories of tribal missions and missionaries, one of the most well known is *Through Gates of Splendor* by Elisabeth Elliot. This details the lives of five missionaries who were killed in the jungles of Ecuador in 1956. Joanne Shetler co-authored the book *And the Word Came With Power,* which recounts her amazing life as a single female laboring for two decades to translate the Bible and bring the gospel to the Balangao tribe of the Philippines. Lastly, see the book by Darlene Deibler Rose, one of the first American women to go to the Baliem Valley of New Guinea. Separated from her husband, she spent four years in a prison camp occupied by the Japanese. *Evidence Not Seen* captures her commitment to see the gospel proclaimed to the ends of the earth.

"Sing to the Lord a new song,
his praise from the ends of the earth,
you who go down to the sea, and all that is in it,
you islands, and all who live in them." (Isaiah 42:10)

CHAPTER 8
THE HINDU WORLD

My first introduction to Hinduism came when I arrived in India and immersed myself into the culture. Sitting on campus at a major university, I struck up a conversation with a student named Avantika. She desired to graduate and get a good, high-paying job—the prototype Indian student! As Avantika and I talked, the conversation turned to spiritual things. I told her that during my short visit I had seen a very religious country. Depictions of gods were seen everywhere. I confessed I felt overwhelmed by all the gods India offered and didn't think I would ever get my bearings on this religion. She laughed and said, "Just focus on the main three." In disbelief I asked, "There are 330 million gods in India … how do I know which are the main three?"

ONE, THREE, OR MILLIONS

A few years later, I spoke at a conference in the U.S. regarding the gods of India. I shared the statistic that there are more gods in India than there are people in the United States. As the evening came to a close, I packed up my things and headed to my car to find a note on my windshield. I opened it up and read, "There is only one God in India!" This illustrates the classic problem in the Hindu religion—the same problem that confronted me during my time in India with Avantika, the problem exposed by the note on my windshield after the seminar: the problem of identifying Hindu deities.[1]

If you take India's temple-laden streets at face value the obvious conclusion is that Hindus worship an infinitude of gods. On the other hand, Avantika distilled the millions down to "the main three." However, reading the Hindu holy books, you will see what the note on my windshield insisted, "In the beginning there was One without a second."[2] The confusing part about the above assertions is all of them are true!

How are these truths reconciled? In Hinduism, Brahman is the unchanging, immanent, and eternal reality. Everything has its source in Brahman. Hinduism asserts, "Brahman is of the nature of truth, knowledge, and infinity."[3] Hindu philosophers have pondered the identity of Brahman for centuries. Whether or not Brahman can be known on a personal level is also up for debate among different schools of thought.[4] Brahman is who my windshield note-writer alluded to.

---

[1] Based on his years of living in India and studying Hinduism, Kevin Thiemann says, "Many use the phrase polytheistic monotheism to understand Hinduism. Almost every Hindu worships a variety of idols and almost all of them also admit there is only one God."

[2] *Upanisads,* trans. Patrick Olivelle (Oxford: University Press, 1996), Chandogya Upanishad 6.2.2, 149.

[3] *Upanisads,* Taittariya Upanishad 2.1, 184-185.

[4] Two of the most important philosophers of Hinduism are Sankara (AD 788-820) and Ramanuja (AD 1017-1137). Both philosophers have different understandings on whether Brahman has attributes or not. For a thorough comparison of the two, see Timothy C. Tennent, *Christianity at the Religious Roundtable* (Grand Rapids, MI: Baker Academic Publishing, 2002).

Brahman manifests himself as other deities so, though literally millions of deities can be seen by the casual observer, they all come back to the one Ultimate Reality, Brahman. The "main three" of these manifestations, referenced by Avantika, are called the *trimurti* or the Hindu trinity: Brahma, Vishnu, and Shiva. Brahma (not to be confused with Brahm*in* which is the name of the high caste or Brahm*an*, the Ultimate Reality) is considered the creator of the world. He created the fathers of the human race. Thus, Brahma is the source of life, though few in India actually worship him today.

The second in this Hindu trinity is Vishnu. He is the most popular of the gods in India, with thousands of temples dedicated to him. He preserves creation, and his ability to deliver messages to and from the dead endears him to the people.[5] Interestingly, Hindus do not directly worship Vishnu as much as his avatars, or manifestations. Of his ten avatars, the two most popular are Ram and Krishna.[6]

The final member of the Hindu trinity is Shiva. He is the destroyer who will bring the world to an end—at which point Brahma will begin the creation process all over again.[7] All the destructive powers of the universe reside in him. Unlike Vishnu, Shiva is the immediate object of worship in Hinduism

---

[5] Troy Wilson Organ, *Hinduism: Its Historical Development* (Woodbury, NY: Barron's Education Series, 1974), 69.

[6] An avatar is a deity who has descended from heaven to earth, an incarnation or manifestation. There are ten avatars that Vishnu manifests himself as: the fish, the tortoise, the boar, the man-lion, the dwarf, Parasurama, Rama, Krishna, Buddha, and one to come. Some consider Jesus to be the tenth. Referring to avatars, the *Bhagavad Gita* states, "Whenever duty decays and chaos prevails, then, I create myself." *Bhagavad Gita* IV:7.

[7] A. L. Herman, *A Brief Introduction to Hinduism: Religion, Philosophy, and Ways of Liberation* (Oxford: Westview Press, 1991), 107.

and may also be worshipped through his wife, Parvati, who has many forms (some of these are Uma, Durga, and Lalita), the most ferocious of them being Kali. Martinson writes, "Kali is perhaps the most terrible of all, running around with disheveled hair, a necklace of skulls, eating human flesh, drinking blood out of a skull cup; she bears fierce weapons and might even hold a severed head in one hand. She is also the bearer of disease."[8]

Many Western Christians have a difficult time explaining the biblical Trinity, but while the average Hindu finds it hard to describe the relationship between their gods, it's not something they feel the need to justify. H. L. Richards suggests, "The average Hindu is not concerned to reconcile the worship of many such figures with belief in one supreme God."[9] Though our Western, linear minds may have a difficult

Hindu Trimurti: Brahma, Vishnu, and Shiva

---

[8] Paul Varo Martinson, *Families of Faith: An Introduction to World Religions for Christians* (Minneapolis, MN: Fortress Press, 1999), 124.

[9] H. L. Richard, *Hinduism: A Brief Look at the Theology, History, Scriptures, and Social System, with Comments on the Gospel in India* (Pasadena, CA: William Carey Library, 2007), 14.

time seeing the consistency of thought behind a single God represented by millions of diversified and often dissimilar deities, we cannot change the fact that millions of Hindus operate with this as the cornerstone of their belief system.

SACRED BOOKS TO DRAW FROM

Recently I asked a friend, "What do you know about Hinduism?" He looked at me with a blank stare and asked, "Didn't their god pop out of a box, and don't they think they get lots of chances?" It's a fair answer considering this man has had no exposure to the religion. Someone whose life work and passion is the study of Hinduism once said, "Trying to grasp Hinduism is like trying to nail Jell-O to the wall!" No doubt Hinduism is quite confusing. Despite this difficulty, the pursuit of understanding it has immense value since there are hundreds of millions of Hindus.

Most scholars identify Hinduism as the oldest religion in the world.

I hope this chapter will shed some light along the path to comprehending it!

One of the things that makes the study of Hinduism even more difficult is the lack of a single sacred text. Hinduism is much more complex because it is supported by a collection of documents that are added to others with appendixes attached to those. In addition, the lack of a particular human founder or date of origin has resulted in a veritable smorgasbord of ideas, opinions, facts, and starting places.

Most scholars identify Hinduism as the oldest religion in the world. Officially, Judaism began with Moses around 1200 BC. The story of Hinduism begins around 1500 BC when Indo-Europeans began to move into regions of northwest India. Thus Hinduism predates Judaism by just a few hundred years.[10] Hindus passed their beliefs down orally until they finally recorded them in a collection known today as the *Vedas* (1500–500 BC), meaning "knowledge." There are four *Vedas,* the most important and oldest of which is the *Rig Veda*—a collection of approximately 1,000 hymns that list thirty-three gods connected with heaven.[11] The priests used these hymns to worship the major gods. This short hymn from the *Rig Veda* has provoked hundreds of commentaries by Hindu theologians:

> Darkness was hidden by darkness in the beginning; with no distinguishing sign, all this was water. The life force that was covered with emptiness, that once arose through the power of heat.... Who really knows? Who will here proclaim it? Whence was it produced? Whence is this creation? The gods came afterwards, with the creation of this universe. Who then knows whence it has arisen? Whence this creation has arisen—perhaps it formed itself, or perhaps it did not—the one who looks down on it, in the highest heaven only he knows—or perhaps he does not know.[12]

---

[10] John Dickson, *A Spectator's Guide to World Religions* (Sydney, Australia: Blue Bottle Books, 2004), 20-21.

[11] The four *Vedas* are the 1) *Rig Veda,* 2) *Sama Veda,* 3) *Yajur Veda,* and 4) *Atharva Veda.*

[12] *The Rig Veda,* trans. Wendy Doniger (England: Penguin Books, 1981) 10.129.3, 6-7.

In an effort to explain the *Vedas,* another text was written—the *Brahmanas.* These rules and expectations produced by the priests expound on the sacred power above, Brahman. Next came the *Aranyakas,* meaning "forest books." These books were believed to hold dangerous powers, prompting the priests to read them in the forest. They were not for general circulation. Then came the highly philosophical and speculative *Upanishads* (1000–300 BC), meaning "sitting near." The teachings of over one hundred individuals are included in them. They contain parables, proverbs, dialogues, and poems. The *Upanishads* develop the concept of reincarnation.[13]

Another sacred text, called *The Laws of Manu,* consists of over 2,600 verses and covers everything from how to punish transgressors to social obligations such as taxes and settling accidents.[14] *The Laws of Manu* deals with how life should be lived in response to all possible situations as well as issues of purity and cleanliness. It can be compared to Leviticus in the Old Testament (except three times the length).

The *Mahabharata,* the longest poem in the world, tells of various battles of the gods. A special song is sung in the *Mahabharata* called the *Bhagavad Gita*, meaning "the song of the Lord." The *Bhagavad Gita* became so popular that it has been extracted from the *Mahabharata* and is the most widely

---

[13] J. L. Brockington, *The Sacred Thread: A Short History of Hinduism* (Oxford: University Press, 1981), 41. Also see David Burnett, *The Spirit of Hinduism* (Grand Rapids, MI: Monarch Books, 2006), 66-80.

[14] *The Laws of Manu,* trans. Wendy Doniger and Brian K. Smith (New Delhi, India: Penguin Books, 1991), xvii.

read of all the holy books in Hinduism. It tells the story of cousins who are ready to fight. The hero of the story, Arjuna, refuses to go to battle. His chariot driver, unbeknownst to him, is really the god Krishna who tries to encourage him in the right way. Arjuna finds himself in a dilemma that mirrors mankind's bondage to sin. Krishna becomes the savior of all. In the song Krishna states, "Arjuna, know that no one devoted to me is lost. If they rely on me, Arjuna, women, commoners, men of low rank, even men born in the womb of evil, reach the highest way."[15]

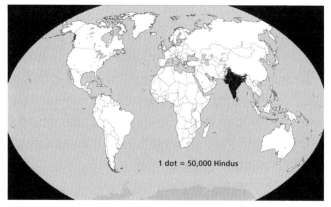

1 dot = 50,000 Hindus

Hindu world map

SALVATION FOR HINDUS

Christians emphasize the need for a person to be "born again." Ironically, Hindus are tired of being "born again." Because of a firm respect for and belief in the law of *karma,* Hindus feel caught in a seemingly endless cycle

---

[15] *The Bhagavad Gita,* trans. Barbara Stoler Miller (New York: Quality Paperback, 1998), IX: 31-32.

of reincarnation. *Karma* refers to the belief that everything one does (or thinks) brings about another event and another existence. The law of karma implies that "all your actions in life 'attach' themselves to you. Sticking to your soul in such a way as to determine your soul's re-existence, your next 'incarnation.'"[16] This either moves you toward salvation (*mukti*) or further away from it. The *Upanishads* claim, "According as one acts, according as one conducts himself, so does he become. The doer of good becomes good. The doer of evil becomes evil."[17]

In Hinduism, you alone reap what you alone sow. Vicarious suffering—suffering in another's place—is an impossibility in Hinduism, though it forms the very essence of the cross of Christ. Our penalty, our karma, was placed on Another who "was pierced for our transgressions, he was crushed for our iniquities; the punishment that brought us peace was upon him, and by his wounds we are healed" (Isaiah 53:5). So how does a Hindu obtain salvation and break the cycle of being "born again"? There are three ways.

First is the way of works. Followers must perform all the religious duties they are aware of and carefully obey the laws and obligations required from the *Vedas.*

Second is the way of knowledge. In Hinduism, knowledge means not the knowing of something, but the awareness of something. The practice of meditation originates here. The goal is to apply self-awareness to bring the body under control in order that total mind and will may eventually unite

---

[16] Dickson, 31.

[17] *Upanisads,* trans. Patrick Olivelle, Brhadaranyaka Upanishad 4.4.5-6, 65.

The ultimate goal of salvation is the return to Brahman.

with the one universal Brahman. Opposite of the way of works, this demands total renunciation of one's life for Brahman, since salvation is rooted in one's very identity with this Ultimate Reality.

Third, and most popular, is the way of faith. Followers become totally devoted to a deity whom they have chosen to worship. This may include a pilgrimage to a holy place, fasting, or obsessive repetition of the god's name. This is called bhakti (devotion), and the worshipper hopes that the god or goddess will reward such devotion with release from the cycle of karma.[18]

The ultimate goal of salvation is the return to Brahman. This reunion is described as an impersonal fusion, illustrated by a drop of rain falling into the ocean and becoming one with it. The Upanishads teach,

> As the rivers flow on and enter into the ocean giving up their names and appearances; so the knower, freed from name and appearance, reaches the heavenly Person, beyond the very highest. When a man comes to know that highest Brahman, he himself becomes that very Brahman.[19]

---

[18] An example of bhakti can be found in the *Bhagavad Gita* where Krishna states, "Men who sacrifice to gods reach the gods; those devoted to me reach me." *The Bhagavad Gita,* VII:23.

[19] *Upanisads,* trans. Patrick Olivelle, Mundaka Upanishad 3.2.8-9, 276.

At this point personhood is annihilated and reincarnation ceases.

FROM THOMAS TO SINGH

Plenty of biblical evidence shows the disciples' dispersion after the commission of the Lord in Matthew 28. The book of Acts gives us a peek into the lives of a few, but we rely on tradition for the rest. One such tale describes the apostles casting lots to determine their missionary destination.[20] Although we know little about where many of them went, there is good evidence Thomas took the gospel to India. A Christian community bearing Thomas's name has existed there since the first century. According to tradition, Thomas arrived in India in the days of King Gundaphorus and began distributing alms to the poor.[21] In southwest India the "Church of Thomas" still exists.

Roberto de Nobili (AD 1577–1656), one of the most famous missionaries to India, served the people for over fifty years. Early on he decided to take the incarnational approach to win the Indians—he became like an Indian. He learned the high-caste Brahmin customs, became a vegetarian, and wore the robe of the gurus. He was the first European to study the classical language of India, Sanskrit. The fruit of de Nobili's dedicated work was the Christian conversion of nearly 200 Hindus.[22] He says,

---

[20] George Park Fisher, *History of the Christian Church* (New York: Charles Scribner's Sons, 1936), 33.

[21] Stephen Neill, *A History of Christian Missions* (London: Penguin Books, 1964), 44.

[22] Neill, 159.

These people have an ardent desire for eternal happiness, and in order to merit it devote themselves to penance, alms, deeds, and the worship of idols. I profit by this disposition to tell them that if they wish to obtain salvation, they must listen to my instructions; that I have come from a remote country with the sole object of bringing salvation to them.[23]

King Fredrick IV of Denmark decided that if Catholics were sending people to India, then so should Protestants. Though his motives may have included a political agenda to protect his territory there, God used him. One initial problem arose—no one from Denmark was willing to volunteer. The king looked to Germany for volunteers and found two: Bartholomaüs Ziegenbalg (1682–1719) and Heinrich Plutschau (1675–1752), the first Protestant missionaries.[24] Initially, Ziegenbalg had reservations; he struggled with illness and

---

[23] Lemuel Call Barnes, *Two Thousand Years of Missions Before Carey* (Philadelphia: American Baptist Publication Society, 1900), 96.

[24] Why is William Carey (1793) commonly referred to as the "Father of Protestant Missions" in light of the many that went before him? Timothy Tennent explains the difference between looking at time from a *kairos* moment (a specially appointed time) versus *chronos* moment (ordinary clock time). Tennent notes, "One of the perplexing curiosities in the history of missions is why William Carey became known as the 'Father of Modern Missions.' Occasionally you will read or hear statements that Carey was the first missionary of the modern period or that he was the first Protestant or even the first Baptist missionary. However, none of these statements are true. … The first Protestant missionaries, Ziegenbalg and Plutschau, translated the New Testament into Tamil by 1715…. William Carey is the father of modern missions because he stepped into a *kairos* moment, which stimulated the founding of dozens of new voluntary missionary *societies* and propelled hundreds of new missionaries out onto the field." Timothy Tennent, *Invitation to World Missions: A Trinitarian Missiology for the Twenty-first Century* (Grand Rapids, MI: Kregel, 2010), 258-259.

felt inadequate with no university degree.[25] After Plutschau signed on, Ziegenbalg was persuaded to accompany him. On July 9, 1706, Ziegenbalg arrived in India at the age of twenty-three and died after thirteen years. Plutschau spent five years in India before returning home to report on the mission and mobilize more manpower. The accomplishments of these two men are astounding. Ziegenbalg translated the entire New Testament and some of the Old Testament (Genesis to Ruth) into Tamil before his death. He also established a Christian community of approximately 350 people.[26] In July of 2006, India honored their memory and the 300th anniversary of their arrival with a weeklong celebration. They even commemorated them with a stamp bearing Ziegenbalg's picture.[27] Then came Carey.

William Carey left England and arrived in India in 1793. The people viewed him with suspicion and he therefore feared deportation by the Indian government. Carey decided to lay low and take a job at a plantation. The next five years proved to be fruitful as Carey learned the Bengali language and translated the New Testament. In his seventh year Carey finally saw his first convert. Carey passionately desired to meet India's spiritual needs without losing sight of their physical needs. Owen Milton, in his book *Christian Missionaries,* explains,

---

[25] Daniel Jeyaraj, *Bartholomaus Ziegenbalg: The Father of the Modern Protestant Mission* (Chennai, India: The Indian Society for Promoting Christian Knowledge, 2006), 58.

[26] Neill, 195, 197.

[27] S. Muthiah, "The Legacy That Ziegenbalg Left," *The Hindu,* India's National Newspaper, July 2, 2006.

There was a practical side to all this as he contributed to the solution of providing for the starving by attending to the need to grow fruit and vegetables. He fought against the hideous custom of *sati*, the burning of widows. He campaigned against infanticide, the killing of lepers, and the various ills with which Indian society and religion were afflicted. In Calcutta he established a leper hospital.[28]

Carey lived by the motto, "Expect great things from God; attempt great things for God." Throughout his thirty years in India he did just that. On top of his personal ministry and social justice pursuits, he also finished the translation of the entire Bible into Bengali, Sanskrit, and Marathi along with the translation of the New Testament into twenty-three other languages.[29] He gave clear instructions as to what he wanted inscribed on his gravestone: "A wretched, poor and helpless worm, on Thy kind arms I fall."

Sundar Singh was born in northern India in 1889 to a religious family. By seven years of age he had memorized the seven hundred verses that comprise the *Bhagavad Gita*.[30] Singh said, "I used to read the Hindu Scriptures till midnight, in order that I might in some way quench my soul for peace."[31] At the age of fifteen, Singh came across a copy of the New Testament and burned it. For some strange reason,

---

[28] Owen Milton, *Christian Missionaries* (Wales: Evangelical Press of Wales, 1995), 49.

[29] Neill, 224.

[30] C. F. Andrews, *Sadhu Sundar Singh: A Personal Memoir* (New York, NY: Harper and Brothers Publishers, 1934), 30.

[31] Andrews, 30.

he could not shake the way he felt afterward; his heart was restless. That night he could not sleep and prayed to Krishna for some revelation. That same night he had a vision of Christ, and he would never be the same.[32] Singh was radically converted and experienced immediate conviction to follow in his Savior's footsteps and live a simple life with no possessions. He took the name *Sadhu,* which means "wandering monk" or "someone who practices strict self-denial." Taking with him only clothes, a blanket, and an Urdu New Testament, he walked across northern India preaching the gospel for the next two years. He became known as the "Apostle of the Bleeding Feet." One biographer said that "in the history of religion, Sundar is the first to show the whole world how the gospel of Jesus Christ is reflected in unchanged purity in an Indian soul."[33] Singh wrote several books challenging Hindus to embrace Christ.[34] He died in the mountains of Tibet at forty years of age. Taking up his cross and following the Savior was no sacrifice but a wonderful privilege. His words reveal his deep passion. He said, "To follow Christ and bear His cross is so sweet and precious that, if I find no cross to

---

[32] Phyllis Thompson, *Sadhu Sundar Singh: A Biography of the Remarkable Indian Holy Man and Disciple of Jesus Christ* (Carlisle, CA: OM Publishing, 1994), 25-26.

[33] T. Dayanandan Francis, *Sadhu Sundar Singh: The Lover of the Cross* (Madras, India: Christian Literature Society, 1990), 1.

[34] Sadhu Sundar Singh's books were written in Urdu and then translated into English. They include *At the Master's Feet* (1922), *Reality and Religion* (1923), *Search after Reality* (1925), *Meditations on Various Aspects of the Spiritual Life* (1926), *Spiritual World* (1926), *Real Life* (1927), and *With and Without Christ* (1928).

bear in heaven, I shall plead before Him to send me as a missionary, if need be, to hell."[35]

Thomas, Ziegenbalg, Plutschau, Carey, and Singh all had one thing in common: their lives underwent "a sudden, complete, marked change." Having been revolutionized by the saving love of God, they took up His ambition and enlisted themselves as laborers in the vast harvest field of India. They looked beyond the intimidating surface of Hinduism to see the people beyond it. God used these men and a host of other men and women throughout history to perpetuate His plan of redeeming all nations. May God continue to raise up ministers to and from this diverse nation to the end that His glory fills the land!

---

[35] Francis, 1.

CHAPTER 9
THE CHINESE WORLD

The year was AD 1266, and the young Italian explorer Marco Polo had just trekked his way across Asia and into modern-day China. After meeting the emperor Kublai Khan, Marco Polo returned to Europe with an extraordinary request. Kublai Khan asked him to send one hundred missionaries back to China to teach the Christian faith to the educated. Kublai Khan wanted these missionaries to be able to show "to the learned of his dominions, by just and fair argument that the faith professed by Christians is superior to and founded on more evident truth than any other."[1] Khan said that if this happened, "he and all his potentates would become men of the Church."[2] This has been called one of history's most open doors! How did the church at Rome respond? Silence. Over twenty years passed until Pope Nicholas IV in 1289 finally sent two men, John of Monte Corvino and another who died en route. John reached China five years later in 1294 (he traveled by sea and spent thirteen months in India) to discover the window of opportunity for influencing

---

[1] Stephen Neill, *A History of Christian Missions* (London: Penguin Books, 1964), 107.

[2] Samuel Hugh Moffett, *A History of Christianity in Asia,* vol. 1, *Beginnings to 1500* (New York: Harper Collins Publishers, 1992), 446.

Kublai Khan and his educated men toward Christianity had been shut. By then the emperor had "grown too old in idolatry."[3] That same year Kublai Khan passed away. Opportunity lost.

A few years ago, my wife and I attended a dinner event in Beijing. In front of us must have been twenty main dishes to choose from. The mayor of a neighboring district approached me to ask a pressing request. "Todd, I would like for you to do something for me. We are lowering the age at which our children will begin to learn English. Schools across the entire country will be implementing language curriculum at the third-grade level. In light of this change, we need 100,000 English teachers to meet the school system's demands. Can you help recruit English speakers from America?" I sat there

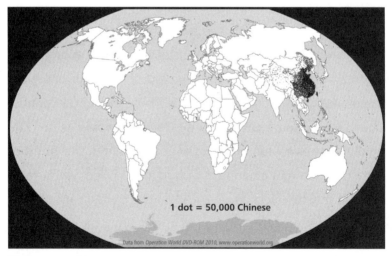

1 dot = 50,000 Chinese

Data from *Operation World DVD-ROM 2010*, www.operationworld.org

Chinese world map

[3]Neill, 108.

stunned at the opportunity. I pray the Western Church waits less than twenty years to respond and will send more than two![4]

THE CHANGING OF CHINA

A group called the Nestorians brought the first Christian witness in China (AD 431). This sect of Christians had been exiled for upholding a belief that conflicted with the historical church doctrine of Christ's personhood. They maintained that His divine and human natures consisted of two persons.[5] Because of their exile, they traveled to Persia and from there, sent missionaries into western China. This means Christianity has been in China longer than Buddhism has been in Japan!

The next major thrust of Christian expansion took place when the Jesuits, a society established by the Roman Catholic Church specifically to propagate and defend the Christian faith, arrived in China in the sixteenth century. The

---

[4] Carla Power of *Newsweek* writes that China's English fever has reached epidemic proportions in light of the 2008 Olympics. She states, "To achieve fluency, non-native speakers are learning English at an ever-younger age. Last year primary schools in major Chinese cities began offering English in the third grade, rather than middle school.... The demand for native English-speakers is so huge that there aren't enough to go around." China is importing English teachers from India. Carla Power, "Not the Queen's English," *Newsweek*, March 7, 2005. Available at newsweek.com.

[5] Nestorius declared that in Jesus there were "two natures and two persons," one divine and one human, thus veering from Christian orthodoxy which holds that the human and divine natures of Christ were united in one person. The Church realized the danger of "dividing the Savior into two beings" and condemned this view at the Council of Ephesus in AD 431. Thus while Nestorius (390–451) was exiled to the Libyan desert, his followers headed east. Justo L. González, *The Story of Christianity*, vol. 1, *The Early Church to the Dawn of the Reformation* (New York: HarperCollins, 1984), 254.

most influential Jesuit in China was Matteo Ricci, who arrived on the edge of the Chinese empire in 1582. Malachi Martin, an expert on the Jesuits, states, "By the late 1600s, Jesuit missionaries to China had made great progress toward converting the emperor of China together with powerful mandarins and nobles. They also had created a multimillion-member Church."[6]

Oh that I could get to them! Oh that I had a thousand tongues to proclaim in every land the riches of God's grace!

The first Protestant missionary to China was an Englishman named Robert Morrison who arrived in 1807. Morrison struggled to learn the language. He faced the added difficulty of a ruling that awarded the death penalty to anyone caught teaching Chinese to a foreigner. Miraculously, by 1819 Morrison translated the entire Bible into Chinese.[7]

This set the stage for Hudson Taylor's arrival in 1854. Born in England, Taylor became a Christian as a teenager. He developed a desire to take the gospel to China and sailed to Shanghai when he was twenty-one. During his five-month voyage from England to China, he wrote a letter revealing his deep conviction about his identity as a laborer in the harvest. Here is an excerpt:

---

[6] Malachi Martin, *The Jesuits: The Society of Jesus and the Betrayal of the Roman Catholic Church* (New York: Simon and Schuster, 1987), 210-211.

[7] Kenneth Scott Latourette, *A History of the Expansion of Christianity,* vol. 6, *The Great Century in Northern Africa and Asia 1800-1914 AD* (New York: Harper and Brothers Publishers, 1944), 297-298.

Shall we think ourselves free from responsibility to obey the plain command, "Go ye into all the world and preach the gospel to every creature"? Is that word of our Savior no longer true, "As My Father hath sent Me ... even so send I you"? Oh that I could get to them! Oh that I had a thousand tongues to proclaim in every land the riches of God's grace! Lord, raise up laborers, and thrust them forth into Thy harvest.[8]

As a pioneer of contextual ministry in China, Taylor's methods seemed eccentric. First, he dressed like a Chinese man and took on Chinese customs. Second, instead of insisting that the people learn English, Taylor learned Mandarin. He also challenged the norm by focusing his efforts on the interior of China. At this time the majority of missionaries resided on the coastlands. To draw more missionaries inland, Taylor founded an organization called the China Inland Mission (CIM) in 1865 which focused on reaching those with no access to the gospel in the interior regions of China. By 1895 the agency had grown to 621 Protestant missionaries.[9] Then disaster struck.

By the beginning of the 1900s, China had grown frustrated with the West because of their acts of imperialism, increased opium trading by Europeans, and proselytizing by missionaries. This vexation climaxed into the Boxer Rebellion, resulting in the deaths of 127 adults and 44 children

---

[8] Dr. Howard Taylor and Mrs. Howard Taylor, *Hudson Taylor in Early Years: The Growth of a Soul* (London: Morgan and Scott, 1911), 195.

[9] Dr. Howard Taylor and Mrs. Howard Taylor, *Hudson Taylor and the China Inland Mission: The Growth of a Work of God* (London: Morgan and Scott, 1920), 539.

from among the Protestant missionary societies.[10] CIM bore the heaviest losses.

In 1949 after years of civil war, fights with the Japanese, and clashes between political parties, the Communists overcame all political opposition. In front of an estimated one million spectators in Beijing's Tiananmen Square, Mao Ze-dong (Chairman Mao) announced the formation of the People's Republic of China. At that time Chinese Catholics numbered 3.2 million and Protestants were around 1.3 million.[11] More than 10,000 foreign missionaries were expelled.[12] It seemed all the work of those who had gone before would be lost. But Tertullian was right, "The blood of Christians is seed."[13] Today, estimates of the number of Christians in China range from between 30 to 100 million![14]

INTRODUCING CONFUCIUS

On the list of opposing forces to the gospel in China, Confucianism and Taoism certainly rank near the top. It is difficult to say if China's native philosophy of Confucianism can be categorized as a religion. The reason for doubt is that

---

[10] Marshall Broomhall, ed., *Martyred Missionaries of the China Inland Mission: With a Record of the Perils and Sufferings of Some Who Escaped* (London: Morgan and Scott, 1901), ix.

[11] David Barrett, George Kurian, and Todd Johnson, *World Christian Encyclopedia: A Comparative Survey of Churches and Religions in the Modern World,* vol. 1 (New York: Oxford University Press, 2001), 191.

[12] Paul Hattaway, *Operation China: Introducing All the People of China* (Pasadena, CA: William Carey Library, 2000), 1.

[13] Boniface Ramsey, *Beginning to Read the Fathers* (New York: Paulist Press, 1985), 126.

[14] Barrett, Kurian, and Johnson, 191.

Confucius's (551–479 BC) main interest was ethical and not religious. Confucius did not talk about supernatural things or beings. He refused to speak on the nature of man and even the way of heaven. The *Analects,* collected by his followers and the only reliable record of his teachings, state, "One can get to hear about the Master's (Confucius's) accomplishments, but one cannot get to hear his views on human nature and the Way of Heaven."[15] The *Analects* also say, "The topics the Master did not speak of were prodigies, force, disorder, and gods."[16]

Born in China as the youngest of eleven children, Confucius married at nineteen and worked in various government positions. At twenty-two he became a teacher and attracted a large following of students; his passions included history and music. He taught until he was fifty-one when he returned to politics as a minister of justice—a position similar to a police commissioner. Confucius later resigned due to lack of cooperation from his superior and spent fourteen years trying to find a position where he could implement his theories of government. He returned to his hometown and spent his few remaining years editing books. He died at seventy-three, disappointed, having no success in spreading his teachings and leaving behind no written work.[17] Only later did his followers compile his sayings and write them down in the *Analects.* So what exactly does Confucius have to do with the philosophy that bears his name?

[15] Confucius, *The Analects,* trans. D. C. Lau (London: Penguin Books, 1979), Book V:13.

[16] Confucius, *Confucius: The Analects.* Book VII:21.

[17] Freya Boedicker and Martin Boedicker, *The Philosophy of Tai Chi Chuan* (Berkeley, CA: Blue Snake Books, 2009), 9.

Confucius felt a burden for the moral responsibility of humanity. He saw himself not as someone who created new ideas, but as one who handed things down from one generation to the next. He once said, "I transmit but do not innovate."[18] He believed the *ren* (translated "humanity") is the good nature found in all mankind. Tapping into one's ren brings about an ideal state of life. Through education, self-cultivation, self-reflection, and adhering to the norms of one's culture, mankind can make this ideal state a reality. Each individual is responsible to transform him or herself and, as each individual is transformed, Confucius believed, society would in turn be transformed. World religion expert Dean Halverson writes, "Confucius, in other words, was humanistic in his orientation in that he found the solution to the cultural crisis in humanity itself, not in anything religious or spiritual."[19] Here is a brief overview of Confucius's belief system:

1. Human nature is good; evil is essentially unnatural.
2. The human will is completely free, and the conduct of man is not predetermined. He is the master of his own choices.
3. Virtue is its own reward. Human conduct is not religiously conditioned. One does not do good for reward or refrain from evil for fear of punishment.
4. No outside help from the gods or anyone else is available. It is a self-effort system.[20]

---

[18] Confucius, *Confucius: The Analects.* Book VII:1.

[19] Dean Halverson, *The Compact Guide to World Religions* (Minneapolis, MN: Bethany House Publishers, 1996), 73.

[20] The four main books to reference for Confucius's system of thought are 1) *The Book of Great Learning,* 2) *The Doctrine of Mean,* 3) *The Analects of Confucius,* and 4) *The Works of Mencius.* Charles Braden, *The World's Religions* (New York: Abingdon Press, 1939), 141.

Around 200 BC the emperors adopted Confucianism as the official ideology of China.[21] Confucius's system of thought became the single most significant factor in shaping the Chinese people.[22] His life, though uneventful, clearly impacted China to this very day.

THE TAO OF WHO

If Confucius's life seemed uneventful, the life of Lao-tzu the founder of Taoism, appears nonexistent by comparison.[23] Some scholars even suggest he was a mythical figure and the book *Tao Te Ching* (Taoism's sacred text) was compiled over the course of several centuries and then attributed to him.[24] Others suggest that Lao-tzu was a historian in charge of the emperor's archives.

Lao-tzu was a contemporary of Confucius, and their respective followers belittled each other.[25] Confucius emphasized society's role in providing harmony, while Lao-tzu took the opposite approach by prioritizing naturalism, letting things take their intended course while humanity retains a

---

[21] Halverson, 73.

[22] Lit-Sen Chang, *Asia's Religions: Christianity's Momentous Encounter with Paganism* (San Gabriel, CA: P and R Publishing, 1999), 43.

[23] I have chosen the Wade-Giles version of Romanization instead of Pinyin, the official system to transcribe Chinese characters. Wade-Giles is closer to English phonics. For Pinyin, it would be Daoism instead of Taoism, Laozi instead of Lao-tzu and Daodejing instead of Tao Te Ching.

[24] The *Tao Te Ching* is the most important book for those who practice religious Taoism. Other classic works for Taoism are 1) *Chuang-tzu,* 2) *Huai-nan-tzu,* and the 3) *Lieh-tzu.*

[25] Lao-tzu, *Tao Te Ching,* trans. D. C. Lau (London: Penguin Books, 1963), ix.

passive role. For example, when asked how one should repay injury, Confucius answered from a societal perspective: "Recompense injury with justice." In contrast, Lao-tzu said, "Recompense injury with kindness."[26] Allowing life to take its course without intervention constituted his philosophy. This is the *Tao* or "the Way." The *Tao Te Ching* says,

> There is a thing confusedly formed, born before heaven and earth. Silent and void, it stands alone and does not change, goes round and does not weary. It is capable of being the mother of the world. I know not its name so I style it "the Tao."[27]

What exactly is the Tao? The *Tao Te Ching* explains that the Tao existed before all things and all things conform to the Tao. In no place is the Tao explicitly defined, and it therefore cannot be explained nor can its eternal power. The Tao is not a supreme being, but a cosmic principle "permeating and infusing all aspects of creation with vitality."[28] One can discover the Tao through gods and divinities that have manifested themselves throughout history. After his death, Lao-tzu was quickly elevated to the status of one of these divinities. The Jade Emperor (creator), the Precious Spirit (great priest), and a number of other divinities flow from the Tao. Humanity can only commit to the Tao and conform to nature. This concept is called *wu-wei* and literally translates "non-doing."

---

[26] Braden, 147.

[27] Lao-tzu, *Tao Te Ching,* 25:56.

[28] Jennifer Oldstone-Moore, *Taoism: Origins, Beliefs, Practices, Holy Texts, Sacred Places* (New York: Oxford University Press, 2003), 34-35.

One of Taoism's most important concepts, in practicality it implies that no action which is contrary to nature should be taken, as this would resist the Tao. The world's troubles arise from humanity's acting and responding. This is where war, struggle, and suffering come from. Instead, the way of the Tao is to find happiness in non-action. Here is a helpful illustration by Lit-Sen Chang, author of *Asia's Religions.*

> A man who was afraid of his own shadow determined to run away from it. But the faster he ran, the faster his shadow followed him. He tried to run faster and faster until he was exhausted, he broke down and, as a result, he died! This fool was not aware that by simply going into the shade of a tree and resting under it, by "non-action," he would have gotten rid of his shadow immediately.[29]

This non-action is what achieves harmony in Taoism rather than effort or good works.[30] Taoism, like Confucianism, has significantly impacted East Asia and pervades many aspects of Chinese culture.[31]

---

[29] Chang, 97.

[30] In a clever attempt to increase Taoism's popularity among children in the West, Benjamin Hoff wrote a book entitled, *The Tao of Pooh.* He minimizes the Taoist faith to its simplest truths, using Winnie the Pooh and his friends to explain. Hoff opens the book with his desire to "write a book that explained the principles of Taoism through Winnie-the-Pooh, and explained Winnie-the-Pooh through the principles of Taoism." *The Tao of Pooh* was on the *New York Times* best seller list for 49 weeks. Benjamin Hoff, *The Tao of Pooh* (New York: Penguin Books, 1982).

[31] As we have seen, both Taoism and Confucianism have truly shaped the Chinese culture into what it is today and the reason for much of Chinese behavior and beliefs. However, the average Chinese person would not describe it in so many words. A Chinese person would not say, "I think thus because I follow Confucius." Rather she would say, "I think thus because I am Chinese."

THE CHURCH IN CHINA

Excited about our first Chinese church service in Beijing, we wondered if it would match what we'd read, heard, and imagined. Our driver dropped us off fifteen minutes early. As we entered the room, what we saw surprised us—hundreds of people already seated. After some singing in Mandarin, the pastor approached the podium and adjusted the microphone. He opened his Bible and, as the audience followed along, gave a challenging message from the life of Christ to live a holy life after His example.

Then I noticed that five men in the front row stood, walked over to the center, and raised a huge block of concrete out of the floor. Over a dozen worshippers approached the gaping hole. For the next several minutes, they descended into it and then emerged. They were being baptized! Afterward we left the sanctuary and walked to another building, the bookstore, where we purchased Bibles and other devotionals. Jess and I were visiting one of the churches governed by the Three-Self Patriotic Movement (TSPM).

Churches operating under the Three-Self umbrella are called "Three-Self churches," but the TSPM itself exists under a government branch, which a department of the Communist Party in turn directs. The TSPM began in the 1950s as the "Three-Self Patriotic Reform Movement." The words "patriotic reform" indicate the importance of this movement in ridding the Chinese Church of foreign influence at that time. Like most other religious bodies, the Three-Self disappeared from view during the Cultural Revolution (mid-1960s to mid-1970s). It was revived in the late 1970s as a continuing means whereby the Communist Party could exercise control over Protestant religious activities.[32] The term "three self" was actually coined by missionaries in the nineteenth century and refers to "self-government, self-support, and self-propagation." In other words, the church should not have foreign leaders directing it, nor foreign money financing it, nor foreign missionaries doing its work.

Many of the Three-Self churches are doctrinally orthodox, and many of the clergy are evangelical in their faith.[33] The government allows them to print and sell Bibles to all members. China currently prints approximately 12 million copies a year.[34] Ironically, I have a friend from Singapore who actually smuggles Bibles *out* of China since Chinese copies cost one-tenth of the price he pays in Singapore. Chinese Christians debate amongst themselves whether it is more beneficial to be a part of a Three-Self church or a house church. Some can't get to a Three-Self church because the distance is too great. Chinese Christians get nervous because Three-Self churches have to be registered by the government. They fear the government might change its policies and crack down on open worship. For this and other complex reasons, many Chinese brothers and sisters opt not to attend TSPM churches. The government sometimes monitors Three-Self churches as to the content of the preaching. For example, a

---

[32] Carl Lawrence, *The Church in China: How It Survives and Prospers under Communism* (Minneapolis, MN: Bethany House Publishers, 1985), 98. Also see David Adeney, *China: The Church's Long March* (Ventura, CA: Regal Books, 1985) and Paul E. Kauffman, *China, the Emerging Challenge* (Grand Rapids, MI: Baker Book House, 1982).

[33] David Aikman, *Jesus in Beijing: How Christianity Is Transforming China and Changing the Global Balance of Power* (Washington, DC: Regnery Publishing, 2003), 137.

[34] Austin Ramzy, "China's New Bestseller: The Bible," *Time,* December 17, 2007.

worshipper in a Three-Self church may seldom hear a message on the Second Coming of Christ, which authorities consider a doctrine at odds with the socialist view of human development.[35] Christians who want to avoid the Three-Self have other options, including the many different unregistered groups commonly referred to as "house churches."

Small groups of believers meeting in their homes even during the 1950s were the origin of China's renowned house churches. After Mao's death China turned from its extremist left-wing policies and opened again to the outside world. In response to the prayers of Christians around the world, God began showing what He had done both to preserve and extend His people in China. From scattered groups of home meetings, the house churches rapidly grew to include multimillion-member "networks" of churches based in countryside villages. These rural house-church networks, similar to denominations, continue to provide the bulk of church numbers in China.

As China has urbanized in the late 1990s and the first decades of the twenty-first century, the "third wave" of urban churches has arisen. "Third wave" refers to lively, mostly younger, house churches which are not associated with either the Three-Self Movement nor with traditional house churches.

Great differences in culture, education, living standards, theology, and practical expressions of faith exist between the different house-church models. One common characteristic is that they are not registered with the government. The house church today cannot be said to be "unified," and it would be inaccurate to talk about the house church

---

[35] Aikman, 137.

movement as though there were one single entity under one leadership. Instead, we can celebrate the diversity, vitality, and evangelical fervor of the many forms of unregistered churches in China now: the traditional, relatively smaller home groups; the big rural networks; and the energetic "third wave" urban churches. It is also no longer accurate to characterize the Church in China as a "suffering Church." While harassment continues, and a handful of brave souls endure prison for Christ's sake, the vast majority of Chinese Protestants live out their faith without much fear of severe reprisals. The Church in China grows and thrives in a nation where an authoritarian system seems to hold all the reins. But those who belong to God know better.[36]

MISSION FIELD OR MISSIONARY FORCE

Is China a mission field or missionary force? The answer is both. It is a mission field because one out of six people on the planet live in China. Though the gospel's spread there is steady and promising, it has been no match for the sheer number of people. And the population is growing. The stirring news of Christianity's expansion represents only a fraction of the people groups that exist in this massive country. Though there is still work to be done, God is clearly using the believers there to advance His kingdom both at home and abroad.

The expansion of the Church maintains a predominantly westward trend—from Jerusalem to Constantinople

---

[36] I am indebted to Elizabeth Lowe, a China ministry consultant, for shaping my understanding of the Church's "third wave" in that country.

(modern-day Turkey) to North Africa through Europe and over to the Americas. Now that the gospel has made its way over to China, some Chinese Christians see their role as messengers to take the gospel full circle—to take it back to Jerusalem. These Christians have made the fifty-one countries between China and Jerusalem a high priority. They are asking God to raise up perhaps as many as 100,000 Chinese believers to be missionaries and go to the regions along the Silk Road back to the Church's origin. The 6,200-mile Silk Road led traders from the Middle East to China. Chinese Christians believe it's time to take those roads back to Jerusalem; thus their vision has become known as the Back-to-Jerusalem Movement.[37]

In 1942 Mark Ma, vice president of a Bible institute in China, felt burdened for the Muslims living in northwest China. He challenged the students at the institute to join him, and they formed a group called "The Band That Spreads the Gospel All Over the Place." American missionary to China Helen Bailey heard of this group and circulated the story via her newsletter to the U.S. This was one of the ways the "Back-to-Jerusalem Band" got its name.[38]

A man by the name of Simon Zhao was a Chinese missionary sent out to the far western parts of the country bordering on Central Asia. He is credited for keeping the Back to Jerusalem vision alive when the Communist Party came to power in 1949, bringing to a close that period in

[37] For a full understanding of the movement, see Paul Hattaway, *Back to Jerusalem* (Carlisle, UK: Piquant, 2003).

[38] Kim-kwong Chan, "Mission Movement of the Christian Community in Mainland China: The Back to Jerusalem Movement," Seoul Consultation, Study Commission IX (2010) 71.

Chinese missions activity.[39] Zhao and his team of twenty were arrested and sentenced to forty-five years in prison. His pregnant wife, also arrested, suffered a miscarriage and ultimately death in prison. Several others of the team died in prison as well. Zhao said that many nights he would face the direction of Jerusalem and pray, "God, the vision that you've given us has perished, but I pray you'll raise up a new generation of Chinese believers to fulfill this vision."[40] After forty years, Zhao was released and passed the Back to Jerusalem vision on to the current Chinese house church leaders.

Today, over two dozen mission agencies and training centers exist in China, all trying to see this effort to completion. No doubt, it is not only a mission field but a missionary force!

---

[39] Timothy C. Tennent, *Theology in the Context of World Christianity: How the Global Church Is Influencing the Way We Think About and Discuss Theology* (Grand Rapids, MI: Zondervan, 2007), 237.

[40] Tim Stafford, "A Captivating Vision: Why Chinese House Churches May Just End Up Fulfilling the Great Commission—An Interview with Paul Hattaway," *Christianity Today,* April 2004.

CHAPTER 10
THE MUSLIM WORLD

I n 1978, historian Michael Hart wrote a book entitled, *The One Hundred: A Ranking of the Most Influential Persons in History*. With his book translated into over fifteen languages, Hart stirred controversy by giving the honor of Most Influential Person in History to Muhammad. He states, "My choice of Muhammad to lead the list of the world's most influential persons may surprise some readers and may be questioned by others, but he was the only man in history who was supremely successful on both religious and secular levels."[1] Who was this man that one out of every four people in the world see as the final prophet of God?[2]

THE MAN AND THE MESSAGE

Muhammad ibn Abdullah was born in AD 570 in Makka (modern-day Mecca, Saudi Arabia). During that time

---

[1] The top six of Michael Hart's list of one hundred are: (1) Muhammad (2) Isaac Newton (3) Jesus Christ (4) Buddha (5) Confucius (6) St. Paul. Michael H. Hart, *The One Hundred: A Ranking of the Most Influential Persons in History* (New York: Citadel Press, 1978), 3.

[2] Luis Lugo, "Mapping the Global Muslim Population: A Report on the Size and Distribution of the World's Muslim Population," The Pew Forum on Religion and Public Life, October 7, 2009. Available from pewforum.org.

in the Arabian Gulf, various clans traveled into Mecca to worship and offer their allegiance to over 360 deities.[3] These gods were displayed in the Ka'bah, a cube-shaped structure located in the center of the city. Mecca was a strategic city in light of its placement along the Red Sea between Yemen and the Mediterranean. Muhammad's father was named Abdullah, which in Arabic means "servant of Allah" (*Allah* is the Arabic word for God). He died soon after Muhammad's birth. When Muhammad was just six years old, his mother, Amina bint Wahb, also passed away, leaving him to be raised by his uncle, Abu Talib.

Muhammad spent his youth tending to caravans, guiding them across the Arabian Desert. On one commercial journey to Syria he even encountered Christian monks.[4] Muhammad, a religious man, would often steal away to fast and pray in solitude. When he was twenty-five years old, Muhammad married Khadija, a rich widow fifteen years his senior.[5] They had six children: two boys (who died very young) and four girls. Only one daughter, Fatimah, outlived Muhammad.

Khadija's wealth enabled Muhammad to devote more time to spiritual meditation. He regularly retreated to a cave on Mount Hira, three miles northeast of Mecca.[6] Muslim tradition asserts that there, in AD 610, the angel Gabriel

---

[3] Malise Ruthven, *Islam in the World*, 3rd ed. (New York: Oxford University Press, 2006), 28.

[4] Anne Cooper, ed., *Ishmael My Brother* (Great Britain: MARC Publications, 1985), 105.

[5] Fazlur Rahman, *Islam* (Chicago: University of Chicago Press, 1966), 11.

[6] Ali Dashti, *Twenty Three Years: A Study of the Prophetic Career of Mohammad* (Costa Mesa, CA: Mazda Publishers, 1985), 23-24.

appeared to him and said, "Recite in the name of your Lord who created, created man from clots of blood! Recite! Your Lord is the Most Bountiful One, who by the pen taught man what he did not know."[7] Muhammad was forty and unable to read or write, so the angel charged him to recite those words.

Muhammad's first converts were his wife and his cousin Ali ibn Abi Talib. Over the next few years, as Muhammad's preaching became more public, he attracted ridicule from upper-class politicians. His stance on idol worship and wealth began to undermine their source of power. His claim to speak directly from Allah showed he must be dealt with. A failed assassination attempt caused Muhammad to seek asylum elsewhere. Medina (then called Yathrib), a city approximately 225 miles north, proved open to Muhammad's teaching, so he and his band of 150 loyal followers snuck out of Mecca in AD 622 and journeyed there in hopes of finding refuge.[8]

Though Medina offered the safety they sought, it also presented a new challenge—one that would shape the identity of this emerging faith. The responsibility to feed, clothe, and educate the small group who'd abandoned everything in Mecca fell upon Muhammad. Since Muhammad's past experience had trained him in the ways of camel caravanning, he knew the routes, the seasons, the habits, and the skills of this timeless Middle Eastern tradition. Forced to use desperate measures, Muhammad led his followers in raiding caravans, taking their loot and coercing conversion at

---

[7] *The Koran,* trans. N. J. Dawood (Great Britain: Penguin Books, 1956), Sura 96:1-5.

[8] The year AD 622 is called "the flight," and for the Muslim calendar it is equivalent to AD 0. Norman Geisler and Abdul Saleeb, *Answering Islam: The Crescent in Light of the Cross* (Grand Rapids, MI: Baker Books, 1993), 76.

sword-point. At first, they preyed on small bands and spilled no blood. Tasting success led the early Muslims to believe Allah was on their side.

Eventually as desert caravans became aware of the dangers of Muslim raiders, they fortified themselves by adding men and arms to their expeditions. One of the most important battles for Muslims, the Battle of Badr, involved a wealthy Meccan caravan which, fearing the raiding Muslims, added 1,000 men for protection. Muhammad spent the night in prayer. The next day his 300 men conquered the multitude. He referred to this battle in the Qur'an, saying, "It was not you, but Allah who slew them. It was not you who smote them: Allah smote them so that he might richly reward the faithful" (Sura 8:17). The Meccan tribe rallied 3,000 men for a counterattack against Muhammad. Seventy Muslims died and Muhammad himself was severely wounded. Rumors about his death spread through the camp.[9] Muhammad wasted no time in recovering his reputation and triumphed in a subsequent battle, the Battle of Ditch. In this war, Muhammad put 600 adult Jewish males to death and sold their women and children into slavery because he suspected they betrayed him to his enemy tribe.[10]

Muslims continued to justify themselves in their extreme and bloody warfare and in fighting during sacred months in which tribal attack was forbidden.[11] Muhammad, defending their actions, said, "People ask you about fighting in the forbidden month. Say: 'Fighting in it is a grave matter,

---

[9] Samuel M. Zwemer, *The Moslem World* (Nashville, TN: Publishing House of the M.E., 1908), 15.

[10] Ruthven, 55-56.

but more grave than this is blocking the path of Allah and rejecting Him'" (Sura 2:217). Their success proved to Muhammad's followers that Allah was indeed an ally of Islam and therefore no undertaking, fighting or otherwise, would lack his support. Muslim raiders offered a choice to all their victims: convert to Islam, pay a tax for protection, or fight. Many chose to convert, and in a mere eight years, Muhammad's following increased a hundredfold from 100 to 10,000. He began to set his sights on Mecca.

On January 30, AD 630, he led his army into the city with an offer for their peaceful surrender. They complied. Muhammad's first act as prophet and king over Mecca was to destroy all idols and proclaim "Allahu Akbar" (Allah is the Greatest). On June 8, AD 632, at age sixty-three, he fell ill with a fever and died. He is buried in Medina.

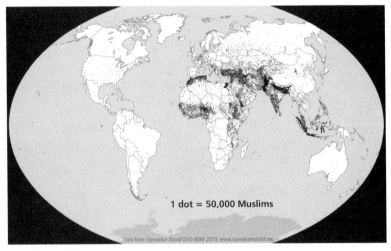

1 dot = 50,000 Muslims

Data from *Operation World DVD-ROM 2010*, www.operationworld.org

Muslim world map

[11] Ruthven, 50-52, 56.

THE SIX TENETS OF FAITH

The word *Islam* means "submission to Allah" and refers to the religion itself. A *Muslim* is "one who submits to Allah" and the individual who practices the faith. To be a Muslim you must abide by the six tenets of Islam. You might be surprised how similar these six tenets sound to doctrines of the Christian faith.

There is one God, who is All-Powerful: Allah is seen as the almighty, the creator, and the sovereign sustainer of everything. Islam holds that there are ninety-nine names of Allah, including: All-Powerful, All-Knowing, and Eternal. He has no partner, and every other god is false. The Qur'an states, "And call not with Allah any other god; there is no god but He" (Sura 28:88). It is important to understand that Allah does not reveal himself, only his will. This means Allah does not enter into a relationship with Muslims. "The Muslim is called to obey Allah, not to know him."[12] The Fatherhood concept of God is completely rejected.

There are angels, good and bad: Allah created angels to praise him and to bow before humans. Satan refused, was cursed, and is now the enemy of man and in authority over all demons.

> And when your Lord said to the angels: "I am going to create a man (Adam) from sounding clay of altered black smooth mud. So, when I have fashioned him completely and breathed into him the soul which I created for him, then fall down prostrating

---

[12] Timothy C. Tennent, *Invitation to World Missions: A Trinitarian Missiology for the Twenty-first Century* (Grand Rapids, MI: Kregel, 2010), 80.

yourselves unto him." So, the angels prostrated themselves, all of them together. Except Iblis (Satan),—he refused to be among the prostrators.... Allah said, "Then get out of here, for indeed, you are expelled." (Sura 15:28-34)

The Qur'an also mentions the angel Gabriel as the angel who appeared to Muhammad in the cave and told him to "recite!" (Sura 2:97-98). The Angel of Death, the angel who will blow the trumpet on the last day, and the angel Michael are also mentioned in the Qur'an (Sura 2:98, 32:11). Other angels, called recording angels, keep account of one's good and bad deeds.

God spoke through the prophets of old: There are twenty-five prophets mentioned in the Qur'an, and many are the same as those found in the Bible. To name a few: Abraham, Isaac, Jacob, Moses, Elijah, Elisha, Jonah, and John the Baptist. Muslims consider these prophets messengers from Allah, and many of their stories also correlate with biblical accounts. However, Islam is adamant the final prophet is Muhammad. The Qur'an states, "Muhammad.... is the Apostle of Allah and the last of the prophets" (Sura 33:40).

God has given us Holy Scriptures: Muslims believe the Holy Books are the recorded words Allah revealed. The five Holy Books Muslims embrace today are: the *Suhufs* (given to Abraham, which are now lost), the *Torah* (given to Moses; our Pentateuch), the *Zaboor* (the Psalms), the *Injil* (given to Jesus and was lost or changed), and the *Qur'an* (given to Muhammad).[13] While three of the five Holy Books

---

[13] Jay Smith, "Six Muslim Beliefs (Iman) and a Christian's Response: For a Muslim Enquirer," May, 1995. Available at debate.org.uk.

support the Christian faith (Torah, Zaboor, and Injil), Muslims believe the Qur'an is the last word of God.

The Qur'an is the highest authority for every Muslim. Taught orally by Muhammad for twenty-three years of his life (from his cave experience at age forty until his death at sixty-three), it was codified in AD 657, almost twenty-five years after his death.[14] The word *Qur'an* means "recitation," referring to when Gabriel recited the words from Allah to Muhammad. It includes 114 chapters called *suras* that together contain 6,219 verses. Most Muslims believe the Qur'an eternally existed in the mind of Allah and is the unalterable word of Allah.[15] That is why, since its original revelation was in the Arabic language, Muslims consider translations an alteration and do not accept them as the true Qur'an. Muslims being groomed for leadership are required to memorize it in full.

What God has predestined will occur: Allah is in complete control and his plans will not be thwarted. Everything happens because he has willed it. It is impossible to have a conversation with a Muslim without hearing the phrase "In sh'allah" (if Allah wills it). It signifies that a Muslim can rest assured because no matter what happens in life, Allah is in control.

God will come and judge the world: Islam attests that everyone will face a day of judgment according to their beliefs and deeds. Tradition holds that when a person dies,

---

[14] Timothy Tennent, *Christianity at the Religious Roundtable: Evangelicalism in Conversation with Hinduism, Buddhism, and Islam* (Grand Rapids, MI: Baker Academic Publishing, 2002), 144.

[15] The Ibadhi sect (the majority group in Oman) strongly rejects the teaching that the Qur'an is eternal. They say only Allah is eternal.

two angels visit him in the grave and ask him a series of questions: "Who is your Lord?" "What is your religion?" and "Who is your Prophet?" They place each individual's good and bad deeds on a scale and weigh them. These factors combine to make a person a favorable candidate for either hell or paradise. Ultimately, though, Allah retains the final word.

THE FIVE PILLARS

Whenever I meet a Muslim, I like to ask, "Are you devout?" It's a difficult question to answer for them. But after a moment of pondering, the response usually goes back to the five pillars of Islam. One's ability to uphold all five defines devotion.

The Creed (Shahada): The creed is Islam's proclamation that "there is no god but Allah and Muhammad is Allah's messenger." In Arabic it is "La ilaha illa Allah Wa Muhammadun rasul Allah." This simple confession, once uttered sincerely, makes one a Muslim. It should be recited aloud without hesitation, understood, and believed in one's heart. These are the first words whispered into a newborn's ears and the last words on the lips of the dying.[16]

Prayer (Salat): Though the Qur'an never explicitly defines the number of times per day one should pray, sacred tradition affirms five.[17] Every Muslim's duty, it should be done with the community of believers at the mosque as much as

---

[16] Cooper, 114.

[17] The times and names of prayer are as follows: (1) Dawn—*Fajr* (2) Just after midday—*Dhuhr/Zuhr* (3) Late afternoon—*Asr* (4) Immediately after sunset—*Maghrib* (5) An hour and a half after sunset, and before midnight—*Isha.*

possible. It is believed Muhammad said, "The reward of the prayer offered by a person in congregation is twenty-five times greater than that of the prayer offered in one's house or in the market alone."[18] The first prayer begins at dawn and the last starts an hour and a half after sunset. In Muslim lands, the call to prayer is a pervasive presence. Crying out all day, it's an inescapable affirmation of Islamic belief. Translated from Arabic, the prayer is,

> Allah is most great, Allah is most great, Allah is most great, I witness that there is no god but Allah: I witness that there is no god but Allah. I witness that Muhammad is his messenger, I witness that Muhammad is his messenger. Come to prayer, come to prayer. Come to prosperity, come to prosperity. Allah is most great. Allah is most great. There is no god but Allah.

Charity (Zakat): Muslims are to be characterized as generous people. Islam requires them to give 2.5 percent of their income to the poor, new converts, or others in need. Today most Muslims fulfill Zakat by giving to their parents or other family members. The Qur'an states giving to one's family yields a double reward: "Righteousness is this, that one should believe in Allah … and give away wealth out of love for him to the near of kin and the orphans and the needy and the wayfarer and the beggars" (Sura 2:177).

Fast (Sawm): For all Muslims who are physically able, fasting during the month of Ramadan (the ninth month of the lunar Hijri calendar) is mandatory. Considered an act of

---

[18] Phil Parshall, *Understanding Muslim Teachings and Traditions: A Guide for Christians* (Grand Rapids, MI: Baker Books, 1994), 63.

worship, Muslims deny themselves food, drink, and sexual relations during the daylight hours for the entire month. During this time they are to do good deeds, spend time memorizing the Qur'an, and make requests of Allah. "There is triumph of mind over matter. The desires to quench thirst, to soften the pangs of hunger, or to light a cigarette are placed in their proper perspective as things which can be postponed, and in some cases given up altogether, if necessary."[19] Muslims believe "when the month of Ramadan comes, the gates of Paradise are opened and the gates of Hell are closed, and the devils are chained."[20] Ironically, many Muslims gain weight during Ramadan because they sleep during the day and celebrate all night with excess food intake.[21] One friend of mine told me that he had to go on a diet after his month of fasting!

One special night comes during Ramadan—the Night of Power. To Muslims, the ear of Allah is never closer than on the Night of Power for it is believed on this night, in AD 610, he handed down the verses of the Qur'an to Muhammad. This one night is more valuable than a thousand months. "And what will explain to you what the Night of Power is? The Night of Power is better than a thousand months" (Sura 97:2-3).

Pilgrimage (Hajj): All Muslims who are physically and financially able have the duty to visit Mecca at least once

---

[19] Kenneth Cragg and Marston Speight, *Islam from Within: Anthology of a Religion* (Belmont, CA: Wadsworth Publishing Company, 1980), 55.

[20] Parshall, 75.

[21] "Gulf Muslims Gain Weight in Ramadan," *Kuwait Times,* August 31, 2008.

in their lifetime. The Ka'bah, the holiest site for all Muslims, is located there. Islam holds that Adam built the original Ka'bah, which Abraham later rebuilt. The Black Stone resides in the southeast corner of the Ka'bah. Its worth lies in the belief that Muhammad himself placed the stone there and that the stone, originally white, has turned black from the sins of the people. During the hajj, pilgrims wear a seamless white robe (signifying the rich and poor are both humbled before Allah) and circle the Ka'bah seven times before kissing the Black Stone. Muslim tradition states, "Every step taken by the pilgrim in the direction of the Ka'bah blots out a sin; and the person who dies on his pilgrimage is enrolled among the martyrs."[22]

Striking similarities exist between the demands of Islam and those of Judaism and early Christianity.

Striking similarities exist between the demands of Islam and those of Judaism and early Christianity. Islamic scholar J. Dudley Woodberry observes that the pillars of Islam are all adaptations from Jewish and Christian forms.[23] The first pillar, confession (*shahada*), was based on Deuteronomy 6:4, "Hear; O Israel: The Lord our God, the Lord is one." The second pillar, prayer (*salat*), is seen in both Jewish and

---

[22] Cooper, 126.

[23] J. Dudley Woodberry, "Contextualization Among Muslims Reusing Common Pillars," *International Journal of Frontier Missions* 13, no. 4 (Oct.-Dec. 1996).

Christian history. Jews practiced formal prayer three times a day, and Christian monks prayed up to seven. Woodberry suggests Islam took a middle position with five times a day. The third pillar, almsgiving (zakat), not only mirrors the New Testament ideal of giving, but also reflects biblical truths that one should give secretly and that God blesses the giver (Matthew 6:1-4, Sura 2:271). The fourth pillar, fasting (sawm) is similar in that Moses, Elijah, and Jesus each fasted for forty days and nights. Paul also fasted frequently. The fifth pillar, the pilgrimage (hajj), is found in Psalm 81:3-4 when the Israelites assembled in Jerusalem for the sacrifices. Festivals gathered the Israelites together in Jerusalem three times a year. Because Christianity and Judaism both pre date Islam, and Muhammad interacted with both Jews and Christians, it's no stretch to imagine the formation of the five pillars was an attempt by Muhammad to earn favor and audience with his monotheistic contemporaries.

THE QUR'AN AND JESUS

My wife and I had just moved to the Middle East. We found an apartment, got a car, enrolled in Arabic class, and headed out to meet some locals. The first person I met was a college student named Abdullah. He spoke good English, and we connected right away. He invited me, his friends, and his brothers to his house for a meal. Halfway through the meal, Abdullah looked up at me and asked, "Todd, in your opinion, what is the most important verse in all the Qur'an?" I almost choked on my piece of lamb! Fresh off the plane and this was the introductory question into my first friendship! Sura 112:1-2 came to my mind and I quoted, "Allah is One. Allah is He on Whom all depend." Abdullah nodded his head in agreement, suggesting I had done well. As we continued to talk, he shared about his work on a class project—an essay on the topic "Who was Jesus?" I asked him what he had concluded. "Jesus is one of the most unique people who has ever been born, lived, and died," he answered. A little shocked, I asked him to elaborate. He explained, "He was born of a virgin, did many miracles, and then ascended to Allah; who else has done these things?" I asked, "What have you been reading?" (thinking he had stumbled onto a New Testament). He responded, "Oh, I found all of that in the Qur'an!"

The Qur'an mentions Jesus by name twenty-five times.

The Qur'an mentions Jesus by name twenty-five times (it mentions Muhammad four), and it affirms His birth, life, and ascension. The following provide a few examples:

Jesus's birth: "O Mary! Allah giveth thee glad tidings of a Word from him: his name will be Christ Jesus, the son of Mary, held in honor in this world and the hereafter." She said: "O my Lord! How shall I have a son when no man hath touched me?" He said: "Even so: Allah createth what he willeth: when he hath decreed a plan, he says 'Be,' and it is!" (Sura 3:45-47)

Jesus's miracles: "He will be a messenger to the children of Israel saying, "I have come to you with a sign from your Lord.... I heal him who was born blind, and the leper, and I bring the dead to life by Allah's leave.... Surely therein is a sign for you if you believe.'" (Sura 3:49)

> *Jesus's ascension:* And when Allah said: "O Jesus, I am going
> to terminate the period of your stay (on earth) and cause you to
> ascend unto me ... then to me shall be your return." (Sura 3:55)

It's clear Christianity and Islam share common ground in elements of Jesus's identity—no Muslim would dispute the virgin birth, Jesus's many miracles, His ascension to Allah, or His expected return. We share other aspects of faith in common as well, such as the following:

- Allah created the earth in six days (Sura 25:59), culminating in the creation of the first man, Adam. He and his wife ate the forbidden fruit and became aware of their nakedness (Sura 20:115-112).
- Allah sent Moses to confront Pharaoh, inflict the plagues on Egypt, and lead the Israelites out of Egypt by parting the Rea Sea (Sura 26:9-75).
- Allah gave Moses the Ten Commandments on two tablets of stone (Sura 7:143-150).
- Noah built the ark (Sura 11:25-49).
- King David committed adultery with Bathsheba (Sura 28:21-25).
- The queen of Sheba visited Solomon (Sura 27:22-44).
- Jonah was swallowed by the great fish (Sura 37:139-148).

Timothy Tennent, in his book *Christianity at the Religious Roundtable,* observes a broader connection between Christianity and Islam: "In addition to specific references to God, Islam shares common theological categories with Christianity, including concepts such as sin, righteousness, divine judgment, heaven, hell, forgiveness, and mercy."[24] So where do our paths separate?

THE PARTING OF WAYS

In AD 615, as persecution of Muslims increased in Mecca, a small group led by one of Muhammad's daughters, Ruqayyah, fled across the Red Sea to modern-day Ethiopia. Ethiopia's Christian king, Negus, granted them protection. The king desired to learn the faith of his new refugees, so they shared elements of the Islamic belief system regarding the one true God and the prophets Jesus and Muhammad. After hearing this, King Negus picked up a stick, drew a line in the sand, and said, "As God is my witness, the difference between your position and ours is not as wide as this line."[25] Timothy Tennent reminds us that though our differences are few, the "theological significance stemming from those few issues is *deeper* than the Red Sea."[26]

It is important to note that Muhammad did not have access to a Bible. No Arabic translations existed in the seventh century. Forced to rely on oral traditions and his own understanding, his picture of Scripture was skewed. For example, you may have heard that Muslims vehemently oppose our idea of the Trinity. Well, Muhammad thought the

---

[24] Tennent, *Christianity at the Religious Roundtable,* 152-153.

[25] Sayed Ali Asgher Razawy, *Restatement of the History of Islam and Muslims* (United Kingdom, World Federation of KSI Muslim Communities). Available at portalislamica.org. Also see Tennent, *Christianity at the Religious Roundtable,* 151-152.

[26] Tennent, *Christianity at the Religious Roundtable,* 166.

members of the Trinity were the Father, Son, and Virgin Mary. The Qur'an says, "And Allah will say: O Isa (Jesus) son of Marium (Mary)! Did you say to men, Take me and my mother for two gods besides Allah...?" (Sura 5:116). So, while a major element of the chasm that stands between us is where we stand on the Trinity, what they oppose is also emphatically opposed by all Christians.

Islam rejects the notion that God would have a son. In the Islamic worldview, this idea lowers Him to the level of an animal. Muhammad was reacting against the polytheistic tribal religions which dominated Mecca, the deities of which procreated sons and daughters through physical relations. Again, it's largely an issue of semantics because Muslims understand the sonship of Christ as originating from a sexual relationship between God and Mary. We, however, understand that sonship has less to do with Christ's physical birth, since He eternally existed with God. Rather, the title "Son" has more to do with the fact that Jesus does the will of the Father and represents Him.[27] The Qur'an states,

> In their ignorance they have falsely ascribed to him sons and daughters. Glory be to him! And high let him be exalted above that which they attribute to him! Sole maker of the heavens and of the earth! How, when he hath no consort, should he have a son? (Sura 6:100-101)

Muslims can't fathom God having a Son, much less ascribing deity to Him. In Islam, the greatest sin someone

---

[27] Colin Chapman, *Cross and Crescent: Responding to the Challenge of Islam* (England: InterVarsity Press, 1995), 191.

could commit is called *shirk*, the attribution of a partner to Allah. The Qur'an asserts, "Allah forgives not [the sin of] joining other gods with him; but he forgives whom he pleases other sins than this: one who joins other gods with Allah, hath strayed far, far away" (Sura 4:116). Indeed, our differences are few, but they run as deep as the Red Sea!

Islam also rejects the crucifixion. Muslims do not believe Christ endured this death. They choose rather to believe Allah raised Jesus to heaven before He was crucified. On the cross, in Jesus's place, hung another man who all wrongly perceived to be Jesus.

> They say, "Verily we have slain the Messiah, Jesus the son of Mary, an apostle of Allah"—yet they slew him not, and they crucified him not, but they had only his likeness. (Sura 4:156-157)

As one Islamic scholar suggested, "The idea of the physical death of the Infinite God is no doubt the worst blasphemy that has been uttered in the world, even a denial of God coming next to it."

When striving to understand Islam, it is important to know Islam and Christianity share a common ground to build upon. They speak of our prophets and retell many of our biblical stories. Yet the Bible is clear: when you reject the divinity of the Son, you also reject the Father! "Whoever denies the Son does not have the Father; the one who confesses the Son has the Father" (1 John 2:23 nasb). Don't be mistaken in believing that our similarities are enough to affirm Muslims and Christians worship the same God. Don't make the opposite mistake of avoiding Muslims out of fear or ignorance. Every Muslim people group around the globe will one day have a representative before God's throne. It will happen! And God is inviting us now to partner with Him to strive toward its completion.

CHAPTER 11
THE BUDDHIST WORLD

"Wake up, Todd, it's time to go." It was an early start to a long day. After a Nepali breakfast with my friend Roshen, we jumped onto the back of his motorcycle. A 180-mile journey loomed ahead of us that would take us from Kathmandu, the capital of Nepal, to Lumbini, Nepal. Once we left the congested city and hit the open road, with the Himalayan foothills in the distance, we rode only a few hours before we reached our destination—the birthplace of Siddhartha Gautama, founder of Buddhism.

I knew we were getting close to this secluded city when I heard a distant beating of air. Coming over a hill I saw, to my amazement, thousands of prayer flags flapping in the wind. Making our way to the Holy Pond, I noted that every possible branch, tree, and light post fluttered with a string of flags attached. This is the site where Buddha's mother washed before giving birth to him. Some people drank the filthy water; some swam in it. I settled for a picture and a few hours of pondering the man whose teachings would give rise to a major world religion.

THE FOUNDER HIMSELF

In 563 BC, approximately 600 years before Christ, Siddhartha Gautama was born of royal parentage and into a life of privilege. His mother, Mahamaya, died seven days after giving birth to Gautama.[1] His father, Suddhodana, loved him dearly and granted his every wish. Suddhodana forbade his son to leave the palace grounds, attempting to shield him from witnessing the tragic realities of old age, sickness, and death. At age sixteen Gautama married his cousin, Yasodhara. The older Gautama grew, the more difficult he became to contain. Around twenty-nine years of age, he snuck out on a secret venture beyond the palace walls and encountered three strange sights: an old man, a very sick man, and a corpse. He asked his chariot driver and only confidant, Channa, the reason for these tragedies. Channa replied, "Master, there is no escape. Old age, sickness, death—such is the lot of all men."[2] Gautama began to wonder how anyone could truly enjoy life with such suffering. He lost all joy. No one at the palace could offer a remedy for old age, sickness, or death. The next time he escaped to the forbidden reality that surrounded his palace, he passed an ascetic practicing self-denial and noticed what calm eyes this man had. Gautama felt the only way to get sufficient answers to his questions was likewise to become an ascetic.

---

[1] Antony Fernando and Leonard Swidler, *Buddhism Made Plain* (Maryknoll, NY: Orbis Books, 1985), 10.

[2] Nancy Wilson Ross, *Buddhism: A Way of Life and Thought* (New York: Vintage Books, 1980), 6.

One morning before his thirtieth birthday, Gautama kissed his sleeping wife and newborn son, Rahula, good-bye and exchanged his luxuriant lifestyle for a begging-bowl and simple robe. He set out on a journey from modern-day Nepal to northern India where he sat under Hindu gurus for six years in search of inner peace.[3] This is known in the Buddhist tradition as the Great Departure. Gautama writes, "While still young, a black-haired young man endowed with the blessing of youth, in the prime of life ... I shaved off my hair and beard, put on the robes, and went forth from the home life into homelessness."[4]

A legend claims that at times during this quest he lived on a grain of rice a day. At first, Gautama studied under a very famous, albeit reclusive, high-caste Brahmin named Alara Kalama. Despite his profound wisdom, Gautama doubted whether Kalama's teaching would ever lead to liberation from suffering. He went to another famous sage, renowned for his methods of bodily discipline, Uddaka Ramaputta.[5] Ramaputta admitted that he never heard of anyone able to solve the problems of old age, sickness, and death.

His questions unanswered, Gautama increased his self-denial of basic necessities and continued his journey. One day, extremely weak and near death, he passed out. When he revived, he came to the obvious conclusion that his extreme methods were not working. Instead he decided to take the middle ground between pursuing pleasure and pov-

---

[3] Vadanya [Chris Pauling], *Introducing Buddhism* (New York: Windhorse Publications, 1997), 6.

[4] Bhikkhu Bodhi, ed., *In the Buddha's Words* (Boston: Wisdom Publications, 2005), 56. *Majjhima Nikaya,* 1, 163.

[5] Ross, 9.

erty. This philosophy became the foundation for Buddhism and is known as the "Middle Way." Gautama rested under a tree to regain strength. There he began meditating. He vowed not to get up until he found what he sought. Buddhists believe that over the course of forty-nine days, his meditation increasingly deepened, and layer after layer of reality peeled away until he achieved a total perception of truth. He saw a great light symbolizing that he had fulfilled his quest—supreme enlightenment. In that moment, Siddhartha Gautama became a Buddha (Enlightened One). Since Gautama was the first man to become a Buddha, followers regard him as *the supreme* Buddha. The tree he meditated under was henceforth called a Bodhi tree (tree of enlightenment). The Buddha (Gautama) declared,

> Vainly I sought the builder of my house, through countless lives. I could not find him.... How hard it is to tread life after life! But now I see you, O builder! And never again shall I build

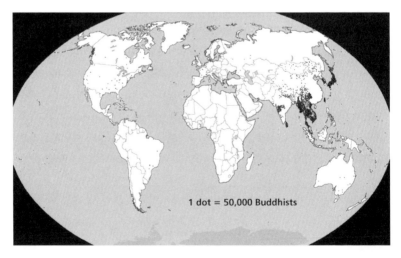

1 dot = 50,000 Buddhists

Buddhist world map

my house. I have snapped the rafters, split the ridgepole, and beaten out desire. Now my mind is free.[6]

For the next forty-five years, Gautama walked the length of northern India propagating his "Middle Way." He died of food poisoning at the age of eighty in an obscure village in Kusinara, India.[7] What exactly did Gautama discover beneath the Bodhi tree?

PATH TO NOTHINGNESS

Siddhartha Gautama's new teaching was a strong reaction against Hinduism. He intensely denounced the two central tenets of Hinduism—the soul and Brahman. Fed up with the high-caste Brahmin priests and their speculative Hindu philosophies, Gautama reserved his harshest criticism for them. He states, "It is like a line of blind men, each holding on to the preceding one; the first one does not see, the middle one also does not see, the last one also does not see. Thus, it seems to me that the state of the Brahmins is like that of a line of blind men."[8] If his new philosophy rejected gods, there would be no need

---

[6] *The Dhammapada: The Sayings of the Buddha,* trans. Thomas Byrom (Boston: Shambhala Publications, 1993), 41-42.

[7] Michael Carrithers, *The Buddha: A Very Short Introduction* (New York: Oxford University Press, 1983), 98.

[8] *Majjhima Nikaya*, 95. The *Majjhima Nikaya* is also called the "Middle-Length Discourses" of the Buddha. A modern translation of the complete *Majjhima Nikaya* is *The Middle Length Discourses of the Buddha: A New Translation of the Majjhima Nikaya,* trans. Bhikkhu Nanamoli and Bhikkhu Bodhi (Boston: Wisdom Publications, 1995). Also see John Dickson, *A Spectator's Guide to World Religions* (Sydney, Australia: Blue Bottle Books, 2004), 55.

for sacrifices. With no sacrifices there would be no need for priests. With no priests, the caste system would be obsolete.[9] Thus, Buddhism's fundamental teaching allows no place for gods; one achieves salvation through one's own efforts.

Gautama did, however, take from Hinduism the concepts of *samsara*, *karma*, and reincarnation (he termed it rebirth).[10] *Samsara* means "passage" and represents life as a continuous movement from one moment to the next. In trying to understand samsara, it helps to picture life as a wheel, cyclical rather than linear. The wheel of samsara has twelve spokes. Timothy Tennent explains:

> Simply put … the entire phenomenal world arises because it is linked with something else. The wheel of *samsara* is constantly turning, but it is sustained by the twelve spokes of (1) ignorance, (2) karmic predispositions, (3) consciousness, (4) name and form, (5) the five senses and mind, (6) contact, (7) feeling and response, (8) craving, (9) grasping for an object,

---

[9] Charles Braden, *The World's Religions* (New York: Abingdon Press, 1939), 123.

[10] Reincarnation in Hinduism and rebirth in Buddhism are actually quite different. In reincarnation, Hinduism embraces the transmigration of a soul from one body to another, and from past to present to future. A helpful analogy is to imagine water in a bowl. This water is poured into another bowl and then into another bowl. The exact same water is transferred from one bowl to another bowl. In contrast, Buddhism denies the existence of the soul; therefore, there is nothing that can transmigrate from the past to the present to the future. Rebirth for Buddhists is often described like a flame of a dying candle being used to light a new candle; both flames are connected, but not exactly the same. "When a person dies and is reborn, the new personality that's reborn is a continuation of the previous personality and is ever-changing. The personality that's reborn is neither exactly the same nor completely different from the previous personality in the previous life." "Rebirth, Reincarnation and Recognition of Past Lives," Know Buddhism, March 3, 2009. Available at knowbuddhism.info.

(10) action toward life, (11) birth, and (12) death. Each of these elements arises because of its dependence on the other link. Because the chain or wheel is circular there is no end to it, and it is, to use the words of the Buddha, "the origin of this whole mass of suffering."[11]

Karma, the law of retribution which results in reward or punishment for humans, keeps one on the spinning wheel in a never-ending cycle.[12] Mankind is screaming, "Get me off this wheel!" and the only hope Buddhism can offer is to break one of the spokes, thus ending the cycle. Gautama believed the two weakest of the twelve spokes were ignorance and craving. In other words, these two held the least power over a person; they were the most easily overcome (for example, by gaining knowledge to replace ignorance or by completely resisting one's cravings). When one breaks the cycle, one enters the state of *nirvana* or "extinction," which is Buddhism's equivalent to salvation. Entering nirvana, they are annihilated. However, since Buddhists reject the concept of the soul, there really is no self to annihilate. It is therefore more accurate to say the "annihilation of the illusion, of the false idea of self."[13]

Mankind is screaming, "Get me off this wheel!"

---

[11] Timothy C. Tennent, *Christianity at the Religious Roundtable: Evangelicalism in Conversation with Hinduism, Buddhism, and Islam* (Grand Rapids, MI: Baker Academic Publishing, 2002), 92.

[12] David Burnett, *The Spirit of Buddhism* (Grand Rapids, MI: Monarch Books, 1996), 12.

[13] Walpola Rahula, *What the Buddha Taught,* 2nd ed. (New York: Grove Press, 1974), 37.

When a monk asked Gautama, "What is there after nirvana?" Gautama answered, "One lives the holy life with nirvana as its final plunge, as its goal, as its ultimate end."[14]

A friend of mine got me a birthday card. Pictured on the front was Siddhartha Gautama with his disciples gathered around him, all of them grinning ear to ear. Gautama opens his present—a cardboard box with the bottom cut out of it. Staring at the ground through the box, Gautama's caption reads, "Just what I wanted, nothingness!"

SAVE ME FROM MY NON-SELF

Buddhists believe that after Gautama became fully enlightened, he taught the way for every individual to attain it. Nancy Ross explains, "What the Buddha had to teach was seemingly, but deceptively, simple. He said, in effect: All humanity is sick. I come therefore to you as a physician who has diagnosed this universal disease and is prepared to help you cure it."[15] Buddhism's cure for this sickness is found in the Four Noble Truths.

The First Noble Truth: All of life consists of suffering (*dukkha*). From birth to old age, one word sums up all life's journey: suffering. No one, whether rich or poor, is able to escape it. It is the universal experience of all mankind. Gautama describes the First Noble Truth, saying, "Now this, monks, is the noble truth about suffering: Birth is suffering, decay is suffering, sickness is suffering, death is suffering.... To be conjoined with things which we dislike; to be separated

---

[14] Rahula, 40.

[15] Ross, 23.

from things which we like—that also is suffering."[16] Gautama did not feel as though his perspective was pessimistic; rather, he considered himself a realist. It is important to note Buddhists do not deny the existence of happiness or enjoyment. However, both these experiences are fleeting and impermanent, abandoning you to sadness again once the situation changes. Hans Schumann, author and scholar of Buddhism, explained, "Everything joyful and dear ends in suffering because it is transitory. It is false happiness, for it has to be counterbalanced with sorrow and tears."[17]

As long as you pursue your desires, you will be bound by a cycle of dissatisfaction and suffering.

The Second Noble Truth: The world tells you to satisfy your every desire. In so doing, people believe, you will find happiness. Buddhism suggests the complete opposite. The cause of suffering *is* one's desires. Without our personal longings, suffering would cease to exist. So, desires must be inhibited and repressed at every turn. As long as you pursue your desires, you will be bound by a cycle of dissatisfaction and suffering.[18] Since life is ever changing, your desires will never be satisfied and the wheel of samsara will continue on an endless course.

---

[16] Friedrich Max Müller, ed., *The Sacred Books of the East,* vol. XIII (Oxford: Clarendon Press, 1881), 95.

[17] Hans Wolfgang Schumann, *Buddhism: An Outline of Its Teachings and Schools* (Wheaton, IL: The Theosophical Publishing House, 1973), 40.

[18] Vadanya, 50.

The Third Noble Truth: One liberates oneself from suffering by eliminating all desire. The Third Noble Truth reveals there *is* freedom from suffering—nirvana. This is the good news for Buddhists. Each person possesses within themselves the ability to overcome. Gautama stated, "By one's self, the evil is done; by one's self, one suffers: by one's self, evil is left undone; by one's self, one is purified. Lo, no one can purify another."[19]

The Fourth Noble Truth: If the First Noble Truth describes the condition of our lives, the Second Noble Truth diagnoses the problem. The Third Noble Truth shows the cessation of suffering is possible. Then the Fourth Noble Truth provides the solution—following the Eightfold Path. The Eightfold Path expounds right behavior, right meditation, and right knowing. This is the most important of all the Noble Truths because in it Gautama reveals the way that leads to liberation. His goal was to lay out a new philosophical code. In contrast to Hinduism, which affirms many roads to liberation from samsara, Gautama developed a specific path or "prescription" to follow in pursuit of enlightenment. He believed these eight steps summarized his new philosophy:

1. Right understanding.
2. Right purpose.
3. Right speech.
4. Right conduct.
5. Right livelihood.
6. Right effort.

---

[19] *The Dhammapada, The Sayings of the Buddha,* trans. Thomas Byrom, 45.

7. Right awareness.
8. Right meditation.

The first two habits in the Eightfold Path deal with *wisdom.* They emphasize the importance of deepening one's understanding of truth. The next three deal with *ethical conduct* and develop the morality of the individual. The final three habits revolve around *mental discipline.* They focus on getting one's thought life under control in order to attain nirvana. John Dickson observes, "You will notice that the Eightfold Path has little to do with prayer, worship of a god, and religious ceremonies. For this reason, some Buddhists avoid calling their way of life a 'religion' at all. The Eightfold Path is all about attaining a realization of 'the way things are' as Buddhism presents it."[20] During the forty-five years Gautama propagated his teaching, practically all of his focus was on the Eightfold Path. He challenged his audiences to follow each step simultaneously since all eight are inextricably linked. Buddhist monk and scholar Walpola Rahula in his book *What the Buddha Taught* explains:

> One may see that it is a way of life to be followed, practiced, and developed by each individual. It is self-discipline in body, word and mind, self-development, and self-purification. It has nothing to do with belief, prayer, worship, or ceremony. In that sense, it has nothing which may popularly be called "religious." It is a Path leading to the realization of Ultimate

---

[20] Dickson, 73.

Reality, to complete freedom, happiness and peace through moral, spiritual, and intellectual perfection.[21]

I recently heard a story regarding a missionary who gave a copy of the New Testament to a Buddhist monk. After a few days, he inquired to see if the monk had read it. To the missionary's surprise, the monk was extremely thrilled with the life of Jesus and proclaimed that Jesus was his new mentor. The missionary, a bit shocked, asked why. The monk responded, "Jesus attained enlightenment in just four life-times. He was born in Matthew, died at the end of Matthew; reborn in Mark, died at the end of Mark; reborn in Luke, died; was reborn in John, and then died a fourth time and attained enlightenment." The Middle Way, the Four Noble Truths, and the Eightfold Path form the lens through which all Buddhists filter life's experiences.

Though we have discussed the background of historic Buddhism accurately, the way Buddhism actually plays out can be very different from country to country. Mark Leighton, an expert in Buddhism, rightly observes,

While "pure" Buddhism has no gods, priests, or sacrifices, what is actually done in "folk" Buddhism may be full of gods, priests, and sacrifices. Buddhism is like a sponge and it absorbs local religions.... So there are temples, idols, incense, and candles. There are spirits, angels, and demons. There are ceremonies to deal with bad karma. There are rituals and rites. One may go to temple A, not get what they want, then they go to shrine B and so forth until they get what they want.

---

[21] Rahula, 50.

Why is it that "pure" Buddhism has little appeal to people in the so-called Buddhist countries? Why do the people have to "corrupt" Buddhism to satisfy their longings and needs? Is it because "pure" Buddhism is lacking? Very few are trying to escape the wheel of suffering but are fatalistically accepting that as impossible, so the only thing to do is to "eat, drink, and be merry" for tomorrow we die![22]

BUDDHISM MADE FAMOUS

Following Siddhartha Gautama's death, Buddhism did not spread rapidly. However, one key event changed its course and propelled the obscure philosophy to the status of a major world religion. One of the greatest kings of India, King Asoka Maurya, converted to Buddhism. King Asoka, a mighty conqueror, not only founded the Indian Empire but expanded it from modern-day Pakistan to Bangladesh. During his reign he ruled almost all of the Indian subcontinent. Horrified by the carnage and ruin caused by war, Asoka sought peace in the passivity of Buddhism. The king and his entire court converted.[23]

Siddhartha Gautama intended, from its inception, for Buddhism to be a missionary philosophy.[24] Soon after his

---

[22] Mark Leighton has worked in the Buddhist world for several years and has a deep knowledge of "folk" Buddhism.

[23] Anuradha Seneviratna, ed., *King Asoka and Buddhism: Historical and Literary Studies* (Sri Lanka: Buddhist Publication Society, 1994), 116.

[24] The distinction between a missionary religion and a non-missionary religion is that a missionary religion is global in scope and global in application. There are three missionary religions in the world: (1) Christianity: "Then Jesus came to them and said, 'All authority in heaven and on earth has been given to me. Therefore go and make disciples of all nations," (Matthew 28:18-19), (2) Islam: "Call all men to the path of our Lord" (Sura 16:125), and 3) Buddhism: "May I be able to disclose the teachings of the Buddha to all the world with all the voice that exists in the world" (Tatagatha Gurath Sutra).

first sermon, Gautama sent out sixty of his early followers, saying,

> O monks, I am liberated from all human and divine bondage and you too are liberated. So start on your way and go forth for the good and the happiness of many in compassion towards the world.... Do not go two by two on the same road. Preach the Law which is charitable in its beginning, in its middle, and its end. [25]

King Asoka captured this heart of Buddhism. Asoka aggressively sent Buddhist missionaries all over Asia and Europe. Even his own son became a Buddhist missionary to modern-day Sri Lanka. Under his rule numerous temples were built and monuments carved to the Buddhist faith. Many still stand. Today there are many nations whose major religion is Buddhism: Japan, Bhutan, Thailand, Sri Lanka, Myanmar, Cambodia, Laos, and Vietnam.

Around the same time as King Asoka's reign, Buddhism began to divide. The two main emergent schools of thought became known as Mahayana Buddhism and Theravada Buddhism.[26] Though differences between them abound, the major separation is over who can be enlightened: How narrow

---

[25] Siddhartha Gautama also stated, "Go forth, for the gain of the many, for the welfare of the many, in compassion for the world. Proclaim the Doctrine glorious, preach a life of holiness, perfect, and pure." Christmas Humphreys, *Buddhism: An Introduction and Guide* (London: Penguin Books, 1951), 61.

[26] A third branch of Buddhism is known as Vajrayana (or Tantrayana) Buddhism, which includes Tibetan Buddhism. The symbol of Tibetan Buddhism is the Dalai Lama. For more information on Tibetan Buddhism see John Powers, *Introduction to Tibetan Buddhism* (Ithaca, NY: Snow Lion Publications, 1995). Also see Robert A. E. Thurman, *Essential Tibetan Buddhism* (San Francisco: Harper San Francisco, 1995).

is the path? More conservative Theravada Buddhism takes a limited stance, saying only the few who adhere to the strict observance of all the rules (basically, only committed monks) can be enlightened. Conversely, Mahayana Buddhism asserts that anyone can attain enlightenment, whether monk, businessman or school teacher, rich or poor, man or woman, old or young. Mahayana Buddhism also adds a provision to aid those in pursuit of enlightenment—the *bodhisattva,* or wisdom being. A bodhisattva is someone who has already achieved enlightenment and yet chooses not to enter nirvana for the sake of others. They turn their back on what they have rightfully earned in order to be a guide. "Now the cosmos is filled with countless bodhisattvas, both here on earth and in various heavenly realms, who can also assist an earthly spiritual pilgrim toward enlightenment."[27]

Another division in Buddhism involves what is considered scripture. Theravada Buddhism states only the Pali Canon (the original teachings of Gautama) should be called sacred. The Pali Canon is divided into three groups known as the *tripitaka,* meaning "three baskets" of teaching. These are (1) Buddha's sermons, (2) rules for monks, and (3) philosophical teachings. The Pali Canon is seventy times larger

---

[27] In Mahayana Buddhism we find a close comparison to the Reformation's central theological contribution, "Salvation by grace through faith." Obviously, it is not in the full Christian understanding of the phrase. However, in this sect of Buddhism a person trusts in their bodhisattva to attain enlightenment. Timothy Tennent suggests, "There is a remarkable sense in which the helplessness of the human condition and the desperate cry for grace continue to push their way to the surface of world religions." For more information on this topic, Tennent denotes an entire chapter to it in *Theology in the Context of World Christianity: How the Global Church Is Influencing the Way We Think About and Discuss Theology* (Grand Rapids, MI: Zondervan, 2007), 158. Also see Tennent, *Christianity at the Religious Roundtable*, 93.

than the Bible.[28] Followers of Theravada Buddhism believe in the historic authenticity of the Pali Canon and are extremely reluctant to adopt any practices that are not prescribed in it.[29] In contrast, Mahayana Buddhists believe other writings could be included beyond the Pali Canon and believe the teachings of the Buddha continued even after his death.[30] They would argue that during Siddhartha Gautama's day, the people were not able to understand the deeper truths and thus these teachings were delayed until people were ready. Mahayana Buddhism makes up approximately eighty percent of Buddhists in the world.

In 1903 a girl by the name of Tshering was born in Bhutan, a small country between China and India. She married at a young age and had five children. A devout Buddhist, she sought diligently to raise her children according to the teachings. In her heart, she silently wrestled, lacking peace and the assurance she would find enlightenment. Her husband died when her children were grown, and this deepened her sense of turmoil over the afterlife. As a widow she could fully devote herself to the teachings of the Buddha by becoming a Buddhist nun. She traveled throughout Bhutan

---

[28] Dean Halverson, *The Compact Guide to World Religions* (Minneapolis, MN: Bethany House Publishers, 1996), 60.

[29] For a succinct understanding of Theravada texts, see Bhikkhu Bodhi, ed., *In the Buddha's Words* (Boston: Wisdom Publications, 2005).

[30] The foremost thinker on Mahayana Buddhism is Paul Williams, who experienced conversion to Christianity. He shares his conversion story in his book *The Unexpected Way* (New York: T & T Clark, 2002). Also see Paul Williams, *Mahayana Buddhism: The Doctrinal Foundations* (London: Routledge, 1994). For a succinct understanding of Mahayana texts, see *A Treasury of Mahayana Sutras: Selections from the Maharatnakuta Sutra,* trans. Garma C. C. Chang (New York: The Pennsylvania State University, 1983).

from one monastery to another performing all the proper rituals and sitting at the feet of the wisest monks her religion offered; her unrest lingered, unabated. But God was going to find her. Dawa, Tshering's grandson, a Buddhist like the rest of the family, feared rebirth because he'd collected quite a list of bad deeds. On the other hand, his college roommate was gentle, loving, caring, and seemed to have hope; his roommate was a Christian. Dawa's curiosity as to the source of his roommate's peace led to many probing conversations. The result was that Dawa gave his life to Christ. Excited, he shared the good news with his family. They disowned him immediately. And then to everyone's astonishment, his grandmother Tshering began to weep and said, "I have searched every monastery, sought every wise monk, pored over the text, and this is the answer I've been looking for. This is it!" I recently spent two weeks with Dawa and he never grew tired telling this testimony to God's grace. God is at work redeeming people from the Buddhist world to Himself!

As we conclude this section on the world's religions, let us not forget the purpose for our study. If we allow God's Word to be our guide, we clearly see that the globally redemptive plan He initiated with Abraham provides the theme for the whole of Scripture. It has caught up every generation of believers in its wake since Genesis 12. This revolution now comes to us and beckons us to see the world as God does. That is our purpose here—not to be more religiously astute, but to have His eyes and therefore to move out and embark upon a life lived with kingdom impact.

THE WORK

"World evangelization requires the whole Church to take the whole gospel to the whole world."

- John Stott

CHAPTER 12
THE WORLD CHRISTIAN

ome things in life are optional, some things are not. Getting married is optional. Loving your wife is not. Wearing shoes is optional. Eating is not. Driving is optional. Driving on the correct side of the road is not. Becoming a Christian is optional. Becoming a World Christian is not.[1]

This section focuses on the work God entrusted to His followers. How do we as believers look at the Word and the world, and then engage in the work God has for us? Make no mistake, though no two journeys are the same, every believer has a strategic part to play in world evangelization. God is inviting us to a World-Christian lifestyle (not to be confused with a *worldly* Christian lifestyle). The World Christian is a believer who has discovered the truth about God's unfulfilled global purpose and His desire to reach all peoples. Such people understand they are now responsible to act, pray, think, and believe according to this truth.[2] World Christians have reached the conclusion that God's *Word* is a missions book, and they embrace God's plan as the theme which unifies Scripture. World Christians see the *world* through the filter

---

[1] C. Peter Wagner, *On the Crest of the Wave: Becoming a World Christian* (Ventura, CA: Regal Books, 1983), 5.

[2] David Bryant, *In the Gap* (Ventura, CA: Regal Books, 1979), 73.

of this biblical theme, which inevitably causes them to grow in knowledge and personal application. They recognize the people and parts of the planet with no access to the gospel. They actively participate in the *work:* reaching out to internationals, praying for the world, giving sacrificially, raising awareness of missions, and going overseas either short-term or long-term. Though an individual's circumstances and surroundings are in constant flux, such things do not define one as a World Christian. The World Christian embraces a lifelong commitment to God's purpose, doing whatever it takes—going or staying—to be strategically involved. World Christians willingly make sacrifices no matter their season of life and continually strive to align their lives with God's redemptive agenda.

World Christians are not called such based on location, nor are they given this title because of an overseas experience they had one summer or for any other single, specific role they fill. World Christians are on a journey, a journey of walking with a missionary God through the good works He has set out for His followers. It is not about a time commitment or task, but a lifestyle of being engaged with God in reaching the world.

COMING TO TERMS

In the past when one spoke of missions involvement, it was primarily in the context of going. Unfortunately, ingrained in the minds of many churchgoers today is the idea that to be used by God among the nations means one thing: living overseas. This perspective is harmfully narrow because it conveniently excludes most people, namely the person holding that view. Today's globalization demands a much broader definition of involvement.

The term "World Christian" actually first appeared in 1919 in a book by Daniel Fleming called *Marks of a World Christian.* Fleming writes,

> One can be a World Christian in the smallest community of America. Reading, prayer, giving, all the manifold forms of holding the ropes for those who have gone abroad, are ways in which one may express one's interest in the world.... For those who stay and those who go, "the field is the world"— not the distant portions only, but the whole world.[3]

How insightful Fleming was in observing the breadth of World Christianity: giving financially, interceding on behalf of the world, taking personal responsibility to care for those on the mission field, and personal missions education are all involved.

David Bryant did not invent the term "World Christian" but he most assuredly did more than anyone else to highlight it. Sixty years after Daniel Fleming's book, Bryant popularized the term in his landmark work entitled, *In the Gap: What It Means to be a*

"When my activities and interests don't vitally link me to the reaching of earth's unreached people, I've succumbed to pea-sized Christianity."

---

[3] Daniel Johnson Fleming, *Marks of a World Christian* (New York: Association Press, 1919), 190.

World Christian. Bryant brought to light what he understood as a major problem with the Church; he calls it "pea-sized" Christianity. This is Christianity with little to no vision. Bryant elaborates,

> When my Christian experience expands no further than *my* salvation or small group, or church, or future, it's pea-sized. When I compartmentalize my walk with Christ in neat packages of prayer, Bible study, worship, fellowship, evangelism, and (somewhere off to the side) missions, it's pea-sized. When my activities and interests don't vitally link me to the reaching of earth's unreached people, I've succumbed to pea-sized Christianity.[4]

Bryant realized that if we serve a global God, then we must have a global vision. This vision is not for a select elite who seem to have life all together, but for every Christian, no matter their current stage of life: the mother of twins in Iowa going to the mosque to meet Muslim women, the young man in Texas mobilizing his church to pray for China, the college student in Nebraska recruiting a summer team to work in Thailand, the seven-year-old boy who just came on my friend's support team for a one-time gift, the newly retired couple from Michigan on their way to India to oversee a school. We are all a part. Everyone can and should be involved.

---

[4] Bryant, 28.

MAXIMUM IMPACT

No one just wakes up one day and says, "I am a World Christian!" It doesn't happen overnight and it doesn't happen without effort. We have an amazing capacity to forget the world. However, by developing our understanding of the biblical basis of missions, putting forth continual effort to grow in knowledge and awareness of the world, and involving ourselves in the work of God, we can catch the World-Christian vision and consistently live it out. J. Herbert Kane, author of *Wanted: World Christians,* says, "If the World Christian

Some World Christians will have the biggest impact by staying, some by going.

lives up to his name, he will believe that the prime responsibility of the Church is the evangelization of the world. He will also believe that this responsibility devolves not just on the pastors, missionaries, and other full-time workers, but on every member of the Christian community. To this end, he will devote a good share of his time and energy."[5]

In the Great Commission, Jesus gave a global sweep of the task the apostles would face. He did not emphasize one particular place or assignment at the expense of another, but commanded, "Go and make disciples of all nations" (Matthew 28:19). Patrick Johnstone reminds us,

---

[5] J. Herbert Kane, *Wanted: World Christians* (Grand Rapids, MI: Baker House, 1986), 160.

> The Great Commission is not just the glamorous "far far away," but the humdrum local outreach in the streets and fields where the believers live, and also to the difficult sections of the community nearby that we would normally seek to avoid. Jesus was not giving a range of alternatives from which we could choose, but showing that every Christian has a global concern, even if his calling is to a specific location whether local or afar.[6]

Don't think you need to fly over salt water to be spiritual. Living as a World Christian is bigger than that. Some World Christians will have the biggest impact by staying, some by going. The World Christian follows God as He redeems all peoples, no matter what continent he is on.

My wife was exposed to the world's needs her freshman year of college. Her immediate response was to spend a summer overseas. The opportunity arose for her to go to Papua New Guinea. To hear her talk about it—it was an incredible summer! But as it drew to a close, Jess started to get excited about returning home and resuming, in her words, "normal Christian life" where everyone looks the same, dresses the same, goes to church, and loves Jesus. Just as Jess was preparing to check "go overseas" off the Christian to-do list, she began to understand the people of Papua New Guinea are always on God's heart. In fact, God had been longing to draw the unreached people of that island to Himself long before she'd arrived, and actually, long before she was born! God changed Jess's definition of "the

---

[6] Patrick Johnstone, *The Church Is Bigger Than You Think: The Unfinished Work of World Evangelism* (Great Britain: Christian Focus Publications, 1998), 21.

normal Christian life" to encompass this ongoing awareness of the lost. Still today, her testimony is "His heart is for the world and that alone is a good enough reason to make it my heart, not just a summer plan." Being a World Christian has nothing to do with location, profession, spiritual gifting, or calling; it has everything to do with the fact that we love and serve a missional God. To follow Him means to conform to His heart, His ambition.

Just as in 1919 Daniel Fleming pointed out the various habits of a World Christian, so today everyone, no matter their location, can take part in key habits: going, sending, praying, welcoming, and mobilizing. Let us take a closer look at each while we take our own spiritual pulse in light of the World-Christian lifestyle.

CHAPTER 13
REVOLUTIONARY GOING

I recently heard of a student who was trying to find out what country God wanted him to minister in. Overwhelmed by options and desperate, he decided to throw a dart at a world map and, no matter where it landed, that was God's intended destination for him. It landed in the ocean.

The first habit we come to in our World-Christian quest is going—being physically present, ministering in a cross-cultural setting. Going may mean a short-term trip or an entire life spent in a foreign land. The goer immerses him or herself in an unfamiliar culture with the intention of furthering the gospel.

WHOLLY AVAILABLE

The book of Exodus opens with God explaining to Moses His plans to send Moses back to rescue the Israelites from the hand of the Egyptians. It says,

> The Lord said, "*I have* indeed seen the misery of *my* people in Egypt. *I have* heard them crying out because of their slave drivers, and *I am* concerned about their suffering. So *I have* come down to rescue them from the hand of the Egyptians

and to bring them up out of that land into a good and spacious land, a land flowing with milk and honey.... And now the cry of the Israelites has reached *me*, and *I have* seen the way the Egyptians are oppressing them. So now, go. *I am* sending you to Pharaoh to bring *my people* the Israelites out of Egypt." (Exodus 3:7-10)

Nine times in this short passage, God references His own desire and concern for the Israelites.[1] During this entire discourse, God refers to Moses only once. "So now, go. I am sending *you*" (Exodus 3:10). Many of us can identify with Moses's reaction in the next verse. It reads, "But Moses said to God, 'Who am I, that I should go to Pharaoh and bring the Israelites out of Egypt?'" (Exodus 3:11). Sounds like us sometimes, doesn't it? God's calling inevitably draws all our insecurities to the surface. We see our struggles, our weaknesses, and our doubts, but we forget God will give us everything we need. God is not part of the equation—God *is* the equation. God's response to Moses is simple: "I will be with you" (Exodus 3:12). God's strength and power stand at our disposal, yet we seldom tap into them.

The promise of God's presence motivates us to move out and gives us the confidence to withstand the inevitable trials connected to going. We are not alone. God was with Abraham in Genesis 12. God offered His abiding comfort to Isaac as he stepped out in obedience (Genesis 26:3). God affirmed Jacob, Isaacs's son, of His presence (Genesis 31:3). As Joshua set out to conquer the Promised Land, he

---

[1] Bob Sjogren, Bill Stearns, and Amy Stearns, *Run with the Vision* (Minneapolis, MN: Bethany House Publishers, 1995), 141-142.

relied on God's guidance (Joshua 1:5). This same assurance comes to believers in Jesus's commissioning, when He says, "Therefore go and make disciples of all nations.... And surely I am with you always" (Matthew 28:19-20). In our missionary endeavors today we find our security in the nearness of God.

God is not interested in our ability but in our availability. Many Christians get excited about possibly stepping out of their comfort zone and crossing a culture. However, something happens between their initial desire and actually boarding a plane. The steps required to make it a reality start to feel overwhelming. They focus on their weaknesses, their inadequacies, the things their family might say, the support they need to raise, or their inability to articulate the Trinity, and many never make it.

These doubts are valid. We *can't* make the global impact we have been called to on our own. But Scripture reminds us, "God chose the foolish things of the world to shame the wise; God chose the weak things of the world to shame the strong. He chose the lowly things of this world and the despised things—and the things that are not—to nullify the things that are, so that no one may boast before him" (1 Corinthians 1:27-29). We bring nothing to the table. It's all God! When Robert Morrison sailed to China to translate the Bible, the ship's captain asked sarcastically, "Mr. Morrison, do you really expect to make an impression on the idolatry of the great Chinese Empire?" "No, sir," Morrison replied. "I expect God will."[2] The truth of our inadequacy ought to produce in us a spirit of dependence, not despair. "Not that

---

[2] Kenneth Scott Latourette, *A History of Christianity,* vol. VI (New York: HarperCollins, 1944), 297.

we are adequate in ourselves to consider anything as coming from ourselves, but our adequacy is from God, who also made us adequate as servants of a new covenant" (2 Corinthians 3:5-6, nasb). Scripture exhorts us to rejoice in our weaknesses because they provide an opportunity for God's strength and sufficiency to be displayed.

BUT WHAT ABOUT ...

Over the last decade of encouraging Christians' involvement in world evangelization, I have found that certain common obstacles surface routinely. At times people use these as excuses, while at other times these reflect the honest issues someone is wrestling with. At the bare minimum, they present barriers that suppress any thought of going. It is beyond the scope of this chapter to give a detailed understanding of each.[3] However, my intention is to let the following list serve as a warning to any would-be revolutionary: If you allow them, these obstacles will have you questioning, like Moses, "Who am I that I should go?" Here are the top five:

Family: What do you do when God says go and family says no? There are two seemingly paradoxical commands in Scripture that God desires us to keep in balance, and we must be careful not to be extreme and one-sided. The tension exists between Exodus 20:12 ("Honor your father and your mother") and Luke 14:26 ("If anyone comes to me and does not hate his father and mother, his wife and children,

---

[3] For a more thorough explanation of these obstacles, see my previous book that dedicates a chapter to each. Todd Ahrend, *In This Generation: Looking to the Past to Reach the Present* (Colorado Springs, CO: Dawson Media, 2010).

his brothers and sisters—yes, even his own life—he cannot be my disciple"). How do these two passages coexist? The way to biblically heed both of these commands is to listen to parents' advice, speak with them in an honorable way, but to ultimately follow God's will when the two contradict.

"No aspect of Christian mission is more puzzling than this problem of a call."

Calling: J. Herbert Kane said, "No aspect of Christian mission is more puzzling than this problem of a call."[4] I couldn't agree more! Scripture alludes to three types of calling.[5] The first is the *mysterious call.* Here the call comes directly (even audibly at times) from God Himself. An example of this is when Peter saw a vision from God in Acts 10:10-20. The Macedonian call provides another well-known example (Acts 16:9). The second call is the *commissioned call.* It's found in Acts 13:1-3 when the leaders of the church in Jerusalem, under the direction of the Holy Spirit, identify Paul and Barnabas as set apart for a particular mission. The leadership commissioned them as missionaries to Antioch. The third call is the *common-sense* call. Believers were sent by virtue of the fact that a need had been made known. For example, in Acts, "it seemed good to the apostles and the elders, with the whole

---

[4] J. Herbert Kane, *Understanding Christian Missions* (Grand Rapids, MI: Baker Book House, 1982), 39.

[5] These three types of calling come from the observations of Paul Borthwick. See Steve Hoke and Bill Taylor, *Global Mission Handbook: A Guide for Crosscultural Service* (Downers Grove, IL: InterVarsity Press, 2009), 67.

church, to choose men from among them and send them to Antioch" (Acts 15:22, esv). The common-sense call is the most-experienced call among missionaries.

These three categories provide a guidepost to navigate the confusion of the call. I have met people who God called in a way that would certainly classify as a *mysterious call.* It is important, however, to note that these are the exception rather than the rule. The *commissioned call* confirms the responsibility of elders to speak direction into an individual's life as their ministry and gifting are discerned. Finally, more information is available to this generation than any other. Through television and the Internet, we have been made aware of the once-distant poverty, disease, and war. No one is ignorant of the world's condition. The natural conclusion for many: "It seems good that I should go."

Support Raising: Raising support is not unbiblical; it's just un-American. When Jesus sent out the twelve disciples for ministry in Matthew 10:9-10, He gave them specific instructions not to take money. Jesus taught that because of the nature of their work, they were worthy to receive compensation. He expected others to provide their physical needs so they could focus solely on the spiritual needs of the people. Not only did He exhort the disciples in this approach, but Jesus Himself, with abundant resources at His disposal, modeled it. The gospel of Luke tells us that various women in the community met His and the disciples' needs. Luke offers examples such as, "Joanna the wife of Cuza, the manager of Herod's household; Susanna; and many others. These women were helping to support them out of their own means" (Luke 8:3). It's no surprise the apostle Paul echoed this way of life in his writings. Paul was clear he had full privileges to receive financial gifts from others.[6] He said, "In the same way, the Lord has commanded that those who preach the gospel should receive their living from the gospel" (1 Corinthians 9:14). Don't fear support raising; it is a viable method God uses to send workers into His harvest.

Bad Theology: Scripture makes known the destiny of a person who dies without accepting Christ, and yet a misunderstanding of this truth keeps many from the mission field. As John's gospel says, "Whoever believes in him is not condemned, but whoever does not believe stands condemned already because he has not believed in the name of God's one and only Son" (John 3:18). Again John asserts that "Jesus answered, 'I am the way and the truth and the life. No one comes to the Father except through me'" (John 14:6). And yet another verse affirms, "For there is one God and one mediator between God and men, the man Christ Jesus" (1 Timothy 2:5). A belief that Jesus is merely *a* way to God rather than the *only* way will never stand up against the difficulties of going. It's increasingly popular, even among Christians, to assume Christianity, Islam, Buddhism, and Hinduism all offer acceptable paths to God; different route, same destination.[7] Nothing slows the momentum for missions more than bad theology.

Relationships: I have met hundreds of mission-minded singles who are on track to go overseas long-term. They have

---

[6] Scott Morton, *Funding Your Ministry: An In-Depth, Biblical Guide for Successfully Raising Personal Support* (Colorado Springs, CO: NavPress, 2007), 42.

[7] Approximately two-thirds of evangelicals (64 percent) think there are multiple paths to salvation. In mainline Protestantism the statistic is as high as 73 percent. The Pew Forum on Religion and Public Life: Surveys, "Many Americans Say Other Faiths Can Lead to Eternal Life," Dec. 18, 2008. Available from pewforum.org.

read all the books about the culture God has directed them to, mobilized others to go with them, and even tried to comfort their parents with the inevitability of living far away. Then they fall in love and missions gets kicked to the curb. They justify a new life direction. Relationships have detoured many potential missionaries.

I counsel the individual pursuing World Christian priorities who finds him or herself in a relationship with a Christian who is not to recognize the difference between being unaware and being disobedient. God's desire to reach all peoples could be a new concept. Your dating partner may have never been exposed to the idea or been challenged to take personal responsibility for world evangelization. Present the opportunity to move toward World Christianity. If their uninvolvement finds its roots in unawareness, this opportunity may remedy the situation. Uninvolvement rooted in disobedience is another story. These people understand God's desire to reach the nations, yet they choose inaction. Hudson Taylor broke off a relationship when the girl made it plain she would not go to China. She asked him, "Must you go to China? How much nicer it would be to stay here and serve the Lord at home!"[8] Not the smartest thing to say to a guy willing to give a thousand lives to China. If you plan on being a missionary, don't marry a Christian, marry a World Christian.

I know many couples where only one spouse has been mobilized to missions during the course of their marriage. Tension builds as their lives begin to diverge. One now wants to go to China—the other wants to go to counseling! I

---

[8] Dr. Howard Taylor and Mrs. Howard Taylor, *Hudson Taylor in Early Years: The Growth of a Soul* (London: Morgan and Scott, 1911), 110.

encourage the mission-minded partner to embrace patience and prayer. No one ever became a World Christian because they were scolded or guilted into it. Be patient and pray for their vision while you make the biggest impact for God's global cause within the context of the family you have.

WHY GO?

I recently decided to read through the New Testament with a very specific purpose. I wanted to see how Jesus and the apostles motivated people to be involved in furthering the kingdom of God. Honestly, I expected to find one or two motivations, but I was surprised to find Scripture offers several.

Love: Jesus takes motivation to the most basic level by inviting us to respond based on our love for Him. Before Jesus ascended to the Father, three times He asked Peter if he loved Him. By the third time Peter was hurt by the question. Peter answered, "Lord, you know all things; you know that I love you." Then Jesus said to him, "Follow me!" (John 21:17, 19). Jesus connected loving Him to following Him. For some, this is all the motivation it takes.

Bloodguilt: God not only expects us to share the good news, He holds us accountable. If a watchman in the Israelite army knew invaders were approaching and did not warn the people, the blood of those killed would be on his hands. "But if the watchman sees the sword coming and does not blow the trumpet to warn the people and the sword comes and takes the life of one of them, that man will be taken away because of his sin, but I will hold the watchman accountable for his blood" (Ezekiel 33:6). Paul picked this idea up and connected it to sharing the gospel. He referred to it a few weeks before he concluded a missionary journey that took him through Asia and Europe. He stated, "Therefore, I declare to you today that I am innocent of the blood of all men" (Acts 20:26). People today grow wary when guilt is used as a motivation for anything: salesmen use it, boyfriends and girlfriends use it, and even parents use it to control behavior. The Bible, however, employs this motivation in an appropriate way to stir God's followers to involvement. It rattles us out of apathy to ask, "If not me, who? If not now, when?"

Hell: Of the thirteen books that Paul wrote, he spoke of hell in all but one (Philemon). Jesus taught about hell more than he did about heaven. Actually, Jesus devoted more teaching to the subject than any other biblical writer. He took his listeners on a virtual tour of hell in the story of the rich man and Lazarus (Luke 16:19-24). He also describes hell using words and phrases such as eternal, torment, weeping, "the worm dieth not," and "the fire is never quenched." He said, "The angels will come and separate the wicked from the righteous and throw them into the fiery furnace, where there will be weeping and gnashing of teeth" (Matthew 13:49-50). Though they faced persecution for the name of Christ, the disciples continued preaching for the sake of those headed to eternal torment.[9]

Obedience: The first recorded conversation between Christ and the disciples is a short one: " 'Come, follow me,' Jesus said, 'and I will make you fishers of men.' At once

---

[9] For a more in-depth study on the topic of hell see R. A. Torrey, *Heaven or Hell* (Springdale, PA: Whitaker House, 1985). Also see William G. T. Shedd, *The Doctrine of Endless Punishment,* reprint (Carlisle, PA: Banner of Truth Trust, 1986).

they left their nets and followed him" (Mark 1:17-18). Why did the disciples drop everything, leave their families, and follow Jesus? Why did Levi the tax collector do the same (Mark 2:14)? Some suggest Jesus had been observing potential followers for some time and chose these particular men because He knew they would respond obediently. Others say this was not Jesus's first conversation with them, so He knew they would be faithful men. Dietrich Bonhoeffer argues that the reason the disciples and Levi left everything to follow Christ was that the command had come from God Himself. When God speaks, there is only one response: complete obedience. Bonhoeffer believed, "Jesus summons men to follow him not as a teacher or a pattern of the good life, but as the Christ, the Son of God."[10] For some, world evangelism is imperative because of the command of Christ. Jesus commanded it, so that settles it.

Compassion: Compassion motivated Christ. When a man with leprosy approached Him, "Filled with compassion, Jesus reached out his hand and touched the man" (Mark 1:41). When Jesus called the twelve disciples to feed the four thousand, He said, "I have compassion for these people; they have already been with me three days and have nothing to eat" (Matthew 15:32). In the parable of the prodigal son, Jesus gave compassion as the reason the father ran to his repentant son. He said, "But while he was still a long way off, his father saw him and was filled with compassion for him; he ran to his son, threw his arms around him and kissed him" (Luke 15:20). Today's compassionate generation seeks

---

[10] Dietrich Bonhoeffer, *The Cost of Discipleship* (New York: Macmillan Publishing Co., 1937), 62.

to fight injustice, poverty, and other wrongs. This trend transcends culture; it stems from the heart of God.

Rewards: You are probably familiar with the story of the rich young ruler who asked Jesus what he must do to inherit eternal life. Jesus told him to keep the commandments, to sell all he had, and give it to the poor—then follow Him. When the young man heard this, he went away sad because he was a man of great wealth. Less known about this story is Peter's immediate response to the encounter: "Peter answered him, 'We have left everything to follow you!'" (Matthew 19:27). Peter reminded Jesus that the disciples had done what the rich young ruler failed to do. They had forsaken families, comfort, and income in order to follow Jesus. Notice Jesus assures him their wise investment will return great eternal rewards. "And everyone who has left houses or brothers or sisters or father or mother or children or fields for my sake will receive a hundred times as much and will inherit eternal life" (Matthew 19:29-30). Christ told Peter his sacrifice paled in comparison to his future rewards.

Purpose: Only two things on this earth will last for eternity—the Word of God and the souls of mankind. Chasing the American dream clearly results in a futile and wasted life when compared to a life lived for an eternal purpose. As Matthew pointed out, "What good will it be for a man if he gains the whole world, yet forfeits his soul? Or what can a man give in exchange for his soul?" (Matthew 16:26). God offers believers the opportunity to use their fleeting lives to make an eternal impact. Peter reminds us, "All men are like grass, and all their glory is like the flowers of the field; the grass withers and the flowers fall, but the word of the Lord stands forever" (1 Peter 1:24-25). The idea of living life for a purpose is a huge motive in the kingdom of God.

Glory: Jesus's earthly ministry revolved around bringing glory to the Father. He did this by accomplishing what the Father desired Him to do. He said to His Father, "I have brought you glory on earth by completing the work you gave me to do" (John 17:4). In the same way, as we complete the work He has for us, we bring glory to the Father. To glorify someone means to make them famous. You reveal the resplendent beauty or magnificence of that person. In everything Jesus did, He strived to bring glory to God. How can we do the same? By bearing spiritual fruit. "This is to my Father's glory, that you bear much fruit, showing yourselves to be my disciples" (John 15:8). If duty is not a motivator, then God offers the delight of bringing Him glory.[11]

Speed His Coming: The disciples asked Jesus a very important question as His ministry neared an end. They asked, "What will be the sign of your coming and of the end of the age?" (Matthew 24:3). In His answer Jesus connects His return with the gospel's spread to all nations: "And this gospel of the kingdom will be preached in the whole world as a testimony to all nations, and then the end will come" (Matthew 24:14). Aligning our lives with the one prerequisite to Christ's return certainly provides a legitimate incentive to go. Jesus's return is a reality we can be a part of. What an incredible motivator.

---

[11] The theologian at the forefront of this concept is John Piper. For more insight into duty versus delight, see, John Piper, *Desiring God: Meditations of a Christian Hedonist* (Sisters, OR: Multnomah Books, 1986); John Piper, *Let the Nations Be Glad! The Supremacy of God in Missions* (Grand Rapids, MI: Baker Books, 1993); John Piper, *Don't Waste Your Life* (Wheaton, IL: Crossway Books, 2003); John Piper, *When I Don't Desire God: How to Fight for Joy* (Wheaton, IL: Crossway Books, 2004).

Why so many different motivations? Why not one overarching motivator for all? Christ doesn't give us a rigid formula to follow. In His infinite wisdom, He allowed all of us to be unique. What stirs my heart may not stir yours. Furthermore, what originally motivates a person to *go* to the mission field might not be the same thing that *keeps* him there. One season of life may call for an entirely different drive than another. It's okay. It's just the way we are designed.[12]

As my wife and I packed our bags and prepared to live in the Middle East, the reality pressing on my mind and heart was that millions of Muslims were headed for hell and few laborers worked among them. The thought of saving some from this hopeless fate drove me to be a witness for Christ. But something interesting happened when I got there. I saw the faces of the people, I made friends, I shared meals, I had long conversations, I laughed with them, I learned their names, and I grew to truly love the people. After about ten months, I realized my motivation had shifted from the truth

---

[12] David Bosch indicates that in every period since the early Church, a tendency arose to take one biblical verse and make that *the* motivation. The particular text embodied the primary motivation for that particular time period. For the patristic period (AD 100-450), it was, "For God so loved the world that he gave his one and only Son, that whoever believes in him shall not perish but have eternal life" (John 3:16). For the medieval Roman Catholic missionary period, including the Crusades (AD 600-1500), it was "Then the master told his servant, 'Go out to the roads and country lanes and make them come in, so that my house will be full'" (Luke 14:23). For the Protestant Reformation (AD 1517-1596), the key text was "I am not ashamed of the gospel, because it is the power of God for the salvation of everyone who believes: first for the Jew, then for the Gentile" (Romans 1:16). For the Enlightenment (AD 1600-1790), it was "During the night Paul had a vision of a man of Macedonia standing and begging him, 'Come over to Macedonia and help us'" (Acts 16:9). Since William Carey (AD 1792), the key missionary text has been, "All authority in heaven and on earth has been given to me. Therefore go and make disciples of all nations" (Matthew 28:18-19). David J. Bosch, *Transforming Mission: Paradigm Shifts in Theology of Mission* (MaryKnoll, NY: Orbis Books, 2005), 339-340.

of hell to compassion. I looked on my Muslim neighbors as friends and desired to see them come to know the Lord.

In my own experience, I have been motivated by hell, compassion, purpose, obedience, and God's glory—all at different stages in my journey. God is so good to speak to us all in different ways and at different times, revealing at each juncture a new facet of His own heart.

WHERE DO I GO?

How do you decide where to go? I once heard a mission speaker challenge his audience, "God gave you a planet; pick a country." While this helps give freedom from the paralysis that often comes from not having a specific direction, it's also helpful to have some decision-making tracks to run on. So, how do you narrow the planet down a bit? Just because you want to go somewhere doesn't mean you should. Here are three guides for those facing this difficult question.

86 percent of Buddhists, Hindus, and Muslims in the 10-40 window do not have a Christian friend.

First, allow the state of the world to potentially help you narrow down your options. Statistics are not everything in discerning God's will, but they do allow us to pray and reach out in a more informed way. Did you know that 86 percent of Buddhists, Hindus, and Muslims in the 10-40 window do not have a Christian friend? That means that without a drastic change, they will never have a chance to embrace the gospel. Someone will have to cross a culture to share Christ with them! Here are a few other statistics worth considering:

> Mauritania is 99 percent Muslim
> Yemen is 99 percent Muslim
> Maldives is 99 percent Muslim
> Turkey is 96 percent Muslim
> Thailand is 85 percent Buddhist
> Cambodia is 83 percent Buddhist
> Myanmar is 80 percent Buddhist
> Bhutan is 75 percent Buddhist
> India is 75 percent Hindu
> Nepal is 75 percent Hindu[13]

Again, God may be leading you to an area where a work has already begun or where missionaries already live. But if you are country-neutral in your decision-making process, why not allow the state of the world to direct you? Why not choose the least-reached people groups or the country furthest removed from any witness?

Second, connect with God. Begin to pray for the various religious blocs of the world. As you pray, you may find a particular country, people group, or religion ignites your heart the most. As you pray for the tribal, Hindu, Chinese, Muslim, or Buddhist world, what is God speaking to you about your involvement? Does your heart break for South America or

---

[13] Jason Mandryk, *Operation World,* 7th ed. (Colorado Springs, CO: Biblica Publishing, 2010).

Europe as you ask God to raise up workers for those areas of the world? God is more excited about getting us to the right spot than we are about getting there. He wants to speak to us. We just need to listen.

Third, connect to others. When people ask me where they should go, I encourage them to meet internationals in their community. While on the home front, we have a great opportunity to test the waters without fully committing to a specific country. Interacting with foreigners among us affords us the luxury of learning about them and their culture. Connecting to others also means networking with mission agencies. These organizations have a history of getting you to the field where you can work in your greatest capacity. They are professionals in determining which people groups may utilize your giftings and which places are accessible to you in light of your education or professional experience. Mission agencies offer great resources to point you to where the greatest needs are and where the greatest opportunities exist.

Thanks to modern technology, you can be anywhere in the world in less than twenty hours. What an amazing time in history to be alive! Even if you feel you should not go long-term, it is a worthwhile investment to spend some time in a cross-cultural setting. Looking at the world, connecting with God, and connecting with others will help clarify the most strategic place for the goer.

A friend of mine attended a conference where the marketing director for Coca-Cola was speaking. He explained that a catchphrase stimulates Coke's vision and helps them be strategic in decision making: "It is the goal of Coca-Cola to place a bottle of Coke within one kilometer of every person on the planet." What a vision! What would it look like if the whole Church felt the same way about the gospel? Let's see if we can beat the Coke truck!

CHAPTER 14
REVOLUTIONARY SENDING

I used to think there were two types of Christians—the *goers* and the *wavers*! Unfortunately, I was not the first or the last to have this perspective. It's not too far from the way many in the church feel. Some think that since they are not one of the select few who are called to board a plane and go to some faraway land they cannot be involved. I now know that couldn't be further from the truth.

Sending is another essential habit of the World-Christian life. The sender makes it possible for missionaries to both make it to the field and stay there. While the erroneous perspective above tends to cultivate a mentality that goers are superior Christians, it is like asking the question, "Which is more important—the rescuer who goes down into the well to save a life or the man at the top holding the rope?" The answer is obvious. Both are vital! You can't have one without the other. In Israelite warfare the sender and goer held equal value. Scripture commanded that "the share of the man who stayed with the supplies is to be the same as that of him who went down to the battle. All will share alike" (1 Samuel 30:24). God's spiritual army is no different. Simply put, missionaries need people on the home front.

In Romans Paul itemizes the process for someone to become a believer. He explains,

How, then, can they *call* on the one they have not believed in? And how can they *believe* in the one of whom they have not heard? And how can they *hear* without someone preaching to them? And how can they *preach* unless they are *sent?* (Romans 10:14-15)

Working backward from the point of conversion, Paul explains the entire process depends upon the *sender.* The one who takes the gospel must be sent out. Neal Pirolo, in his book *Serving as Senders,* observes, "Paul acknowledged that there are others besides those who go who must be involved in this worldwide evangelization endeavor: those who are serving as senders."[1] The nations do not have a chance to hear the gospel without people on the home front funding, praying, and communicating with those who are going.

The habit of sending is not only integral, but diverse as well. A sender may help in one or all of the following areas: finances, logistics, and prayer coordination.

Finances: The most obvious aspect of sending is giving of one's financial resources to support the missionary. Financial contributions need not be enormous. The World Christian budgets missions into her lifestyle regardless of her income. An effective sender continually evaluates his resources in order to meet the missionary's changing needs. One of our supporters told my wife and me, "The family voted, and we decided to put our vacation money toward your specific need in the Middle East." Special one-time gifts, even random packages, photos, or letters of encouragement

---

[1] Neal Pirolo, *Serving as Senders* (Carlisle, UK: OM Publishing, 1996), 4.

are all part of sending and can provide the lift to keep the missionary on the field. To the missionary, supporters are the unsung heroes.

Logistics: The sender who helps in logistics deals with things that may arise during preparation: packing the missionary's belongings, travel plans, and the concerns of the missionary once on the field. When a missionary returns on furlough, plenty of practical things must be dealt with as well. Where will the missionaries stay? What will be their transportation? What will their speaking schedule be like while home? This type of sender helps to solve these issues.

Prayer Coordination: The mission field is a spiritual battlefield with extraordinary things at stake. On the home front, the prayer coordinator communicates specific concerns and enlists others to be involved in praying for missionaries. It is this sender's responsibility to stay in steady communication with the missionary so prayer requests and needs are known.

Being a sender is difficult. Dealing with the day-to-day, behind-the-scenes tasks of mission work may even seem fruitless, but it is not without reward.

THE CLOG IN THE DRAIN

In our culture it is easy to feel entitled to live at whatever standard matches one's income. We reason that if a couple makes $70,000 a year, they should live at $70,000. When a person gets a raise, the natural tendency is their standard of living gets a raise too! Western Christians live in one of the most prosperous periods of history, and yet missionaries struggle to find funding. During the Great Depression in 1933,

Christians gave an average of 3.3 percent of their income. Today, Christians give an average of 2.5 percent![2] Affluence is the sender's greatest enemy—43 percent of American consumers spend more than they earn each year.[3] No wonder the Bible devotes more passages to money than it does to faith and prayer combined.[4]

Affluence can skew our perspective. It blurs the line between needs and wants. Listen to this story of a professional baseball player:

> *The Bible devotes more passages to money than it does to faith and prayer combined.*

> A New York Yankees ballplayer had just signed an $89 million contract. He had held out for a long while before signing, hoping that the management would match the $91 million offer of another team. The Yankees did not budge. His wife later said, "When I saw him walk in the house, I immediately knew that he had not succeeded in persuading them to move up to ninety-one million. He felt so rejected. It was one of the saddest days of our lives."[5]

---

[2] Gene Edward Veith, "Who Gives Two Cents for Missions? We Do, to Our Shame," *World Magazine* 20, no. 41 (October 22, 2005).

[3] Kim Khan, "How Does Your Debt Compare?" Available at moneycentral.msn.com. Also see Paul Borthwick, *Simplify* (Colorado Springs, CO: Authentic Publishing, 2007).

[4] Randy Alcorn, *Money, Possessions, and Eternity* (Carol Stream, IL: Tyndale House, 2003), 16-17.

[5] Ravi Zacharias, *Jesus Among Other Gods: The Absolute Claims of the Christian Message* (Nashville, TN: W Publishing Group, 2000), 43-44.

I laughed out loud when I first read this. How ridiculous it seemed for someone to be so out of touch with reality that they cannot enjoy an $89 million contract! Then I thought of my friend Damtew from Ethiopia, the director of Nomads for Christ. He told me he had nine staff ready to be deployed, but they had been unable to raise their support of $20 per month. I suddenly felt as out of touch with reality as the millionaire athlete's wife. David Platt, in his book *Radical,* says,

It is a constant battle to resist the temptation to have more luxuries, to acquire more stuff, and to live more comfortably. It requires strong and steady resolve to live out the gospel in the middle of an American dream that identifies success as moving up the ladder, getting the bigger house, purchasing the nicer car, buying the better clothes, eating the finer food, and acquiring more things.[6]

Human nature remains consistent across the board. Our cravings are never satisfied, no matter what we attain. Because we always strive for the next level, we deceive ourselves with the words, "I'll give when I have a little more." I know that has been my excuse at times. In the moment it seems logical, except *more* is elusive and its definition keeps changing. Of those on the list of the four hundred richest people in America, only seventeen made it onto the other list—the most generous.[7] Affluence is deceptive. In *Neither Poverty nor Riches,* Craig Blomberg observes, "It is arguable

[6] David Platt, *Radical: Taking Back Your Faith from the American Dream* (Colorado Springs, CO: Multnomah Books, 2010), 136.

[7] Jon Swartz, "Band of Billionaires Pledge to Give to Charity," *USA Today,* August 6, 2010.

that materialism is the single biggest competitor with authentic Christianity for the hearts and souls of millions in our world today, including many in the visible church."[8] Statistics show that for every $100 of disposable income a North American evangelical makes, he gives 50 cents to missions. That number drops dramatically to a nickel per $100 when you're talking about what goes toward unreached people groups.[9]

We have been blessed with so much. The only problem is the blessings we hold soon take hold of us. Scripture warns believers about the dangers of affluence:

> Be careful that you do not forget the Lord your God, failing to observe his commands.... Otherwise, when you eat and are satisfied, when you build fine houses and settle down, and when your herds and flocks grow large and your silver and gold increase and all you have is multiplied, then your heart will become proud and you will forget the Lord your God.... You may say to yourself, *"My power and the strength of my hands have produced this wealth for me."* (Deuteronomy 8:11-14, 17)

Money gets a tight grip, and it can easily become the primary motivation behind our every decision. God invites us to simplify, to give more, and in so doing, to advance His work. Peter Marshall suggests, "Give according to your income lest God make your income according to your giving."[10]

---

[8] Craig Blomberg, *Neither Poverty nor Riches: A Biblical Theology of Material Possessions* (Downers Grove, IL: InterVarsity Press, 2001), 132.

[9] John Holzmann, "Jesus Said Our Hearts Are Where Our Treasure Is," *Mission Frontiers.* Available at missionfrontiers.org.

[10] Oswald J. Smith, *The Challenge of Missions* (London: Marshall, Morgan and Scott Publishing, 1959), 59.

MEASURING OUT THE TITHE

Tithing is first mentioned in Genesis when Abraham gave a tenth of his spoils from a retaliation raid to the priest Melchizedek (Genesis 14:17-20). Later the Mosaic law commanded the Israelites to give the first 10 percent of their income to God as a celebration of what He had done (Leviticus 27:30). The tithe was not a gift to God; it already belonged to God. As the Psalms state, "The earth is the Lord's, and everything in it" (Psalm 24:1).[11] The Levites received this tithe and rightfully used it for their needs and for the needs of the poor. God told the people, "When you have finished setting aside a tenth of all your produce in the third year, the year of the tithe, you shall give it to the Levite, the alien, the fatherless and the widow, so that they may eat in your towns and be satisfied" (Deuteronomy 26:12).

Jesus only mentions the tithe twice in the New Testament, and in both cases it's spoken of negatively (Matthew 23:23; Luke 18:10-14).[12] The apostle Paul makes no reference to the Old Testament law of the tithe. Instead, the New Testament just admonishes its readers to give generously, joyfully, not under compulsion, and as God leads. Jesus

---

[11] Richard Stearns, *The Hole in Our Gospel* (Nashville, TN: Thomas Nelson, 2009), 211.

[12] Jesus said, "Woe to you, teachers of the law and Pharisees, you hypocrites! You *give a tenth* of your spices—mint, dill and cummin. But you have neglected the more important matters" (Matthew 23:23). He also said, "Two men went up to the temple to pray, one a Pharisee and the other a tax collector. The Pharisee stood up and prayed about himself: 'God, I thank you that I am not like other men—robbers, evildoers, adulterers—or even like this tax collector. I fast twice a week and *give a tenth* of all I get.' But the tax collector stood at a distance. He would not even look up to heaven, but beat his breast and said, 'God, have mercy on me, a sinner.' I tell you that this man, rather than the other, went home justified before God" (Luke 18:10-14).

states, "Give, and it will be given to you. A good measure, pressed down, shaken together and running over, will be poured into your lap. For with the measure you use, it will be measured to you" (Luke 6:38). Paul told Timothy to command the rich to "do good, to be rich in good deeds, and to be generous and willing to share" (1 Timothy 6:18). Also, to the Corinthian church Paul wrote, "Remember this: Whoever sows sparingly will also reap sparingly, and whoever sows generously will also reap generously. Each man should give what he has decided in his heart to give, not reluctantly or under compulsion, for God loves a cheerful giver" (2 Corinthians 9:6-7). It's clear that Jesus and Paul prioritized giving. So why would they hesitate to enforce this well-established biblical tradition? Richard Foster explains,

> The tithe simply is not a sufficiently radical concept to embody the carefree unconcern for possessions that marks life in the kingdom of God. Jesus Christ is the Lord of *all* our goods, not just 10 percent. It is quite possible to obey the law of the tithe without ever dealing with our mammon lust. We can feel that our monthly check to our church meets the new law of Jesus, and never once root out the reigning covetousness and greed.[13]

Given that our standard of living is four times higher than the global average, it can be hard to argue we give as generously as God might desire. The New Testament charges believers to give because they love Christ and want to see

---

[13] Richard Foster, *Freedom of Simplicity: Finding Harmony in a Complex World* (New York: Harper One, 2005), 59.

His kingdom, not theirs, expand. In *Run with the Vision,* the authors observe,

> Living as a sender doesn't mean taking a vow of poverty—since poverty isn't necessarily spiritual and wealth isn't necessarily unspiritual. But being good stewards of money as we seek first the kingdom of heaven is definitely a mark of a World Christian sender.... The lifestyle of a globally significant sender isn't mostly about money. It's about character.[14]

THE HIGH CALLING OF A SENDER

The command of Christ to take the gospel to all nations binds both the one who goes and the one who stays. Both must live a life of self-denial in order to see the gospel spread. The one who goes leaves behind everything familiar. The sender, on the other hand, must keep God's mission at the forefront, in the midst of everything familiar. Paul Borthwick explains, "On the most basic level, sacrifice could mean being willing to live at a lower standard of living than we are capable of so we can give more away.... On a deeper level, sacrifice means realizing that all we have is the Lord's, and we should be willing to let Him direct our giving."[15]

The concept of sending someone is seen nine times in the New Testament. All of them are in a missionary context. In one of the most challenging passages about sending we read,

---

[14] Bob Sjogren, Bill Stearns, and Amy Stearns, *Run with the Vision* (Minneapolis, MN: Bethany House Publishers, 1995), 196.

[15] Paul Borthwick, *A Mind for Missions: Ten Ways to Build Your World Vision* (Colorado Springs, CO: NavPress, 1987), 114.

Dear friend, you are faithful in what you are doing for the brothers, even though they are strangers to you. They have told the church about your love. You will do well to send them on their way in a *manner worthy of God*. It was for the sake of the Name that they went out. (3 John 5-7)

The apostle John sets the standard for our sending—in a manner worthy of God. Here we see the same spirit of giving Jesus and Paul taught about: giving generously, not under compulsion, and joyfully. When the opportunity arises to serve a missionary, how do you respond? Do you quickly volunteer, encourage, and equip, or do you screen their calls about support? As senders, how can we involve ourselves in a *manner worthy of God*? John continues, reminding us that they are going out "for the sake of the Name." Tom Stellar states, "This elevates the importance of sending as high as can be imagined.... The Name of God is at stake in how we treat our missionaries. God receives glory when we support them substantially with our prayers, our money, our time, and myriad other practical ways."[16]

"How different our standard is from Christ's. We ask how much a man gives. He asks how much he keeps."

In the Sermon on the Mount, Jesus challenged his

---

[16] John Piper, *Let the Nations Be Glad! The Supremacy of God in Missions* (Grand Rapids, MI: Baker Books, 1993), 227.

audience, "Do not store up for yourselves treasures on earth, where moth and rust destroy, and where thieves break in and steal. But store up for yourselves treasures in heaven" (Matthew 6:19-20). Andrew Murray echoed this same idea when he said, "How different our standard is from Christ's. We ask how much a man gives. He asks how much he keeps." Sending is not a second-class calling. Rather, to bolster those in frontline battle through prayer, to reinforce field work with needed supplies, to minister to missionaries with encouragement, to serve as senders however we can—this is a grand opportunity! To exclude ourselves from such a lofty pursuit is to miss out on the incredible reward of advancing the kingdom in a way, for the most part, hidden to others, but greatly pleasing to the Lord.

CHAPTER 15
REVOLUTIONARY PRAYING

I t seemed like an easy assignment. I had only attended Bible study a few times when the leader tried to help me take a more prominent role in the group. Before the study he pulled me aside and gave me a task. He said, "When Bible study starts, I want you to go around the room asking people if they have any special prayer requests. Once you have done this, I would like you to pray for them." I thought, *I can do this*! As the guys filtered in, the leader signaled me to begin. With my pen in hand and paper ready, I started with the person to my immediate right. "Do you have any prayer requests?" I asked. His answer thoroughly confused me: "Unspoken." This concept, so new to me, left me unsure how to respond. Apparently it was trendy to be so veiled about prayer needs because the next guy had two unspokens! I felt my confidence slipping. Total bewilderment replaced my prior certainty in my ability to tackle this role. How am I supposed to pray about private needs?

Jesus employs no such secrecy about that which burdens His heart. He is explicit in His prayer request, telling the disciples, "The harvest is plentiful but the workers are few. *Ask* the Lord of the harvest, therefore, to send out workers into his harvest field" (Matthew 9:37-38). He gives His followers the prayer request that the vast field would be supplied with workers! The disproportion between need and laborers greatly concerns Christ, and He asks us to take on the burden in prayer.

The World Christian sets time aside regularly to pray for the world. In a culture where we can easily become consumed with our own immediate needs, such as family, friends, and finances, Jesus exhorts us to look up and see the greater need—the enduring need of lost souls to hear the good news and the shortage of people to tell them.

All Christians pray. But remember the definition of a World Christian: a believer who has discovered the truth about God's unfulfilled global purpose and His desire to reach all peoples. The difference between the prayer life of a Christian and that of a World Christian is that a World Christian prays in light of God's unfulfilled global purpose. World Christians look for ways to join God's mission, and so this aspect of spiritual life gets filtered through a mis-

A battle rages throughout the earth in which the glory of God and the souls of men are at stake.

sional understanding. Through prayer we come alongside the missionary on the field. Through prayer we hold the hungry infant in our arms. Through prayer we fight injustice. Through prayer we bring down the strongholds of the enemy. Through prayer we push back the darkness in the world.

Let us not underestimate the ministry and power of

prayer. Our efforts to reach the lost are not carried out in neutral territory. People who pray know a battle rages throughout the earth in which the glory of God and the souls of men are at stake. Prayer *is* our greatest weapon. Jason Mandryk, author of the definitive prayer guide for the nations, *Operation World,* explains,

> When we seek to rescue unreached peoples and lost souls from the grip of the Evil One, we must expect violent opposition in the heavenlies. The gates of hell will not prevail against the Church, but they must be stormed; they will not open of their own accord. It is no accident that the passage of the armor of God in Ephesians 6 ends with the exhortation to be "praying at all times in the Spirit, with all prayer and supplication" (Ephesians 6:18 esv).[1]

WE WRESTLE NOT

How often do you pray, and what do you pray about? What are you asking the God of heaven and earth for? The

---

[1] One of the greatest resources for prayer is the book *Operation World* (also see operationworld.org). This tool guides the reader to pray for every country in the world, utilizing its easy-to-follow calendar that allots various countries for each day. *Operation World* presents relevant statistical divisions of each country: people groups, languages, percentage of languages with Scripture, percentage of Christians, and number of missionaries present and missionaries sent. It lists several prayer points with each country. The statistics and requests enable the Church to pray knowledgeably and specifically and inform the Church of facts about people groups. Another resource is the Joshua Project (joshuaproject.net), a Web-based research initiative that highlights unreached people groups of the world. Maps, photos, informative articles, and presentations on the world fill the site and can be downloaded and utilized for prayer. Jason Mandryk, *Operation World,* 7th ed. (Colorado Springs, CO: Biblica Publishing, 2010), xxiv.

One who created the vast galaxies in which billions of stars exist, who organized every minute of every life for all history toward His good purposes—it is He who invites us to bring our requests to Him. How do we respond to this amazing invitation? We ask for: A better job? A bigger house? A larger savings account? A newer car? Is that *all* we know to ask?

One of my favorite parables in the gospels tells of the widow and the unjust judge found in Luke 18:1-8. Jesus describes a judge who did not fear God or care about people. A widow kept coming to this judge with a petition to be freed from her adversary. The more he refused, the more she approached him. Eventually the judge conceded, "Even though I don't fear God or care about men, yet because this widow keeps bothering me, I will see that she gets justice, so that she won't eventually wear me out with her coming!" (Luke 18:4-5). Jesus's intention in the parable is not to highlight the similarities between the unjust judge and God, but to emphasize an important difference. If a persistent widow can cause an *unjust* judge to answer, how much less does it take a gracious judge (our God) to respond? Martin Luther captured this idea when he wrote, "Prayer is not overcoming God's reluctance, but laying hold of His willingness." So, why don't we pray? Jesus' widow parable goes on to address our hearts as Jesus says, "However, when the Son of Man comes, *will he find faith* on the earth?" (Luke 18:8). What an interesting way to end the passage. When Jesus returns, will he find faith on the earth? Jesus makes a connection between the regularity of our prayers

God has given us His burden to adopt as our own.

and our belief that God wants to answer us. In other words, we can talk about time management, and we can discuss possible self-absorption or self-reliance as the source of a poor prayer life, but the root of the issue is a deep-seated lack of faith that God is interested in us or our requests. For that matter, it represents a lack of faith that He is necessary at all. Indifference and self-reliance set in to replace a dependence on a benevolent God. Scripture teaches the complete opposite. God has given us His burden to adopt as our own, and when we petition Him to meet that request, His generosity inclines Him to do so. When the Son of Man comes, will He find that *you* have faith?

LESSONS FROM HISTORY

Andrew Murray says, "The man who mobilizes the Church to pray will make the largest contribution in history to world evangelization." History shows us that when individuals get serious about connecting to God, He gets serious about moving. He moves in us and through us on behalf of the world. The following represents a small sampling from history of those who saw the vastness of the harvest and beseeched the Savior to move—revolutionaries who involved themselves in prayer and whose impact reached far beyond their own lives.

Nikolaus Zinzendorf: Zinzendorf was born at the turn of the eighteenth century.[2] He attended the College of Halle

---

[2] John R. Weinlick, *Count Zinzendorf: The Story of His Life and Leadership in the Renewed Moravian Church* (Bethlehem and Winston-Salem: The Moravian Church in America, 1984).

in Germany and formed a group called the Order of Grain of Mustard Seed, which endured even after his death. Each member of this society wore a ring engraved with the words "None of us liveth unto himself." Zinzendorf possessed an unyielding passion for the world, and the precept he lived by was, "May the Lamb that was slain receive the reward of His suffering." He later established a community of believing Moravians and set up a watch of continuous prayer that ran uninterrupted for one hundred years. The Moravians sent hundreds of missionaries out all over the world.

John Wesley: In 1726 at Oxford in England, John Wesley and his brother Charles became the leaders of a small band known as the Holy Club.[3] The club's purpose was to study the Bible deeply. They fasted twice a week and memorized key passages. The Wesleys' highest priority, though, was the two hours they spent in prayer each day.[4] People around them gave them the nickname *Methodists* in light of the methods they employed to grow spiritually. Today there are millions of Methodists in all corners of the world. John Wesley traveled an average of seventy miles per day on horseback for fifty-four years, preaching fifteen sermons per week to tens of thousands of people. Yet he savored every opportunity to get alone with his Savior and pray. He said, "God does nothing but in answer to prayer."

Samuel Mills: When Samuel Mills arrived as an incoming freshman at Williams College, Massachusetts, his roommate described him as having an "awkward figure and

---

[3] Stanley Ayling, *John Wesley* (Nashville, TN: Abingdon Press, 1979).

[4] Wesley L. Duewel, *Touch the World through Prayer* (Grand Rapids, MI: Zondervan, 1986), 155.

ungainly manner and croaking sort of voice."[5] But Samuel Mills had Asia on his mind. Ironically, up to this point, America had not sent a single missionary. Even if a willing candidate stepped forward, no mission agency existed in 1806. In a field just off campus, Mills met with other younger men for Bible study and prayer. One day a violent storm approached during their study. The five students frantically sought shelter next to a haystack. Crouching there, they feared death. After the storm passed, they refocused their lives for God in reference to the spread of the gospel to Asia. From then on, these five students called themselves the Society of the Brethren and sought to mobilize even more students. Their battle cry for Asia was "We can do this if we will." As the direct fruit of their efforts, America's first missionary launched in 1812 and the first six mission agencies in the United States were formed. How? Mills knew that as a child of God he was connected to the Lord of the harvest who desired to answer his requests on behalf of the world. Mills prayed knowing God would answer him. Mills exhorted, "Though you and I are very little beings, we must not rest satisfied until our influence is felt in the remotest corner of this ruined world."

C. T. Studd: In the 1880s, C. T. Studd was the captain of the Cambridge cricket team, a premier athlete, and set to go pro.[6] Then something happened to permanently alter Studd's heart and plans: D. L. Moody came to speak. That provided the spark that ignited Studd's heart for the world.

---

[5] Clarence P. Shedd, *Two Centuries of Student Christian Movements: Their Origin and Intercollegiate Life* (New York: Association Press, 1934), 50.

[6] Norman P. Grubb, *C. T. Studd: Athlete and Pioneer* (Grand Rapids, MI: Zondervan, 1933).

Not content to go alone, he prayed that other students would be stirred to go. His prayers resulted in six of his teammates committing to work in China. Known as the Cambridge Seven, these young adults traveled all over England for eighteen months before they launched. Through their recruitment 165 others committed to join them. Studd's journey first took him to China, then India, and finally to Africa. He is quoted as saying, "We Christians too often substitute prayer for playing the game."

Robert and Grace Wilder: In 1881, Robert Wilder entered Princeton and launched a student organization called Princeton Foreign Missionary Society.[7] A handful of students met Sunday afternoons in his home to pray for the world. Wilder received an invitation to participate in a summer project where young men from eighty-nine universities would spend four weeks in intense discipleship. His sister, Grace, encouraged him to go by committing to pray daily for one hundred of the 251 students to become missionaries. He agreed and, upon arrival, began mobilizing as many as possible toward missions through prayer. By the time the project ended, exactly one hundred students committed to long-term service. That year, while the other students headed back to their campuses, Robert Wilder and John Foreman set out to visit 162 colleges to educate students regarding God's Word and God's work in the world. A key part of their recruitment strategy was prayer. God raised up a mass of laborers: 2,106 students responded. That year, the greatest

[7] Robert P. Wilder, *The Great Commission: The Missionary Response of the Student Volunteer Movements in North America and Europe; Some Personal Reminiscences* (London: Oliphants Publishers, 1936).

mobilization movement in history was birthed—the Student Volunteer Movement (SVM). By 1940, the SVM had recruited 75 percent of all missionaries on the field.[8] The success of this movement is credited to the foundation laid in prayer by Robert and Grace Wilder.

When we hear these stories, we feel tempted to say, "That's great for them, but that's not me. I work from eight to five, have kids, and am barely reading my Bible." Scripture does not let us get away with that excuse—it's full of people just like us who God used. Take for example a prophet in the Old Testament named Elijah. He wanted desperately to get the attention of his disobedient nation and prayed for a drought. God answered his request and no rain fell for over three years. Scripture reminds us, "Elijah was a man just like us. He prayed earnestly that it would not rain, and it did not rain on the land for three and a half years" (James 5:17). At times Elijah doubted God, at times he stumbled, and at times he sinned. Yet through Elijah's prayers, God awakened a nation. Can you imagine that? Does that kind of radical outcome feel within your reach? If effective prayer seems impossible to attain, hear the words of prayer warrior Hudson Taylor, who said, "Many Christians estimate difficulty in light of their own resources, and thus they attempt very little and they always fail. All giants have been weak men who did great things for God because they reckoned on His power and presence to be with them."

---

[8] North American Students and World Advance, Addresses Delivered at the Eighth International Convention of the Student Volunteer Movement for Foreign Missions, Des Moines, Iowa, Dec. 31, 1919 – Jan. 4, 1920, 62.

THE HEART OF GOD

If you could ask Jesus to teach you anything, what would it be? Personally, I think I would want to learn how He multiplied the bread to feed the 5,000! Well, in all of the Scriptures we see only one time when the disciples asked Jesus to teach them something. Their request: "Lord, teach us to pray" (Luke 11:1). Isn't it interesting that after three years with Jesus they desired to pattern their prayer life after His? Maybe after following Him around for a few years, they realized things happened when He prayed. Listen to Christ's response: "This, then, is how you should pray: 'Our Father in heaven, hallowed be your name, your kingdom come, your will be done on earth as it is in heaven'" (Matthew 6:9-10). Jesus was saying that when you pray, you should ask God to bring the activity of heaven down to earth. In other words, pray that what is going on up there would go on down here. In heaven, all eyes focus on Jesus in a multicultural worship service! Ask God to make this a reality on earth. I have a friend, Keith, who attended a very loud concert with his young son. All of a sudden, his son put his head on Keith's chest. "What are you doing?" Keith asked. His son replied, "I am trying to see if I can hear your heartbeat despite all the noise." That's what prayer does for us. The noise of the world drowns out the heartbeat of God. As your prayer life deepens, your heart breaks for the things that break God's heart. Andrew Murray said, "Some people pray just to pray, and some people pray to know God."

After conquering France, Napoleon declared himself emperor and set out to overtake the rest of Europe. As his forces moved into the Mediterranean, he knew one particular island would be costly to invade. Laying siege to the island, Napoleon's army suffered many casualties. In celebration of the victory, Napoleon dined with his generals. During the dinner a young soldier entered the room and approached the emperor's table. Shocked by the boldness of the soldier to approach his emperor, the generals stood to remove him. Napoleon looked at the battle-worn soldier and asked his purpose. He turned and faced Napoleon and simply said, "Napoleon, give me this island." The soldier's audacious request shocked the whole room. Without saying a word, Napoleon summoned for a piece of paper and something to write with. It took a few seconds for Napoleon to write his response. The soldier read the note, thanked him, and walked out. The generals waited in anticipation. "I granted his request," Napoleon finally said. Astonished, the other men murmured among themselves as to this young soldier's identity. Napoleon hushed them all, "The reason I gave him the island was that *I was honored* by the magnitude of the request."

God wants us to make bold requests which bring glory to His name. Our prayers have impact! Do you believe your prayers can eradicate poverty, bring justice to the oppressed, change world leaders' hearts, and see people groups reached? Dick Eastman, in *The Hour That Changes the World,* reminds us, "Nothing is beyond the reach of prayer because God Himself is the focus of prayer."[9] We engage confidently in prayer knowing His desire for the nations exceeds our own. He has begun it, and He will bring it to completion.

---

[9] Dick Eastman, *The Hour That Changes the World: A Practical Plan for Personal Prayer* (Grand Rapids, MI: Baker Book House, 1978), xi.

CHAPTER 16
REVOLUTIONARY WELCOMING

few Thanksgivings ago, I walked into my in-laws' home and thought, *What on earth is that smell? It's definitely not turkey and dressing!* Their Thanksgiving tradition always involves a huge production of deep-fried turkey, stuffing, casseroles, and a slew of other holiday delicacies whose aroma immediately sweeps away all who encounter it. No, something felt wrong. The smells were far from my memories of Thanksgiving. Entering the kitchen I met the answer. "Hello, I am Hussein. Do you like falafel?" The sight of an international student cooking shocked me. My expectations of good ol' holiday overindulgence went out the window as I stood there looking at this Saudi Arabian.

Later, I asked my in-laws how a Middle Eastern Muslim ended up in their kitchen. They explained their desire to reach out to internationals. They had contacted the local university and were immediately matched up with the International Student Association's president, Hussein. He became a regular presence at the house and a good friend. My in-laws asked him what he wanted for Christmas. His response—a study Bible. He started going to church with them and even went to Sunday school and Bible study. I believe he even drove the weekly car pool to the study! To my knowledge Hussein never became a believer, but he did not leave America without at least having the opportunity—an opportunity that is scarce in his homeland.

The World-Christian lifestyle includes welcoming. Millions of internationals come to America to raise their family, work, and study. Welcomers see this as a gold mine of opportunity because they recognize the exponential impact to be made for the kingdom by reaching out to internationals both practically and spiritually.

THE FOREIGNER AND ISRAEL

Israel dealt with foreigners who lived in the Promised Land. God knew the dangers of Israel becoming arrogant toward the foreigners (called aliens in the text). To keep their hearts from hardening, God gave specific instructions through the Mosaic law. Over forty times in the Old Testament, He commanded Israel to love the foreigners among them. "Do not oppress an alien; you yourselves know how it feels to be aliens, because you were aliens in Egypt" (Exodus 23:9). "The alien living with you must be treated as one of your native-born. Love him as yourself, for you were aliens in Egypt" (Leviticus 19:34). Deuteronomy later says of God, "He defends the cause of the fatherless and the widow, and loves the alien, giving him food and clothing. And you are to love those who are aliens, for you yourselves were aliens in Egypt" (Deuteronomy 10:18-19; see also Deuteronomy 26:11-12; Leviticus 23:22). God did not want the Israelites to forget what it felt like to be foreigners in a foreign land. Similarly we should remember our past, how we were strangers to God and yet He invited us into fellowship with Himself. Chawkat Moucarry, an Arab Christian who has spent many years living abroad, explains,

> Because the people of Israel were God's chosen people, they were in danger of despising the non-Israelites living in the land. Hence the Law of Moses included very specific teaching on how the Israelites should behave towards them. It highlighted the fact that Israel's election did not in any way mean that God neglects the other nations, who are represented, as it were, by the strangers in Israel. On the contrary, it says that God cares for them and sees to their needs, beginning with the most basic.[1]

In light of God's love for all people and the opportunity He has given us to meet the internationals surrounding us, every believer should reach out to foreigners, consider them our neighbors, and love them enough to share the gospel with them.

FROM ACROSS THE OCEAN TO ACROSS THE STREET

Today, around the globe, 200 million people live and work in countries other than their countries of origin.[2] God is at work orchestrating lives that they may hear the gospel. America hosts the largest number of internationals of

---

[1] Chawkat Moucarry, *The Prophet and the Messiah: An Arab Christian's Perspective on Islam & Christianity* (Downers Grove, IL: InterVarsity Press, 2001), 284.

[2] Duncan Mavin, "One Big ATM," *The Financial Post Magazine,* October 7, 2008. Don Mills Canada: National Post.

any country. The world waits at our doorstep! What a perfect opportunity to extend God's grace and love to the world! You don't need a passport, you don't need to raise support, and you will most likely not get arrested.

I recently enjoyed the privilege of sharing the gospel with a few international students from Saudi Arabia. It's amazing to think of the hardship I would face should I go to Saudi Arabia and attempt to do the same! Yet here we have complete freedom to share with otherwise unreached people! Approximately 30 million immigrants make up 11 percent of America's population. More Muslims than Methodists and more Buddhists than Episcopalians live in Chicago.[3] Over 750,000 international students study here from 188 countries of the world, and 60 percent are from the 10-40 window.[4] Additionally, international students currently studying at universities in the United States will fill half of the world's top positions in education, the military, politics, and business. The nations are no longer across the ocean, distant and unknown; they are across the street! We work with them, study with them, and our children play on the soccer

200 million people live and work in countries other than their countries of origin.

---

[3] Rajendra K. Pillai, *Reaching the World in Our Own Backyard* (Colorado Springs, CO: Waterbrook Press, 2003), 12.

[4] The top ten countries represented in American universities are (1) India, (2) China, (3) South Korea, (4) Japan, (5) Taiwan, (6) Canada, (7) Mexico, (8) Turkey, (9) Indonesia, and (10) Thailand.

team with them. The president of Yale University challenged the incoming freshman class, saying,

> When I greeted my first freshman class thirteen years ago, only one student in fifty came from a foreign country other than Canada. Today, that number is one in twelve.... It means that each of you can, without much effort, become close friends with at least one classmate from a country quite different from your own. You each have a chance to begin your exploration of the world—its peoples and their diverse values.... But forming friendships is only the beginning of the work that each of you needs to do to become an informed global citizen capable of bringing the world closer together.[5]

Sadly, the ministry of welcoming gets overlooked. Roughly 80 percent of internationals never see the inside of an American home. With high hopes they come to study, but soon loneliness sets in. So they live in their isolated communities with other internationals. The hospitality so common in their homeland is just as foreign to America as they are. Many never hear the gospel. Returning home, they view Americans as distant and self-absorbed.

The nations are no longer across the ocean, distant and unknown; they are across the street!

Welcoming is the Great Commission reversed.

---

[5] Lisa Espineli Chinn, *Crossing Cultures Here and Now* (Downers Grove, IL: InterVarsity Press, 2006), 7-8.

Instead of us being sent abroad, the nations come to us! So, everyone can be a welcomer. It only demands a little time, some energy, and a willingness to say hello. Christians should make it a priority to cultivate friendships with internationals. Why not introduce yourself and initiate a conversation at the mall, the grocery store, or the waiting room at the doctor's office? At first, it might feel intimidating, but imagine yourself in a foreign culture. You would be so grateful for the slightest gesture of hospitality, even if it wasn't all that smooth. There are tons of questions you can ask to get started: Where are you from? How do you like it here? How is it different from your country? Was learning English harder than you thought? Are you finding your way around? Can I help in any way? Welcomers stand willing to serve and to reach out in hopes that Christ will be glorified. Try it and you will quickly see how easy it is to get involved. Soon you will be loving internationals and making an eternal impact in nations you may never even visit.

THE GREAT OPPORTUNITY

One fall day my wife was out shopping and initiated a conversation with a Jordanian Muslim woman named Fatima. They talked for a few minutes and exchanged numbers. Before leaving Jess asked if Fatima had ever experienced Halloween. She hadn't. Jess invited Fatima, her husband, and their young son Muhammad to join us. My daughter's costume had already been purchased—a hot dog. Talk about a smooth impression—we'd invited Muslims over for Halloween and our daughter was going as a pork product! So, after some dinner together (which Fatima did not eat because she found it too spicy), we hit the neighborhood to knock on doors. Ironically, Fatima received the most compliments on her "costume"; people just loved the head scarf and robe she wore!

It was a great night, albeit a little bumpy at times. Kareem, Fatima's husband, enjoyed answering our door and giving candy to the neighborhood kids. Fatima told Jess she hadn't heard Kareem laugh so much. Later he sent me this letter:

> Dear Todd,
> I sent this to express for you how much great time we spent at your house. You can't imagine how when a person is a stranger in a country and suddenly finds welcoming people who are being kind for him just because he is a human being and for nothing else. We saw a lot of new nice traditions and had nice conversations, and I really am planning to keep this friendship going with a special couple that I didn't have the chance even in my country to find such people as kind as you are. Next weekend you have to come to our house!
> Kareem

Now I consider him one of my best friends, and our discussions often center around spiritual things. He's told me about many of his conversations with family back home. He shares his positive experiences, how much his friends love God, and the kindness of Americans. I pray that one day he will be telling his family in Jordan about how he found true life in Jesus. Every time I'm around this family I am reminded of the strategic nature of reaching internationals.

After interviewing over 3,000 internationals about

their experience in America, Mark Rentz from the American Language and Cultural Program concluded, "All of the respondents said it was not their academic experience that they remember. Instead, the most valuable experience to them was their time with Americans and the opportunity to experience life in America."[6] Think of the impact if believers took initiative and reached out to our international neighbors on a deeper level, not just showing them life in America, but life in Christ!

TWO-WAY STREET

Some interesting phobias exist out there—some are accepted, and some will get you made fun of in high school. For example, it is okay to suffer from acrophobia (the fear of heights), but it's maybe a little less cool to have arachibutyrophobia, the fear of peanut butter sticking to the roof of your mouth. Definitely seek attention if you suffer from hippopotomonstrosesquippedaliophobia, the fear of long words (oxymoronic, isn't it?). Whatever phobia you may have, no Christian should suffer from xenophobia, the fear of foreigners. The xenophobe frets, "I don't know their culture. I can't pronounce their name correctly. I won't understand their broken English." The xenophobe avoids them at all cost. He doesn't know them, which is why he fears them. My friend recently had an eye-opening experience at a conference discussing immigration in America. He realized during the con-

---

[6] Tom Phillips and Bob Norsworthy, *The World at Your Door: Reaching International Students in Your Home, Church, and School* (Minneapolis, MN: Bethany House Publishers, 1997), 27.

ference that the person who cooked his meal, the maid at the hotel, and the taxi driver who drove him to the airport were not native to this country. If we take the time, we too will see the international presence in the United States. Xenophobes of the future will practically be housebound if they want to avoid foreigners. Let's embrace the opportunity God granted us as a nation to host a multitude of cultures, and let's reach out!

A unique ministry climate exists among internationals because they live away from their families and away from their homeland. Generally, this different environment makes them more receptive to new ideas and worldviews. In surveys of internationals who became believers in the United States, two reoccurring themes appear.[7] First, a Christian befriended them; not merely an acquaintance or a name without a face, but someone who expressed real love to them, served them, and genuinely wanted to spend time with them. Through this friendship, the international saw Christ. Second, someone took the time to provide a Bible in their language and was willing to work through their questions. In most cases this was their first time to actually read it for themselves. A patient Christian friend and the Word of God can be an incredible witness to internationals.

We gain so much personally by reaching out to internationals. God uses the friendship in several ways. We mature in the way we view ourselves and the world. My own perspective has been most affected by their hospitality. The way they treated my family and me in their home caused

---

[7] Rick Rood, "Reaching the World That Has Come to Us," Probe Ministries. Available at leaderu.com.

me to reevaluate the way I host others. International ministry changed my outlook on the world. My preconceived notions of people shatter as I experience the world from a new perspective. Suddenly, rather than casually dismissing the news about a devastating earthquake in China, I find myself feeling compassionate, even connected to the tragedy.

Practically speaking, we also benefit by having connections any time we travel! A friend of mine named Tim began encouraging people in his church to reach out to internationals in their community. One day he received a phone call. The caller said, "Tim, we invited Ahmed, from Bahrain, over for Thanksgiving, and we want everything to go well. Can you come too and help us host him?" Tim agreed. From that point on, Tim and Ahmed became great friends. Coincidently, Tim was preparing to go to Bahrain to study Arabic. Before he left, Tim had the opportunity to meet Ahmed's father who had come to the States for a visit. Ahmed's father, anxious to show his gratitude to the people who had welcomed his son, gave Tim his business card and said, "You've helped my son here in the U.S., so when you come to Bahrain, you will be like my son. I will help you with anything you need."

A few months later, after Tim settled in a bit in Bahrain, he decided to look up Ahmed's father, who ran an architecture firm. Over coffee, Ahmed's father extended the request again; he communicated his willingness to help in any way—money, housing, anything. Tim had one problem. He could only obtain a tourist visa. This made it impossible to get a driver's license, buy a car, or even set up a bank account. Hearing this, Ahmed's father assured Tim he could help. The next day, Tim went with him to the Office of Foreign Affairs. At the gate, the guard saluted Ahmed's father. Inside, the secretary stood and saluted him. Then, in the office of the assistant to the director, the man behind the desk stood and saluted Ahmed's father. Finally, the director of foreign affairs himself stood to salute him. Astonished, Tim asked him, "Why are all these policemen saluting you, the manager of an architecture firm?" He informed Tim that in his previous job, he was the director of foreign affairs! He handed Tim's passport to his old assistant, the current director of foreign affairs, who immediately issued Tim a two-year visa. This relationship proved to be an incredible blessing to Tim's team in Bahrain.

You can help reach the nations by befriending internationals. We have the opportunity to influence those who can spread the gospel further than we might be able. Not only is the gospel advanced, but we grow in our understanding of the world and its peoples.

I have a friend who really desired to utilize his senior year of college for ministry. His options included living off campus in a house with friends or moving into the international dorm on campus. He opted for the international dorm. His simple strategy was to leave his door open. One day, in walked Samuel from China. Through the friendship, God began stirring Samuel's heart and he gave his life to the Lord. He became consumed with the Word, prayer, and evangelism. Over Christmas break he traveled back to China and led his mother to Christ. Back in America Samuel joined a church, got baptized, and even pledged a fraternity to increase his own ministry opportunities. That summer he led a short-term mission trip to Thailand. In fact this summer he will lead a short-term trip back to China. When I asked Samuel for his permission to include his story in this book he agreed on one condition, "As long as you include in my story my passion for the Chinese people." May the Church not miss this strategic and significant opportunity to participate in God's plan by reaching the world at our door.

CHAPTER 17
MOBILIZING TO THE REVOLUTION

As I sat in the car with my kids while my wife ran into the store, I started fiddling with my wedding ring. All of a sudden I dropped it. As if in slow motion, I watched it bounce a couple of times before finally slipping between the seat and the console—that abyss from which nothing ever escapes. As I peered into the black hole, I could make out a straw wrapper and a few peanuts. I think there was even a parking ticket. I tried for a painful few minutes to wedge my hand down the dark crevasse, but to no avail. I even got out of the car and tried from different angles. It was impossible. Either the front seat would need to be dismantled, or I would buy a new ring. Then an idea occurred to me. I pulled my three-year-old daughter out of her car seat and told her to look down into the crevasse of despair. In one motion she reached her hand down, grabbed the ring, and gave it back to me. Then she grabbed the parking ticket.

That incident educated me on a truth of mobilization. Little fits where big doesn't. My daughter, with her teeny arm, had no problem accomplishing a task that proved impossible for me. I used to believe all I needed to do was to get my friends to hear an incredible message from someone about missions and they would get a heart for the world. Not true. God placed them in *my* life for *me* to mobilize. God has placed people in your life only you can mobilize. Even though you may not have a tear-jerking story of reaching an unreached nation or consider yourself a good communicator, little fits where big doesn't. Everyone can mobilize.

The final habit in the World-Christian lifestyle is mobilization. A mobilizer has a passion for the world and a passion to pass it on. Simply put, a mobilizer recruits. Mobilizers recruit to all the habits of the World-Christian lifestyle; they desire to raise up welcomers, prayers, givers, and goers. The mobilizer even mobilizes others to mobilize!

First used in a military context by Europeans in the 1850s, the word *mobilize* literally means "to put into movement." When used in the context of missions, mobilization is inspiring, informing, and activating believers for the completion of world evangelization. It does not require creating something out of nothing, but transforming existing energies, capabilities, and resources for the cause.[1] Have you ever wondered where missionaries come from? The answer—from mobilizers. Behind every missionary, there stands a mobilizer. Thomas Richards, a missionary biographer, acknowledges, "The business of the recruiting officer may not blazon the pages of history, but it wins battles."[2] Phil Parshall, a missionary and author, explains the crucial role of mobilizers,

---

[1] Bill Taylor, "Mobilizing Missionaries for a Different World," *Connections Magazine* 4, no. 3. (October 2005): 3.

[2] Thomas C. Richards, *Samuel J. Mills: Missionary Pathfinder, Pioneer and Promoter* (Boston: The Pilgrim Press, 1906), 78.

Someone must sound the rallying call. Those who desire to see others trained, prepared, and released to ministry are known as mobilizers. Mobilizers stir other Christians to active concern for reaching the world. They coordinate efforts between senders, the local churches, sending agencies, and missionaries on the field. Mobilizers are essential. To understand the role of mobilizers, think of World War II as a parallel. Only 10 percent of the American population went to the war. Of those, only 1 percent were actually on the firing lines. However, for them to be successful in their mission, the entire country had to be mobilized!

YOU'RE IT

God raises up people to work in His harvest. Praise Him for allowing our participation! Because the overwhelming evidence of Scripture points to God's ultimate end—the presence of "every nation, tribe, people and language, standing before the throne and in front of the Lamb" (Revelation 7:9)—the responsibility falls on all Christians to play a part. Therefore, all believers need to be mobilized. The mobilizer's heart burns for the world and his most strategic spot is on the home front. Many today equate *missions* with *missionary*. As we have seen, that is simply not the case. Mobilization is not just what you do until you get to graduate and be a missionary. It is an essential role in its own right.

Imagine yourself seeing a huge, raging fire in the distance. You could run to get a bucket, fill it with water, run to the blaze, and dump water. Then you could run again and dump more water on the fire. And again, and again. But perhaps, on first seeing the danger of the fire, you could run and wake up one hundred sleeping firemen—who would do at least a hundred times what you could have done yourself.[3]

God may be calling you, for the sake of the world, to stay behind and wake up the sleeping fireman. For some, going overseas is actually far less strategic! Take John Mott and Robert Speer, for example.

John Mott (1865–1955) grew up in Postville, Iowa, and attended Cornell University. His mission vision began when he heard a guest speaker, J. E. K. Studd, teach on the kingdom of God.[4] After college, instead of going to the mission field, Mott stayed behind to mobilize. He became the director of the Student Volunteer Movement, which he led for thirty-two years.[5] The SVM mobilized approximately 20,000 missionaries to the field and 80,000 supporters.[6] In 1946, under the endorsement of President Harry Truman, John Mott received the Nobel Peace Prize for his life's work.

Robert Speer (1867–1947) grew up in Huntingdon, Pennsylvania. A contemporary of John Mott, he attended

---

[3] Bob Sjogren, Bill Stearns, and Amy Stearns, *Run with the Vision* (Minneapolis, MN: Bethany House Publishers, 1995), 205.

[4] J. E. K. Studd was one of the three famous Studd brothers, along with George and Charles Thomas (C. T.). J. E. K. Studd traveled to campuses in America telling the story of the Cambridge Seven, the high-profile athletes who had committed to missions after graduation. J. E. K. Studd met John Mott at Cornell University. For more information on John R. Mott see Basil Mathews, *John R. Mott: World Citizen* (New York: Harper and Brothers Publishers, 1934).

[5] C. Howard Hopkins, *20ᵗʰ Century Ecumenical Statesman, John R. Mott: 1865-1955* (New York: Eerdmans Publishing Company, 1979), 569.

[6] Michael Parker, *The Kingdom of Character: The Student Volunteer Movement for Foreign Missions 1886-1926,* 2ⁿᵈ ed. (Pasadena, CA: William Carey Library, 2008), 56.

Princeton University and gave his time and attention to play-ing football. Mobilized in college by two students en route to India, Speer decided not to go to the foreign field.[7] Instead he pursued another field where he thought he would be most strategically used—mobilization. For the next forty-six years, Speer directed the Presbyterian Church's missionary endeavors. He inspired goers and senders to the work. When he took the position, the board raised $110,000 per year for world evangelization. By the time he retired, that number had increased to $16 million.[8] Throughout his mobilization career, he authored sixty-seven books.

John Mott and Robert Speer loved to mobilize, so much so that the president of the Y.M.C.A. stated that during his student generation, "Mott and Speer were almost one word of two syllables."[9] Neither Mott nor Speer traveled overseas for any significant amount of time. Neither one of them saw themselves as a missionary in the traditional sense of the word, but how strategic these two men were! Dr. Ralph Winter, renowned mission scholar and founder of the U.S. Center for World Mission, said, "What if Mott had decided to be a missionary rather than a mobilizer? Probably no two people in history are traceably responsible for more

---

[7] Robert Wilder and John Forman, both a part of the Student Volunteer Movement, mobilized Speer. Speer summarizes what took place the day he was mobilized, "I can see still the little room in the North Middle Reunion at Princeton, where a little group of us met years ago in our sophomore year and faced this question, and one by one sat down at a table and wrote our names under the words: 'I am willing and desirous, God permitting, to become a foreign missionary.'" W. Reginald Wheeler, *A Man Sent from God: A Biography of Robert E. Speer* (Westwood, NJ: Revell Publishing, 1956), 53.

[8] Wheeler, 70.

[9] Wheeler, 127.

missionaries going to the field than John Mott and Robert Speer."[10] Every World Christian has been mobilized, and every World Christian can do it!

BECOMING A MOBILIZER

Robert Speer and John Mott

Usually within fifteen minutes of conversation, someone's passion surfaces. As Luke says, "For out of the overflow of his heart his mouth speaks" (Luke 6:45). My wife bumped into her friend Rachel, whom she hadn't seen in six months. Within two minutes Jess knew about the Christian yoga class Rachel had started and received an invitation to the Thursday night class. Everyone is a mobilizer, but not everyone is a missions mobilizer. If you are not passionate about God's purpose in the world, you cannot be a missions mobilizer. If it doesn't burn in you, it will not burn in others. There are some

Everyone is a mobilizer, but not everyone is a missions mobilizer.

---

[10] Ralph D. Winter and Steven C. Hawthorne, eds., *Perspectives on the World Christian Movement,* 4th ed. (Pasadena, CA: William Carey Library, 2009), 734.

simple yet profound principles for every person desiring to recruit others to missions.

Get educated: At first I was clueless. I couldn't tell you what God was doing in the world, where the least-reached people groups resided, or even how to find the answers to those questions. I couldn't mobilize because I didn't have much to pass on. The people we seek to mobilize depend upon our guidance for their own mission education. Every mobilizer must be a wealth of information, ever deepening their own vision, passion, and personal walk with God.

Find Christians who are not aware: The mobilizer needs people to mobilize. We all have something in common; we know uninvolved Christians. Start where you are: your small group, Sunday school class, campus ministry, or high-school youth group. People are not mobilized overnight. No two journeys look the same. For some it may take months of exposure and prayer; others, years. A man who spent his life motivating others toward missions, A. T. Pierson, once said, "Christians need to be converted to missions, just as the lost do to Christ."[11] Seek out uninvolved Christians and patiently endure the process, allowing yourself to be used by God in any capacity to see their conversion to missions take root.

Find Christians who care: As mobilizers, we are usually in the minority. The majority of our audience often seems apathetic to the message. We face disappointment and discouragement as a normal, inevitable part of the work! These things only become dangerous when we experience them in isolation. They can overwhelm us when we are not

---

[11] Arthur Tappan Pierson, *The Crisis of Missions: Or, the Voice Out of the Cloud* (New York: Robert Carter, 1886).

connected to other mobilizers with whom we can relate. Pursue community with like-minded people who can encourage you, keep you accountable, and build you up. Mark my word, a sense of team is critical.

MOBILIZING OTHERS

God cannot lead people on the basis of facts they do not know.[12] Think of the tragic implications of this truth on missions. If a high-school teacher remains unaware of the opportunity in China for volunteers to teach conversational English to Chinese youth for a summer, she will never end up on that summer trip. How pressing is the need for mobilizers who effectively activate and connect people to fulfill their role in world evangelization! In my own mobilization, I stick to three big-picture ideas for guidance:

Motivation: Millions of Christians wake up each day with little room for anything outside their own scope of life: family, job, managing finances, and hobbies. Scripture reminds us that without vision people perish (Proverbs 29:18). Relatively few believers have been introduced to the concepts of unreached peoples, the 10-40 window, and how their life can make an impact. Logically, they lack the impetus to apply themselves in any strategic missional way. They need someone to give them vision, an introduction to those life-changing, direction-altering truths. They need motivation. Motivation is like a spark that can be kindled in many ways—a book, a speaker, a video, a Bible study,

---

[12] David Bryant, *In the Gap* (Ventura, CA: Regal Books, 1979), 35.

a conversation with the Hindu next door, a prayer meeting. Each person is moved differently, so good mobilizers take the assorted approach to motivating others.

Personally, I spend most of my own mobilization efforts in motivating others. In large and small group environments, I share the biblical basis for missions to those who oftentimes have never heard it. In casual conversation over coffee, I find I tell stories about friends on the mission field, share verses that have deepened my understanding of God's heart, or talk about what I have been learning from my most recent missions reading material. The spark takes a lot of different forms, but motivation is always the first step of mobilization.

Information: Proverbs 19:2 warns, "It is not good to have zeal without knowledge." That's why information must supplement motivation. The danger in excluding this critical step is that the flame sparked by motivation can dim or die out. Every new World Christian needs to learn the same basic categories: needs of the world, world religions, mission agencies, key terms, and sources for further information.

As soon as possible, I try to meet one-to-one with those who show interest after their initial (motivational) exposure. I give tracks to run on, such as what missions books they need to read, who they should talk to, and what overseas opportunities exist. The right information can fan the flame into a raging fire.

Attention: Just as a fire burns out without someone to stoke it, so missions zeal will die without someone to fuel it. After I have provided information to an individual, my job isn't finished. My focus shifts to mentoring. I open up my schedule to meeting with that person regularly. We pray for the world, meet internationals, and I continue to develop the new World Christian's scriptural understanding of missions. For two years I have poured into a few guys, seeing their passion increase. Recently we traveled to the Middle East to experience what God is doing on the front lines. Attention is the most time-consuming part of mobilization, but there is no substitute.

I've found an over-arching rule that applies to all three principles. Habak-kuk states, "Then the Lord replied: 'Write down the revelation and *make it plain* on tablets so that a herald may run with it'" (Habakkuk 2:2). God instructed Habakkuk to write down His vision in a way

> *"Every Christian a World Christian, and every World Christian a mobilizer."*

people could understand, to make it plain for them. Motivation, information, and attention must involve common-sense communication. Growing into a consistent World Christian can be daunting, so we must remember to break it into chunks our audience can digest.

After I spoke at an event on mobilizing this genera-tion, Dr. Ralph Winter approached me and noted, "Motiva-tion, information, and attention are M.I.A., Missing In Action. Believers engaged in harvest work are M.I.A., because we often fail to apply motivation, information, and attention in our mobilization efforts." To mobilize effectively, these three ideas must be utilized. Claude Hickman captures the awe-some potential of mobilization in his statement, "Every Chris-tian a World Christian, and every World Christian a mobilizer."

Every Christian is orchestrating his or her life around God's heart for the world and, at the same time, passing on vision to new believers and the next generation. Incredible!

Dorothy in *The Wizard of Oz* was a mobilizer.[13] She started off to Oz by herself. On the journey she met a scarecrow who needed a brain. She then found a tin man in need of a heart. Finally, she came across the lion who lacked courage. They each had a unique need which required Dorothy to handle them differently. In the same way, as a missions mobilizer you will come across people at different stages of the journey, each with diverse needs. Some, like the scarecrow needing a brain, have misguided perceptions about the world. They need information to correct their thinking. Others, like the heartless tin man, lack a heart for the world. You might need to pray with them or even expose them to the needs of the world so they grow in compassion. You will also encounter individuals who, like the lion, need confidence. They don't think they have anything to offer in world evangelization. They may need help discerning their contribution or the encouragement to step out. On their journey to Oz, Dorothy and her small band encountered disappointments and setbacks, but she was the catalyst to keep them going. Dorothy showed them the way and helped them on the way!

---

[13] This illustration is adapted from Claude Hickman, *Live Life on Purpose: God's Purpose. Your Life. One Journey.* (Enumclaw, WA: Pleasant Word Publishing, 2003), 188.

CHAPTER 18
THE REVOLUTION WITHIN

I n 1473 a child was born who would change the way humanity viewed the world. Nicolaus Copernicus's ideas challenged the status quo. Born in Poland, the youngest of four children, his wealthy father died before Copernicus's teenage years. His uncle, a successful church cleric, took the children under his protection and encouraged Copernicus to pursue church law and medicine. Feeling obligated, Copernicus agreed; however, his passions were mathematics, astronomy, and astrology. During his university years, he began to collect books on these subjects and, at random times, looked over the problems of astronomy. He eventually obtained degrees in law and medicine. Though consumed with his professional responsibilities, his passion for astronomy never died. He spent his nights studying the stars, and what he observed changed the way we view the world.

For thirteen hundred years, people believed the Earth was the center of the universe. The sun, moon, and stars all revolved around man. Copernicus believed the sun was the center—not the earth. Through his research, Copernicus realized the earth orbited around a fixed point: the sun. To the majority of scientists and theologians, this was not just false, but heretical.

On the day he died, May 24, 1543, Nicolaus Copernicus's book was released, *De Revolutionibus.* This six-volume work reached Copernicus only a few hours before his death. In it he states, "In the center rests the sun. For who would place this lamp of a very beautiful temple in another or better place than this wherefrom it can illuminate everything at the same time."

The Copernican Revolution opened new ways of interpreting the world. This revolution paved the way for scientists like Galileo. Internationally renowned scholar on science and philosophy Thomas Kuhn asserts, "The Copernican Revolution was a revolution in ideas, a transformation in man's conception of the universe and of his own relation to it.... The Copernican Revolution is among the most fascinating episodes in the entire history of science."[1]

THE REVOLUTION AND YOU

Thousands of years before Nicolaus Copernicus was studying space, God was orchestrating humanity. What Copernicus observed scientifically, God was revealing to Abraham theologically; that the Son was the center of the universe, not humanity.

God asked Abraham to follow Him in faith. Because he stepped out in obedience, the father of our faith experienced a marked change. His life no longer looked the same—he

---

[1] Thomas S. Kuhn, *The Copernican Revolution: Planetary Astronomy in the Development of Western Thought* (Boston: Fellows of Harvard College Publications, 1957), 1-3.

joined God's revolution. Isaac and Jacob were next. Whatever their lives would have looked like detached from God's purpose, no one knows. The trajectory of their lives underwent a complete change. Others in the Old Testament followed: Moses, Joshua, David, Elijah, Elisha, Daniel, Isaiah, and Jeremiah. The legacy of revolutionaries for God's kingdom continues. In the New Testament, Jesus invited the disciples to join this revolution

The legacy of revolutionaries for God's kingdom continues.

begun with Abraham. They left everything and followed. Paul the apostle was next. This Pharisee of Pharisees experienced a total transformation on the road to Damascus, and he made it his ambition to preach Christ where Christ was not known (Romans 15:20). Do you see how each life that is surrendered to God's purpose is a life of immeasurable impact? Biblical history is really one long narrative, carried out by the transformed lives of men and women living for a unifying idea—the spread of God's radical love and truth to the ends of the earth.

The early Church fathers including Clement, Irenaeus, Tertullian, and Origen all labored to see the revolution continue beyond the apostles. Through medieval Christianity, Anselm of Canterbury and Thomas Aquinas were influential philosophers and theologians who carried on their revolutionary heritage. God raised up men such as Martin Luther, Ulrich Zwingli, and John Calvin during the days of the Reformation to keep the gospel pure and to guide those who were being led astray by errant theology. Over the past four hundred years, William Carey, Hudson Taylor, Cameron Townsend, and Donald

McGavran provided the much needed-reemphasis on the nations by laying down their lives in the pioneering efforts that advanced the kingdom beyond borders. Their revolutionary example also blazed the trail for men and women like John Mott, Robert and Grace Wilder, Luther Wishard, Jim Elliott, Amy Carmichael, and Helen Roseveare. An all-consuming vision for the nations transformed each one. God's desire for our own generation brings the revolution to our doorstep today.

We have been grafted into that which God began in Abraham: the privilege of participating with God in the grandest story of all time.

We find ourselves in a long line of surrendered lives who embarked on the Abrahamic Revolution. Now it comes to you. As Paul said, "He redeemed us in order that the blessing given to Abraham might come to the Gentiles through Christ Jesus" (Galatians 3:14). There it is—the purpose of our redemption!

By virtue of our own salvation, we have been grafted into that which God began in Abraham: the privilege of participating with God in the grandest story of all time.

"We have not made the Revolution, the Revolution has made us." When we say yes to His purpose, a sudden and marked change occurs. Believers did not create missions. We did not generate the idea of spreading God's redemptive love to the far corners of the earth. Rather, the fullness of our identity as children of God develops under the influence of

His mission. We read God's Word in a new context, we see the world with new eyes, and we take on a new lifestyle; a lifestyle with purpose. We conform with the mission that God set in motion with Abraham. The Revolution makes us.

Like Abraham, you are invited to abandon your ambitions in exchange for His. God has never strayed from His plan, and He has never veered from His method—using people. Join the legacy of those who have said yes to God. Come be a part of the *Abrahamic Revolution!*

BIBLIOGRAPHY

Adeney, David. *China: The Church's Long March.* Ventura, CA: Regal Books, 1985.

Ahrend, Todd. *In This Generation: Looking to the Past to Reach the Present.* Colorado Springs, CO: Dawson Media, 2010.

Aikman, David. *Jesus in Beijing: How Christianity Is Transforming China and Changing the Global Balance of Power.* Washington, DC: Regnery Publishing, 2003.

Alcorn, Randy. *Money, Possessions, and Eternity.* Carol Stream, IL: Tyndale House, 2003.

Andrews, C. F. *Sadhu Sundar Singh: A Personal Memoir.* New York: Harper and Brothers Publishers, 1934.

Ayling, Stanley. *John Wesley.* Nashville, TN: Abingdon Press, 1979.

Barnes, Lemuel Call. *Two Thousand Years of Missions before Carey.* Philadelphia: American Baptist Publication Society, 1900.

Barrett, David, George Kurian, and Todd Johnson. *World Christian Encyclopedia: A Comparative Survey of Churches and Religions in the Modern World,* vol. 1. New York: Oxford University Press, 2001.

The Bhagavad-Gita. Translated by Barbara Stoler Miller. New York: Quality Paperback, 1998.

Blomberg, Craig. *Neither Poverty nor Riches: A Biblical Theology of Material Possessions.* Downers Grove, IL: InterVarsity Press, 2001.

Bock, Darrell. *Acts.* Grand Rapids, MI: Baker Academic, 2007.

Bodhi, Bhikkhu, ed. *In the Buddha's Words.* Boston: Wisdom Publications, 2005.

Boedicker, Freya and Martin Boedicker. *The Philosophy of Tai Chi Chuan.* Berkeley, CA: Blue Snake Books, 2009.

Bonhoeffer, Dietrich. *The Cost of Discipleship.* New York: Macmillan Publishing, 1937.

Borthwick, Paul. *A Mind for Missions: Ten Ways to Build Your World Vision.* Colorado Springs, CO: NavPress, 1987.

Borthwick, Paul. *Simplify.* Colorado Springs, CO: Authentic Publishing, 2007.

Bosch, David J. *Transforming Mission: Paradigm Shifts in Theology of Mission.* MaryKnoll, NY: Orbis Books, 2005.

Braden, Charles. *The World's Religions.* New York: Abingdon Press, 1939.

Brockington, J. L. *The Sacred Thread: A Short History of Hinduism.* Oxford: University Press, 1981.

Broomhall, Marshall. *Martyred Missionaries of the China Inland Mission: With a Record of the Perils and Sufferings of Some Who Escaped.* London: Morgan and Scott, 1901.

Bruce, F. F. *The Book of Acts.* Grand Rapids, MI: Eerdmans Publishing, 1988.

Bryant, David. *In the Gap.* Ventura, CA: Regal Books, 1979.

Burnett, David. *The Spirit of Buddhism.* Grand Rapids, MI: Monarch Books, 1996.

Burnett, David. *The Spirit of Hinduism.* Grand Rapids, MI: Monarch Books, 2006.

Burnett, David. *World of the Spirits.* Grand Rapids, MI: Monarch Books, 2000.

Cardoza-Orlandi, Carlos F. *Mission: An Essential Guide.* Nashville: Abingdon, 2002.

Carey, William. *An Enquiry into the Obligations of Christians to Use Means for the Conversion of the Heathens.* England: Ann Ireland, 1792. Reprint, Dallas, TX: Criswell Publications, 1988.

Carrithers, Michael. *The Buddha: A Very Short Introduction.* New York: Oxford University Press, 1983.

Chan, Kim-kwong. "Mission Movement of the Christian Community in Mainland China: The Back to Jerusalem Movement." Seoul Consultation, Study Commission IX, 2010.

Chang, Lit-Sen. *Asia's Religions: Christianity's Momentous Encounter with Paganism.* San Gabriel, CA: P and R Publishing, 1999.

Chapman, Colin. *Cross and Crescent: Responding to the Challenge of Islam.* England: InterVarsity Press, 1995.

Chinn, Lisa Espineli. *Crossing Cultures Here and Now.* Downers Grove, IL: InterVarsity Press, 2006.

Codrington, R. H. *The Melanesians: Studies in Their Anthropology and Folklore.* Oxford: Clarendon, 1891.

Confucius. *Confucius: The Analects.* Translated by D. C. Lau. London: Penguin Books, 1979.

Cooper, Anne, ed. *Ishmael My Brother.* Great Britain: MARC Publications, 1985.

Cragg, Kenneth and Marston Speight. *Islam from Within: Anthology of a Religion.* Belmont, CA: Wadsworth Publishing Company, 1980.

Dashti, Ali. *Twenty-Three Years: A Study of the Prophetic Career of Mohammad.* Costa Mesa, CA: Mazda Publishers, 1985.

The Dhammapada: The Sayings of the Buddha. Translated by Thomas Byrom. Boston: Shambhala Publications, 1993.

Dickson, John. *A Spectator's Guide to World Religions.* Sydney, Australia: Blue Bottle Books, 2004.

Dillenberger, John, ed. *Martin Luther: Selections from His Writings.* Garden City, NY: Anchor Books, 1961.

Douglas, J. D. *Let the Earth Hear His Voice: International Congress on World Evangelization: Lausanne, Switzerland: Official Reference Volume, Papers and Responses.* Minnesota: World Wide Publications, 1975.

Duewel, Wesley L. *Touch the World through Prayer.* Grand Rapids, MI: Zondervan, 1986.

Eastman, Dick. *The Hour That Changes the World: A Practical Plan for Personal Prayer.* Grand Rapids, MI: Baker Book House, 1978.

Elliot, Elisabeth. *Through Gates of Splendor: The Event that Shocked the World, Changed a People, and Inspired a Nation.* Carol Stream, IL: Living Books, 1956.

Fernando, Antony and Leonard Swidler. *Buddhism Made Plain.* Maryknoll, NY: Orbis Books, 1985.

Fiedler, Klaus. *The Story of Faith Missions from Hudson Taylor to Present-Day Africa.* Oxford: Regnum Books International, 1994.

Filbeck, David. *Yes, God of the Gentiles, Too: The Missionary Message of the Old Testament.* Wheaton, IL: Billy Graham Center, 1994.

Fisher, George Park. *History of the Christian Church.* New York: Charles Scribner's Sons, 1936.

Fleming, Daniel Johnson. *Marks of a World Christian.* New York: Association Press, 1919.

Foster, Richard. *Freedom of Simplicity: Finding Harmony in a Complex World.* New York: Harper One, 2005.

Francis, T. Dayanandan. *Sadhu Sundar Singh: The Lover of the Cross.* Madras, India: Christian Literature Society, 1990.

Geisler, Norman and Abdul Saleeb. *Answering Islam: The Crescent in Light of the Cross.* Grand Rapids, MI: Baker Books, 1993.

Glasser, Arthur. *Announcing the Kingdom: The Story of God's Mission in the Bible.* Grand Rapids, MI: Baker Academic, 2003.

González, Justo L. *The Story of Christianity.* Vol. 1, *The Early Church to the Dawn of the Reformation.* New York: HarperCollins 1984.

González, Ondina E. and Justo L. González. *Christianity in Latin America: A History.* New York: Cambridge University Press, 2008.

Grubb, Norman P. *C. T. Studd: Athlete and Pioneer.* Grand Rapids, MI: Zondervan, 1933.

Halverson, Dean. *The Compact Guide to World Religions.* Minneapolis, MN: Bethany House Publishers, 1996.

Hart, Michael H. *The One Hundred: A Ranking of the Most Influential Persons in History.* New York: Citadel Press, 1978.

Hattaway, Paul. *Back to Jerusalem: Three Chinese House Church Leaders Share Their Vision to Complete the Great Commission.* Carlisle, UK: Piquant, 2003.

Hattaway, Paul. *Operation China: Introducing All the People of China.* Pasadena, CA: William Carey Library, 2000.

Hawthorne, Steve. "Mercy to Babel: God Answers Man's Desire for Security and Significance." Available from thetravelingteam.org.

Hefley, James and Marti Hefley. *Uncle Cam.* Huntington Beach, CA: Wycliffe Bible Translators, 1984.

Herman, A. L. *A Brief Introduction to Hinduism: Religion, Philosophy, and Ways of Liberation.* Oxford: Westview Press, 1991.

Hickman, Claude. *Live Life on Purpose: God's Purpose. Your Life. One Journey.* Enumclaw, WA: Pleasant Word Publishing, 2003.

Hoff, Benjamin. *The Tao of Pooh.* New York: Penguin Books, 1982.

Hoke, Steve and Bill Taylor. *Global Mission Handbook: A Guide for Crosscultural Service.* Downers Grove, IL: InterVarsity Press, 2009.

Holzmann, John. "Jesus Said Our Hearts Are Where Our Treasure Is." *Mission Frontiers Magazine.* Available at missionfrontiers.org.

Hopkins, C. Howard. *20th Century Ecumenical Statesman, John R. Mott: 1865-1955.* New York: Eerdmans Publishing Company, 1979.

Howard, David M. *Student Power in World Evangelism.* Downers Grove, IL: InterVarsity Press, 1970.

Humphreys, Christmas. *Buddhism: An Introduction and Guide.* London: Penguin Books, 1951.

Jeyaraj, Daniel. *Bartholomaus Ziegenbalg: The Father of the Modern Protestant Mission.* Chennai, India: The Indian Society for Promoting Christian Knowledge, 2006.

Johnson, Alan. "The Frontier Mission Movement's Understanding of the Modern Mission Era." *International Journal of Frontier Missions* 18, no. 2, (Spring 2001).

Johnstone, Patrick. *The Church Is Bigger Than You Think: The Unfinished Work of World Evangelism.* Great Britain: Christian Focus Publications, 1998.

Kaiser, Walter C. *Mission in the Old Testament: Israel as a Light to the Nations.* Grand Rapids, MI: Baker Books, 2000.

Kane, J. Herbert. *Understanding Christian Missions.* Grand Rapids, MI: Baker Book House, 1982.

Kane, J. Herbert. *Wanted: World Christians.* Grand Rapids, MI: Baker House, 1986.

Kauffman, Paul E. *China, the Emerging Challenge.* Grand Rapids, MI: Baker Book House, 1982.

Khan, Kim. "How Does Your Debt Compare?" Available at moneycentral.msn.com.

Know Buddhism. "Rebirth, Reincarnation and Recognition of Past Lives." March 3, 2009. Available at knowbuddhism.info.

The Koran. Translated by N. J. Dawood. Great Britain: Penguin Books, 1956.

Köstenberger, Andreas J. and Peter T. O'Brien. *Salvation to the Ends of the Earth: A Biblical Theology of Mission.* Downers Grove, IL: InterVarsity Press, 2001.

Kuhn, Thomas S. *The Copernican Revolution: Planetary Astronomy in the Development of Western Thought.* Boston: Fellows of Harvard College Publications, 1957.

Kuwait Times. "Gulf Muslims Gain Weight in Ramadan." August 31, 2008.

Kyle, John, ed. *Should I Not Be Concerned? A Mission Reader.* Downers Grove, IL: InterVarsity Press, 1987.

Latourette, Kenneth Scott. *A History of Christianity,* vol. 1. New York: HarperCollins, 1938.

Latourette, Kenneth Scott. *A History of the Expansion of Christianity.* Vol. VI, *The Great Century in Northern Africa and Asia 1800-1914 AD.* New York: HarperCollins, 1944.

Lawrence, Carl. *The Church in China: How It Survives and Prospers under Communism.* Minneapolis, MN: Bethany House Publishers, 1985.

The Laws of Manu. Translated by Wendy Doniger and Brian. K. Smith. New Delhi, India: Penguin Books, 1991.

Lewis, Jonathon, Meg Crossman, and Stephen Hoke. *World Mission: An Analysis of the World Christian Movement, Part 1: The Biblical–Historical Foundation.* Pasadena, CA: William Carey Library, 1987.

Lugo, Luis. "Mapping the Global Muslim Population: A Report on the Size and Distribution of the World's Muslim Population." The Pew Forum on Religion and Public Life, October 7, 2009. Available from pewforum.org.

Mandryk, Jason. *Operation World,* 7th ed. Colorado Springs, CO: Biblica Publishing, 2010.

Martin, Malachi. *The Jesuits: The Society of Jesus and the Betrayal of the Roman Catholic Church.* New York: Simon and Schuster, 1987.

Martinson, Paul Varo. *Families of Faith: An Introduction to World Religions for Christians.* Minneapolis, MN: Fortress Press, 1999.

Mathews, Basil. *John R. Mott: World Citizen.* New York: Harper and Brothers Publishers, 1934.

Mavin, Duncan. "One Big ATM." *The Financial Post Magazine.* October 7, 2008.

McDowell, Michael and Nathan Robert Brown. *World Religions at Your Fingertips.* New York: Penguin Group Publishing, 2009.

McGavran, Donald Anderson. *Bridges of God: A Study in the Strategy of Missions.* London: World Dominion Press, 1957.

McManus, Erwin Raphael. *An Unstoppable Force: Daring to Become the Church God Had in Mind.* Loveland, CO: Group Publishing, 2001.

The Middle Length Discourses of the Buddha: A New Translation of the Majjhima Nikaya. Translated by Bhikkhu Nanamoli and Bhikkhu Bodhi. Boston: Wisdom Publications, 1995.

Milton, Owen. *Christian Missionaries.* Wales: Evangelical Press of Wales, 1995.

Moffett, Samuel Hugh. *A History of Christianity in Asia.* Vol. 1, *Beginnings to 1500.* New York: HarperCollins Publishers, 1992.

Morton, Scott. *Funding Your Ministry: An In-Depth, Biblical Guide for Successfully Raising Personal Support.* Colorado Springs, CO: NavPress, 2007.

Moucarry, Chawkat. *The Prophet and the Messiah: An Arab Christian's Perspective on Islam & Christianity.* Downers Grove, IL: InterVarsity Press, 2001.

Müller, Friedrich Max, ed. *The Sacred Books of the East,* vol. XIII. Oxford: Clarendon Press, 1881.

Muthiah, S. "The Legacy That Ziegenbalg Left." *The Hindu, India's National Newspaper,* July 2, 2006.

Neely, Alan. *Christian Mission: A Case Study Approach.* New York: Orbis Books, 1997.

Neill, Stephen. *A History of Christian Missions.* London: Penguin Books, 1964.

Newbigin, Lesslie. *The Open Secret: An Introduction to the Theology of Mission.* Grand Rapids, MI: Eerdmans, 1995.

Noll, Mark A. *A History of Christianity in the United States and Canada.* Grand Rapids, MI: Eerdmans Publishing, 2003.

North American Students and World Advance, Addresses Delivered at the Eight International Convention of the Student Volunteer Movement for Foreign Missions, Des Moines, Iowa, Dec. 31, 1919–Jan. 4, 1920.

Oldstone-Moore, Jennifer. *Taoism: Origins, Beliefs, Practices, Holy Texts, Sacred Places.* New York: Oxford University Press, 2003.

Organ, Troy Wilson. *Hinduism: Its Historical Development.* Woodbury, NY: Barron's Education Series, 1974.

Parker, Michael. *The Kingdom of Character: The Student Volunteer Movement for Foreign Missions 1886–1926,* 2nd ed. Pasadena, CA: William Carey Library, 2008.

Parshall, Phil. *Understanding Muslim Teachings and Traditions: A Guide for Christians.* Grand Rapids, MI: Baker Books, 1994.

Peters, George W. *A Biblical Theology of Missions.* Chicago: Moody Press, 1972.

The Pew Forum on Religion and Public Life. "Many Americans Say Other Faiths Can Lead to Eternal Life." Dec. 18, 2008. Available from pewforum.org.

Phillips, Tom and Bob Norsworthy. *The World at Your Door: Reaching International Students in Your Home, Church, and School.* Minneapolis, MN: Bethany House Publishers, 1997.

Pierson, Arthur Tappan. *The Crisis of Missions.* New York: Robert Carter, 1886.

Pierson, Arthur Tappan. *The Divine Enterprise of Missions.* London: Hodder and Stoughton, 1893.

Pillai, Rajendra K. *Reaching the World in Our Own Backyard.* Colorado Springs, CO: Waterbrook Press, 2003.

Piper, John. *Desiring God: Meditations of a Christian Hedonist.* Sisters, OR: Multnomah Books, 1986.

Piper, John. *Don't Waste Your Life.* Wheaton, IL: Crossway Books, 2003.

Piper, John. *Let the Nations Be Glad! The Supremacy of God in Missions.* Grand Rapids, MI: Baker House, 1993.

Piper, John. "Personal Tribute to the Late Ralph Winter." Desiring God Ministries. Available from desiringgod.org, 2009.

Piper, John. *When I Don't Desire God: How to Fight for Joy.* Wheaton, IL: Crossway Books, 2004.

Pirolo, Neal. *Serving as Senders.* Carlisle, UK: OM Publishing, 1996.

Platt, David. *Radical: Taking Back Your Faith from the American Dream.* Colorado Springs, CO: Multnomah Books, 2010.

Power, Carla. "Not the Queen's English." *Newsweek*, March 7, 2005. Available at newsweek.com.

Powers, John. *Introduction to Tibetan Buddhism.* Ithaca, NY: Snow Lion Publications, 1995.

Rahman, Fazlur. *Islam.* Chicago: University of Chicago Press, 1966.

Rahula, Walpola. *What the Buddha Taught.* 2nd ed. New York: Grove Press, 1974.

Ramsey, Boniface. *Beginning to Read the Fathers.* New York: Paulist Press, 1985.

Ramzy, Austin. "China's New Bestseller: The Bible." *Time*, December 17, 2007.

Razawy, Sayed Ali Asgher. *Restatement of the History of Islam and Muslims.* United Kingdom: World Federation of KSI Muslim Communities.

Richard, H. L. *Hinduism: A Brief Look at Theology, History, Scriptures, and Social System with Comments on the Gospel in India.* Pasadena, CA: William Carey Library, 2007.

Richards, Thomas C. *Samuel J. Mills: Missionary Pathfinder, Pioneer and Promoter.* Boston: The Pilgrim Press, 1906.

Richardson, Don. *Eternity in Their Hearts: Startling Evidence of Belief in the One True God in Hundreds of Cultures Throughout the World.* Ventura, CA: Regal Books, 1981.

Richardson, Don. *Lords of the Earth: An Incredible but True Story from the Stone-Age Hell of Papua's Jungle.* Ventura, CA: Regal Books, 1977.

Richardson, Don. *Peace Child: An Unforgettable Story of Primitive Jungle Treachery in the 20th Century.* Ventura, CA: Regal Books, 1974.

The Rig Veda. Translated by Wendy Doniger. England: Penguin Books, 1981.

Ritchie, Mark A. *Spirit of the Rainforest: A Yanomamo Shaman's Story.* Chicago: Island Lake Press, 1996.

Rood, Rick. "Reaching the World That Has Come to Us." Probe Ministries. Available at leaderu.com.

Rose, Darlene Deibler. *Evidence Not Seen: A Woman's Miraculous Faith in the Jungles of World War II.* New York: HarperCollins Publishers, 1988.

Ross, Nancy Wilson. *Buddhism: A Way of Life and Thought.* New York: Vintage Books, 1980.

Ruthven, Malise. *Islam in the World,* 3rd ed. New York: Oxford University Press, 2006.

Sailhamer, John H. *The Pentateuch as Narrative.* Grand Rapids, MI: Zondervan, 1992.

Schumann, Hans Wolfgang. *Buddhism: An Outline of Its Teachings and Schools.* Wheaton, IL: The Theosophical Publishing House, 1973.

Seneviratna, Anuradha, ed. *King Asoka and Buddhism: Historical and Literary Studies.* Sri Lanka: Buddhist Publication Society, 1994.

Shedd, Clarence P. *Two Centuries of Student Christian Movements: Their Origin and Intercollegiate Life.* New York: Association Press, 1934.

Shedd, William G. T. *The Doctrine of Endless Punishment.* Reprint. Carlisle, PA: Banner of Truth Trust, 1986.

Shetler, Joanne and Patricia Purvis. *And the Word Came with Power: How God Met and Changed a People Forever.* Portland, OR: Multnomah, 1992.

Singh, Sadhu Sundar. *At the Master's Feet.* Westwood, NJ: Fleming H. Revell, 1922.

Singh, Sadhu Sundar. *Meditations on Various Aspects of the Spiritual Life.* Edinburgh: R and R Clark, 1926.

Singh, Sadhu Sundar. *Reality and Religion: Meditations on God, Man and Nature.* London: MacMillan, 1923.

Singh, Sadhu Sundar. *The Search after Reality: Thoughts on Hinduism, Buddhism, Muhammadanism, and Christianity.* London: MacMillan, 1925.

Singh, Sadhu Sundar. *With and Without Christ.* New York: Harper and Brothers Publishers, 1928.

Sitton, David. *To Every Tribe With Jesus: Understanding and Reaching Tribal Peoples for Christ.* Sand Springs, OK: Grace and Truth Books, 2005.

Sjogren, Bob, Bill Stearns, and Amy Stearns. *Run with the Vision.* Minneapolis, MN: Bethany House Publishers, 1995.

Sjogren, Bob. *Unveiled at Last: Discover God's Hidden Message from Genesis to Revelation.* Seattle, WA: YWAM Publishing, 1992.

Smith, Gary V. *The Prophets as Preachers: An Introduction to the Hebrew Prophets.* Nashville, TN: Broadman and Holman Publishers, 1994.

Smith, Jay. "Six Muslim Beliefs (Iman) and a Christian's Response: For a Muslim Enquirer." May 1995. Available at debate.org.uk.

Smith, Oswald J. *The Challenge of Missions.* London: Marshall, Morgan and Scott Publishing, 1959.

Stafford, Tim. "A Captivating Vision: Why Chinese House Churches May Just End Up Fulfilling the Great Commission—An Interview with Paul Hattaway." *Christianity Today,* April 2004.

Stearns, Bill and Amy Stearns. *20/20 Vision: Practical Ways Individuals and Churches Can Be Involved.* Minneapolis, MN: Bethany House, 2005.

Stearns, Richard. *The Hole in Our Gospel: What Does God Expect of Us? The Answer That Changed My Life and Might Just Change the World.* Nashville, TN: Thomas Nelson, 2009.

Swartz, Jon. "Band of Billionaires Pledge to Give to Charity." *USA Today,* August 6, 2010.

Taylor, Bill. "Mobilizing Missionaries for a Different World." *Connections Magazine* 4, no. 3 (October 2005).

Taylor, Dr. Howard and Mrs. Howard Taylor *Hudson Taylor and the China Inland Mission: The Growth of a Work of God.* London: Morgan and Scott, 1920.

Taylor, Dr. Howard and Mrs. Howard Taylor. *Hudson Taylor in Early Years: The Growth of a Soul.* London: Morgan and Scott, 1911.

Tennent, Timothy C. *Christianity at the Religious Roundtable: Evangelicalism in Conversation with Hinduism, Buddhism, and Islam.* Grand Rapids, MI: Baker Academic Publishing, 2002.

Tennent, Timothy C. *Invitation to World Missions: A Trinitarian Missiology for the Twenty-first Century.* Grand Rapids, MI: Kregel, 2010.

Tennent, Timothy C. *Theology in the Context of World Christianity: How the Global Church Is Influencing the Way We Think About and Discuss Theology.* Grand Rapids, MI: Zondervan, 2007.

Thompson, Phyllis. *Sadhu Sundar Singh: A Biography of the Remarkable Indian Holy Man and Disciple of Jesus Christ.* Carlisle, CA: OM Publishing.

Thurman, Robert A. E. *Essential Tibetan Buddhism.* San Francisco: Harper San Francisco, 1995.

Torrey, R. A. *Heaven or Hell.* Springdale, PA: Whitaker House, 1985.

The Traveling Team. "From Surfing the Beach to Serving in the Jungle: A Brad Buser Interview." *Ignition Magazine,* 2010.

A Treasury of Mahayana Sutras: Selections from the Maharatnakuta Sutra. Translated by Garma C. C. Chang. New York: The Pennsylvania State University, 1983.

Lao-tzu. *Tao Te Ching.* Translated by D. C. Lau. London: Penguin Books, 1963.

Upanisads. Translated by Patrick Olivelle. Oxford: University Press, 1996.

Vadanya [Chris Pauling]. *Introducing Buddhism.* New York: Windhorse Publications, 1997.

Van Rheenen, Gailyn. *Communicating Christ in Animistic Contexts.* Pasadena, CA: William Carey Library, 1991.

Van Rheenen, Gailyn. *Missions: Biblical Foundations and Contemporary Strategies.* Grand Rapids, MI: Zondervan Publishing, 1996.

Veith, Gene Edward. "Who Gives Two Cents for Missions? We Do, to Our Shame." *World Magazine* 20, no. 41 (October 22, 2005).

Wagner, C. Peter. *On the Crest of the Wave: Becoming a World Christian.* Ventura, CA: Regal Books, 1983.

Walls, Andrew F. *The Cross-Cultural Process in Christian History: Studies in the Transmission and Appropriation of Faith.* Maryknoll, New York: Orbis Press, 2002.

Weinlick, John R. *Count Zinzendorf: The Story of His Life and Leadership in the Renewed Moravian Church.* Bethlehem and Winston-Salem: The Moravian Church in America, 1984.

Wheeler, W. Reginald. *A Man Sent from God: A Biography of Robert E. Speer.* Westwood, NJ: Revell Publishing, 1956.

Wilder, Robert P. *The Great Commission: The Missionary Response of the Student Volunteer Movements in North America and Europe; Some Personal Reminiscences.* London: Oliphants Publishers, 1936.

Williams, Paul. *Mahayana Buddhism: The Doctrinal Foundations.* London: Routledge, 1994.

Williams, Paul. *The Unexpected Way.* New York: T & T Clark, 2002.

Winter, Ralph. "Momentum Is Building: Many Voices Discuss Completing the Task by 2000 A.D." *International Journal of Frontier Missions* 3, no. 1-4 (1986).

Winter, Ralph D. and Steven C. Hawthorne, eds. *Perspectives on the World Christian Movement,* 4th ed. Pasadena, CA: William Carey Library, 2009.

Woodberry, J. Dudley. "Contextualization among Muslims Reusing Common Pillars." *International Journal of Frontier Missions* 13, no. 4 (Oct.-Dec. 1996).

Wright, Christopher J. H. *The Mission of God: Unlocking the Bible's Grand Narrative.* Downers Grove, IL: InterVarsity Press, 2006.

Wright, Christopher J. H. *The Mission of God's People: A Biblical Theology of the Church's Mission.* Grand Rapids, MI: Zondervan Publishing, 2010.

Y Facts. "Percentage of Students who have Served in Missions." Brigham Young University. Available from yfacts.byu.edu.

York, Doug. "Eyjafjallajökull Is Considered a Small Volcano? What Happens if the Big One Erupts?" April 17, 2010. Available at news.gather.com.

Zacharias, Ravi. *Jesus Among Other Gods: The Absolute Claims of the Christian Message.* Nashville, TN: W Publishing Group, 2000.

Zumwalt, John Willis. *Passion for the Heart of God.* Choctaw, OK: HGM Publishing, 2000.

Zwemer, Samuel M. *Into All the World: The Great Commission, a Vindication and an Interpretation.* Grand Rapids, MI: Zondervan, 1943.

Zwemer, Samuel M. *The Moslem World.* Nashville, TN: Publishing House of the M.E., 1908.

NOTES

NOTES

NOTES

NOTES

NOTES

NOTES

NOTES

NOTES

For more information, to request the author to speak, or
for more copies of this book see:

www.abrahamicrev.org

1-800-372-8520

todd@thetravelingteam.org

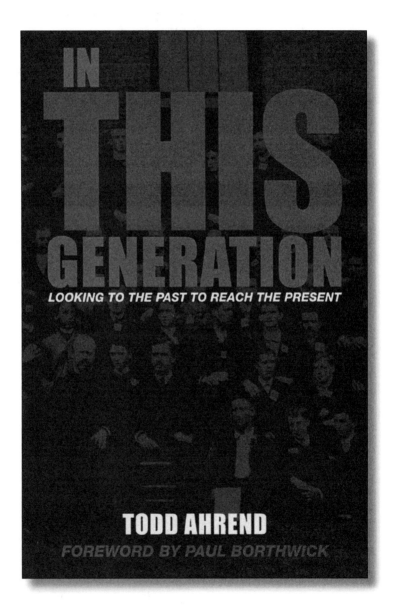

THEY CHANGED THE WORLD ...AND SO CAN WE!

Todd Ahrend takes you on a journey into the greatest missions movement in history. For anyone today who longs for the evangelization of the world, this is the place to begin.

The lessons learned from the historic Student Volunteer Movement provide a priceless well of wisdom and practical methods that God's church can drink from once again.

To reach the world for Christ in THIS generation, look to those who almost accomplished it in their own.

"In This Generation is so right on! Loaded with perspective and wisdom. Thoroughly biblical, historical, visionary, challenging, and practical... I will have every man I disciple read this book, discuss it with them and apply it!"
—Roger Hershey, Campus Crusade for Christ

"Todd combines his personal wisdom gained over a decade of mobilizing students with a historical survey of the Student Volunteer Movement... Reading this book gives you access to the mind and passion of a master mobilizer."
—Joey Shaw, Minister of International Mission, The Austin Stone Community Church, Texas